BLOOD & SACRIFICE

WILLIAM PITT CHAMBERS

BLOOD &
SACRIFICE

THE
CIVIL WAR
JOURNAL
OF A
CONFEDERATE
SOLDIER

EDITED BY RICHARD A. BAUMGARTNER

BLUE ACORN PRESS

Blue Acorn Press
P.O. Box 2684
Huntington, W.Va. 25726

Copyright 1994
by
Richard A. Baumgartner

First Edition Published August 1994
ISBN 1-885033-01-X

Second Printing June 1997

Maps by Richard A. Baumgartner

For
Ted and Carol

CONTENTS

INTRODUCTION

Peering through a loophole in the parapet of a battered trench, Sergeant William Pitt Chambers' view of the scarred, shell-torn ground in front of him conjured a fitting metaphor to the condition of the Confederacy's Vicksburg army by July 1863.

The ravages of civil war already had cut wide swaths through Chambers' home state of Mississippi. Bottled up in besieged Vicksburg, its ragged defenders slowly sank into the depths of despondency as heat, hunger, disease and the danger of shells and bullets continually aimed in their direction sapped the power to resist. Hasty burials were the reward to those who were killed. The wounded and sick suffered in agony in makeshift hospitals. Those in the line watched, worked, waited. And always they were hungry. When rations were issued, nothing went to waste. If a mule died, the lean meat often was devoured with relish. A few men resorted to eating dogs and rats.

Drawing upon the inner strength of deep religious convictions, "Pitt" Chambers found the will to endure privations previously unknown in his life – and managed to record such experiences in a journal he kept of his service as an infantryman through more than three years of war. It is fortunate he did, for so few wartime accounts possessing much historical or literary merit were written by Southern soldiers, especially those serving in the Confederacy's western armies. It is more remarkable that Chambers' inked pages even survived the war at all. In 1864, while stored in a friend's trunk, much of the journal was looted by Federal troops at Meridian, Miss., and thrown away. But by a long stroke of luck, nearly all the crumpled, soiled pages were found in a deserted Federal camp-site, rescued and returned to their author a year later. By the end of hostilities the manuscript had grown in length to several hundred pages, much of it "in a hardly legible form," Chambers wrote, "and none of it fit for other eyes than my own."

Twenty-five years later Chambers, then 50 years old and feeling a compunction to place his mutilated manuscript in more permanent form, copied the journal by hand, in some places fleshing out principal events by memory from "the meager notes taken by the wayside." He further prefaced his account by writing that "no claim is made that this is a history of any movement of [an] army, only so far as it concerns the personal narrative of the writer. Nor is he vain enough to consider that his career as a soldier is more worthy of record than that of hundreds of thousands of others; but humble as it is, he does think it may afford a little help to him who would write a full history of the unfortunate struggle. To such, and to my children, this volume is dedicated ..."

Chambers was born December 14, 1839, the son of John and Mercy Welch Chambers, and grew up near the Leaf River in sparsely populated northeast Covington County, Miss. Of Scotch descent, his father was born in New York City and moved to Mississippi some 30 years before the war, operating a small farm about 55 miles southeast of Jackson, the state capital. Although educational advantages in this rural setting were extremely limited, William Chambers developed studious habits marked by a voracious appetite for reading, and in 1859 began teaching school. He was thus employed when Mississippi, on January 9, 1861, seceded from the Union – the first state to follow South Carolina's lead.

Despite no proximity to railroad or telegraph facilities, Covington County already boasted a militia company known as the "Covington Fencibles," which had been organized, armed and equipped under state law. Early in the spring of 1861 a reorganization of this company took place, the ranks filled, new officers elected and its service tendered to both state and Confederate authorities. Eventually it became Company F, 27th Regiment of Mississippi Infantry Volunteers. Prior to the start of the 27th Regiment's training, however, another company called the "Harvey Desperadoes," was organized with John W. Harvey as captain. Taking leave of his teaching duties, Chambers joined the "Desperadoes," but when its services were not accepted the company disbanded, most of its members going to other commands.

On February 22, 1862, a third company was organized at Williamsburg, Miss. It was composed of a larger proportion of men with families, many of them middle-aged, than either of those preceding it from the county. Nicknamed the "Covington Rebels," the volunteers of Company B elected T.D. Magee their captain, George C. Buchanan as first lieutenant, Arch Fairley as second lieutenant, and James A. Graham as junior second lieutenant. Joseph F. Duckworth was appointed orderly sergeant. That same day the "Rebels" were mustered in as State Troops for a period of 12 months by Colonel Vernon L. Ferrell of Governor John J. Pettus' staff. With this group, William Chambers went off to war as a private one month later.

In April 1862 the author's company and four others were combined to form the 6th Battalion Mississippi Volunteers, an organization existing until December 2 of that year when, with the assembly of five additional companies, it was redesignated the 46th Mississippi Regiment. Interestingly, six months passed after Company B's muster-in before the company was issued its first muskets on August 29. Prior to that, many of the men armed themselves with shotguns brought from home. Initial service under fire was performed at Vicksburg, where Chambers witnessed buildup of the Hill City's defenses, Federal gunboats attempting to run Vicksburg's river batteries, and an alarmingly quick deterioration of his health. Before summer ended, sickness and disease claimed the lives of 18 of Chambers' company comrades.

With length of service came promotion to Chambers, who was appointed third sergeant in Company B on April 2, 1863, and sergeant major in early April 1864. For brief periods he also served as the regiment's adjutant and ordnance sergeant — duties he disliked for the time and paperwork involved, which separated him from his company ties, book reading and journal keeping. At his own request in June 1864, he was returned to Company B as sergeant, and at the end of the conflict he held the rank of orderly sergeant.

As the war ground on and undermined his confidence in many of the South's military and civilian leaders, Chambers' fervent religious beliefs continuously were tested and ultimately proved to be the anchor of his devotion to duty. His faith was severely strained at Vicksburg during the month preceding the city's fall in 1863, but underwent a transformation late that year at Dalton, Ga., where religious revivalism in Confederate camps reached its zenith. Physical and spiritual strength derived from unswerving belief in God, as well as the Confederacy's ideals as he perceived them, helped the author through many trying ordeals, especially in dealing with the battlefield deaths of friends and his own wounding in the battle of Allatoona, Ga., on October 5, 1864.

Like so many other soldiers wearing gray, Chambers fought for what he believed was the South's right to self-government and self-determination. Defense of slavery was not a primary motivating factor in his resolve to remain in the ranks, and he was content to maintain the status quo then existing in his home state where black slaves comprised a large percentage of the population. He espoused common sentiments of the day regarding blacks, feeling by 1864 that wholesale destruction wrought throughout the South and the gross wastage of human life were not worth "nominal freedom ... to some four or five millions of an inferior race, that will probably be invested with the right of suffrage without intelligence to use it." Such prejudice was typical then, even among the Northern soldiers Chambers was trying to kill. When, in early 1865, the Confederate Congress debated whether to bolster dwindling manpower by organizing and arming black fighting units, Chambers' reaction was negative. Of the proposal he wrote in his journal simply, "It is not right."

Just as the author's account provides an open window to the hopes, dreams and fears of one Confederate enlisted man, it also chronicles nearly the entire history of his company and regiment through three years of daily life in camp, on the march and in battles fought in Mississippi, Georgia and Alabama. Known in the army as "Pitt," Chambers describes with particular poignancy the deaths of three comrades at Vicksburg, Allatoona and Atlanta, where, at the latter place, his best friend and messmate was killed by a stray bullet while cooking breakfast. Due to his injuries suffered at Allatoona, the author missed the carnage of Franklin, Tenn., and the virtual destruction of the Army of Tennessee 16 days later at Nashville.

After the war Chambers returned to Covington County, married Sarah Ann Robertson in 1866, moved to the hamlet of Kinterbish, Ala., near the Tombigbee River, and resumed teaching. Two daughters were born to the couple there, May in August 1878 and Janie in October 1880. A decade later Chambers began the work of transcribing a pocket diary he kept early in his service and the journal, assimilating the two with some elaboration into the story presented here. He completed the work by August 1891.

Shortly before the death of his wife in January 1900, Chambers moved back to Mississippi with his daughters, the eldest of whom followed her father in the teaching profession. They settled in Hattiesburg, where Chambers was employed as deputy in the Forrest County chancery clerk's office. He continued writing short stories, essays, poetry and Sunday school notes, at the same time maintaining close ties with former comrades after his election as adjutant of Hattiesburg's camp of United Confederate Veterans. He served in this capacity until January 11, 1916, when he suddenly was stricken with influenza. He succumbed to the illness six days later at the age of 76, and was buried next to his wife in Hattiesburg's Oaklawn Cemetery.

Eleven years earlier, Chambers presented a copy of his manuscript to Dr. Dunbar Rowland, director of the Mississippi Department of Archives and History in Jackson, where it remains today. In 1925, the department published the donated copy under the title "My Journal" in Volume V, Centenary Series of the *Publications of the Mississippi His-*

torical Society. In that format the journal ran continuously for 153 pages with no chapter breaks, and often with misused or unnecessary punctuation — perhaps the fault of the author or possibly the original typesetter.

In any case, Chambers' account has remained largely obscure but deserving of more widespread readership among students of the Confederate experience and the War Between the States. This new edition by Blue Acorn Press resurrects Chambers' story, supplementing the text with a Notes section designed to provide complementary details and background to events, places and persons mentioned by the author, and reprints a 1914 article he wrote for *Confederate Veteran* about the 46th Mississippi's fight at Fort Blakely in April 1865. Twenty chapter breaks and titles have been added, and punctuation/capitalization modified to correct mistakes or oddities for ease of reading. As well, 26 photographs, illustrations and maps, not part of the original 1925 publication, are included to enhance this thoughtful, informative and historically important journal of a Confederate soldier.

Richard A. Baumgartner
Huntington, West Virginia

ACKNOWLEDGMENTS

The editor is indebted to a number of people who greatly facilitated research leading to publication of *Blood & Sacrifice*. Among these, Sara Clark, archivist at the Mississippi Department of Archives and History, provided copies of William Pitt Chambers' military service records and muster rolls, census records, death certificate and cemetery records. Michael J. Winey and Randy Hackenburg, photo curators at the U.S. Army Military History Institute (USAMHI) in Carlisle, Pa., helped locate many of the photographs preserved in that institution's albums of the Military Order of the Loyal Legion of the United States, Massachusetts Commandery (Mass. MOLLUS). And Dr. Kenneth T. Slack, bibliographer of the Rosanna A. Blake Library of Confederate History at Marshall University in Huntington, W.Va., was indispensable for his cheerful assistance, suggestions and patience.

1862

CHAPTER 1

Severing the Ties of Home

March 25th. This morning I left the home of my parents to become a soldier in the army of the South. The thought that I may never return has been with me all day, depressing my spirits to some extent.

Late last afternoon, as the twilight came on, I walked to the spot where stood the house in which I was born and where my brother and I played in our happy childhood. That brother now sleeps in a newly made soldier's grave, the house is gone and the soil has been turned by the plow; but the same skies and the same stars were there that first caught my infant gaze.

I left Williamsburg, Miss., about one o'clock p.m. today, in company with about a dozen others belonging to the "Covington Rebels," a company of infantry commanded by T.D. Magee. We go as State troops, were mustered in for twelve months, and will rendezvous at Meridian, Miss. We will take the cars at Brandon.[1]

We have marched about seven miles and are encamped in the pine woods one mile east of Dry Creek. We are commanded by Sergeant Duckworth and some of the squad are drinking and quite noisy.

26th. After an early start this morning, we arrived at the "Widow Magee's" about ten o'clock a.m., where we met all the company who will go at this time. Another squad, under Lt. Graham, will start next Saturday.

A fine dinner was prepared at this place, to which we did ample justice, and after which we marched away, accompanied by our captain and 1st and 2nd lieutenants. Many sweet faces of old Covington's fair daughters bade us a tearful farewell. Will they ever see their loved ones again? We are encamped tonight near Old Hickory P.O. in Simpson County. There are sixty-five men in the company.

27th. We left camp in fine spirits this morning, and arrived at the hamlet of Fayette Hill at about ten o'clock a.m., where we halted about three hours. Four miles further we crossed Strong River, and are encamped in the pine woods at a place known as "Swor's Springs" in Rankin County and ten miles from Fayette Hill.

I am somewhat unwell and cannot sleep. I am thinking of those who are praying tonight for my salvation. May their prayers be answered, and may it be my lot to die the death of the righteous.

28th. Starting early this morning we marched about two miles and arrived at Cato, after crossing Campbell's Creek. This is a small village, owing its existence to, perhaps, some sulphur springs. There has been an academy of some local note here, but no school is open now.

Some six or eight miles further we crossed a range of high hills, locally known as the "Rocky Mountains." The rocks seem to be gray sandstone and the hills are covered with short-leafed pine, oak and hickory. After the hills, the soil changed and we crossed the "Limestone Belt." Several fine plantations and handsome residences, as well as large areas of uncultivated land lay along the route.

We arrived at Brandon at 3:30 p.m. While this little city can boast of some nice buildings, I must confess I was somewhat disappointed in the place. There is a good court house (of wood) with several brick buildings near it. Most of the trade seems to be supplying the volunteers with camp outfits. About 5 o'clock we started to the depot, one and a half miles distant. Some of the men were drunk, and we were inclined to fight as we left the city. At this place we met Lt. Joel R. Baugh of the "Covington Fencibles."

We are camped about 200 yards from the depot and at 9 o'clock p.m. Capt. Magee left for Jackson. We may not move until Monday.

29th. Remained in camp today, returning to the city in the afternoon to purchase some articles omitted yesterday. We formed a mess, consisting of Stephen Robertson, J.V. Reddock, J.R. Powers, Thos. J.H. and Lotan Sullivan, J.T. Howell and myself, reserving a place for Z.A. Easterling.

I spent an hour in the "City of the Dead" and copied

some of the inscriptions found there. There are some fine tombstones, evidencing taste, skill and affluence.

Learning that some sick soldiers were to come down on the train tonight, Stephen Robertson and I went to the depot after supper to await their coming. While we waited, we spoke much of the changes one year had wrought in our lives, and of the friends and relatives who had passed away in that time.

No soldiers came tonight. We will probably leave here in the morning.

30th. Today is Sunday, but it has been a busy day to us all. We boarded the train at 7:30 o'clock this morning. I was seated at a window and as the train was moving away, a beautiful young lady, standing near the track, handed me a small Confederate flag. To this was fastened a slip of paper, on which was penciled: "Compliments of Anna Collier to a Soldier. This represents Mississippi. Hurrah for the Confederacy and Davis! May an ever watchful eye be over thee! Anna Collier. Near Brandon."

This was my first ride on the train. I sat by the window and gazed outside the whole trip. We were frequently cheered by persons along the road, and when ladies cheered I waved my little flag.

The stations, as I remember them, are: Pelahatchie, in Rankin County; Morton and Forest in Scott County; Lake, Newton and Hickory in Newton County; Chunkey near the line, and Tunnel Hill in Lauderdale County. None of these were very populous towns or, seemingly, of much commercial importance. Just after passing the last-named place, we went through a tunnel several hundred feet in length. The sudden transition, from daylight to darkness, produced a novel sensation to me.

At 1:30 o'clock p.m. we arrived at our destination — Meridian, Miss. We found the platform and the vicinity thronged with soldiers, while on every side barrels of molasses and other government stores were piled in great confusion. At 3:30 we came to this spot, about 350 yards west of the depot and erected our tents.

I expected to find a "town" at Meridian, but was sadly

disappointed. In fact, there is not a fine building in the place, no stores and no streets. Our camp is on a gentle elevation at the edge of the woods. To the east and south is a dark blue range of hills with two or three higher peaks. Some day I hope to visit those hills and climb those peaks.

Thus ends my first Sunday in camp. It has been spiritually unimproved.

31st. Remained in camp, completing yesterday's work. In the afternoon I wrote letters, one to Miss Collier, one to father and one to W.C. Robertson of Company I, 7th Miss. Regt. at Corinth, Miss. Lts. Buchanan and Fairley left for Mobile this afternoon.

We find one regiment, the 36th, encamped near the junction of the railroads above town. A few hundred yards back of us are four or five other companies, and about 150 yards to the right are the "Rankin Farmers," W.K. Easterling, captain.

It is uncertain we can form a regiment.

April 1st. Marking and numbering our tents today exempted me from any other duty. For the first time "drilling" was attempted. Vegetation is much further advanced than when I left home. I love the trees and the flowers.

2nd. Today we had "squad drill" under the most experienced men in our company. At one o'clock p.m. Lt. Graham and 18 more men came in. There are about ten others yet to come in. Lts. Buchanan and Fairley returned from Mobile about 4:30 p.m., having nice uniforms and swords.

At 5 o'clock I went to see the "dress parade" of the 36th Regt. Saw some nice looking ladies who had gone there for the same purpose as myself.

Lotan Sullivan is sick and may have measles.

Tonight we sang some old songs that evoked memories more pregnant with pain than pleasure.

3rd. Somewhat rainy. We were mustered into the Confederate service at 1 o'clock p.m. today. The adjutant of the 36th Regt. drilled us some in the forenoon, and Sergeant Clarke of the "Rankin Farmers" drilled us in the afternoon.

I saw a coffin being taken to one of the companies in

our rear this afternoon. Some soldier died away from home and most likely without the gentle ministrations of a mother or a sister. News from home informs me that J.C. Reddock is dead. He leaves a helpless family.

It is raining tonight.

4th. The forenoon was "wash day." Tried squad drill again this afternoon. I guess we are an awkward lot, both men and officers.

It is supposed a battle is being fought near Corinth, Miss. The enemy is said to be within a few miles of that place and our forces have gone to meet him; hence, tomorrow's news is awaited with anxiety. [2]

Capt. Magee started to Jackson this evening. Wrote letters home, as Lotan Sullivan (whose disease turned out to be chicken-pox) will start home on furlough tomorrow in company with B.F. Speed.

5th. Drilled today. The news from Corinth is meagre and unsatisfactory. Rumors have been rife for two or three days respecting operations near New Orleans, but nothing seems to be known. [3]

Tonight J.V. Reddock and I stayed with a relative of his, Mr. Richard McLemore, who lives about two and a half miles east of town. Mr. McLemore is an elderly man in easy circumstances, and has a pleasant family. After lying down at night I contrasted my surroundings with that of thousands of others enlisted in the same cause as myself, who were deprived of both food and shelter and exposed to the perils of the battlefield.

I attended preaching at the Baptist Church today, but am ashamed to say that I slept during most of the service. Willis Williams conducted the exercises. He expects to go to the front in a few days. In last Sunday's entry I omitted to state that I heard S.R. Bankston, a Protestant Methodist, preach on "Prayer" at night. It is said that he is a candidate for chaplain in our regiment when we form one.

6th. Sunday again. Did not attend preaching because it was too late to do so when we returned from Mr. McLemore's. Have read some in "Nelson on Infidelity," a book borrowed from my host of last night, and some in the New

Testament. I went to the camp of the 36th Regt. to call on a Mr. Speed this afternoon. Found a young man of intelligence. Just before my arrival, a young man in one of the companies, who had left home in disobedience to his parents' commands, suddenly died.

Capt. Magee returned from Jackson this afternoon, having secured no equipment except canteens.

7th. Drilled today. We are improving a little. I talked with a staff officer, who says that 2,000 wounded soldiers are expected at Columbus, Miss., tomorrow and that 175 of the sick at Corinth were brought to Lauderdale Springs today. A terrible battle is evidently on hand and I impatiently long to be in it. Lt. Fairley and a Dr. McInnis, who is with our company, will start at midnight for the scene of action.[4]

8th. Intense excitement today. It was raining and we drilled none at all. Read some. Received a pleasant letter from Miss Collier, which I answered immediately.

Reports of a great battle are coming in. It was rumored that 2,000 Federal prisoners would pass here on the morning train. An excited crowd, including many ladies, thronged the depot long before six o'clock in the midst of a drenching rain. The prisoners did not come, however. Several persons from Simpson County, Miss., among them some of Capt. Magee's relatives, are in our camp tonight on their way to Corinth.

Going to the depot about ten o'clock I found a party of gentlemen from Laurence County on their way to Virginia. They said that a telegram had been received at Brookhaven, Miss., from Gordonsville, Va., stating that in an engagement near that place all but 9 of the "Laurence Rifles" (13th Miss. Regt.) were killed or wounded.[5]

As the twelve o'clock train came up the scene beggars description. There still were no prisoners, but many were aboard the train who claimed to have been in the fight. One old gentleman, from Scott County, had a coffin containing the body of his son, who fell in the fight of Sunday. Multitudinous and contradictory reports of the operations of the armies are heard. It is certain, however, that a desperate battle was fought Sunday and Monday, somewhere between

Corinth and the Tennessee River. Gen. Albert Sydney Johnston is killed, and rumor has it that the Federal General
Buell is also dead. Gen. Prentiss of the Federal army is a
prisoner.[6]

9th. A great change in the atmosphere, it now being quite
cool. We have drilled again today. We were also "inspected"
by the medical authorities, and four of the company were
discharged as unfit for military service. Seven others, however, came in.

10th. This afternoon for the first time we essayed "company drill." Several of the boys are sick.

About 200 prisoners, mostly from Ohio, came down on
the six o'clock train this morning. They were fine looking
men and seemed to be gentlemen. They were captured in
Sunday's fight. Nearly every train brings wounded men, one
of whom was Gen. Chas. Clarke of this state.[7]

It was thought an arrangement had been affected by
which the troops were to receive the telegraphic dispatches
every night, but it is probably an abortion, so far as the
enlisted men are concerned.

11th. Today was set apart as a day of washing and rest.
As I had already performed that necessary task I had leisure
to visit the high hills already spoken of. Crossing Sowashee
Creek, a beautiful stream of water, I soon reached the foot
of the hills. A Sabbath-like stillness pervaded the scene, and
the birds made the air vocal with their songs. Ascending the
rugged side, I at last stood on the summit of the loftiest
elevation in sight and the scene before me amply repaid me
for my trip. Some two miles north of me lay the town of
Meridian, its scattered cottages contrasting with the dark
green background, while the white tents of the soldiers
appeared like tombstones in some "City of the Dead."
Beyond, the pine forests seemed to grow in terraces till the
last one literally blended with the smiling valley of the
creek with its myriads of quivering leaves, and to my ears
was borne the sweet songs of the birds as they chanted their
vernal hymn of gladness.

We drilled some in the afternoon, but were stopped by
the rain. I learned that a schoolmate, Wm. M. Reddock, was

e engagement of "Shiloh" Sunday morning.
personal friends were hurt.

usy day. A heavy rain and wind storm last
ᴣ inconvenience, and I was thoroughly
ᴧ ᴜᴜᴇ trying to keep our tent from blowing down.

ᴧ large detachment — said to be 2,300 in number — of Federal prisoners passed here today from Jackson. Among them were over 100 commissioned officers, including Gen. Prentiss and staff and several regimental commanders. They were a fine looking body of men, Gen. Prentiss, of course, being the most observed. Aside from his rank he would have, perhaps, attracted notice in any crowd. The common soldiers did not impress me so favorably as those that passed a few days ago.

It is said the 36th Regt. has marching orders, and that we will at once form a battalion. Z.A. Easterling came in today, bringing me letters from home. Stephen Robertson started home on furlough.

13th. Lt. Fairley returned from Corinth last night and this a.m. handed me letters from W.C. Robertson. Attended preaching at the Presbyterian Church. I did not learn the preacher's name. It was a good sermon based on the 20th Psalm, and the central idea was that God would answer prayer offered in behalf of a nation as readily as he would those offered in behalf of individuals.

The 36th Regt. was armed this afternoon with old Western rifles made larger in the bore. It is now said we will organize next Tuesday. Lt. J.M. Sublett of the "Yazoo Pickets" is a candidate for major. Night comes and ends my third Sunday in camp.

14th. Two more companies arrived last night. They are the "Gaines Invincibles," Capt. Taylor, and the "Jeff Davis Rebels," Capt. Jones, and are from Wayne and Yazoo counties, respectively. They have seen some service, and have come from New Orleans to aid in the organization of the new battalion. The organization has been postponed till next Saturday, as by the arrival of these two companies we will be entitled to a lieutenant colonel.

Had an ambrotype likeness of myself made today by Mr.

Lipscomb.

Every train from the north carries wounded men. Gen. Gladden's corpse passed yesterday. Gen. Buell, reported killed at Shiloh, is probably not dead.[8] So many and such contradictory reports reach us concerning army operations that the reliability, and possibly the interest of these pages, will be enhanced by giving them no place at all.

15th. Drilled today, though several of the boys are ill and I am far from well. Our guns were appraised today, the Government intending to purchase them. I omitted to mention that before leaving home we armed ourselves with double-barreled shot guns.

The 36th Regt. left for Corinth at six o'clock p.m. today. One of the companies was from this county, and many of their families were present when they left. It is hard to sever the ties of home, but

> "Ne'er be it said, in future years,
> 'Mid bursting sighs and burning tears,"

that *one* son of the South faltered in the discharge of duty. Sang a few old songs tonight.

16th. Too unwell to drill. Had a letter from J.N. Easterling, Company I, 7th Miss. Regt. We were paid for our guns today. Have read a great deal and written some.

17th. Kept my bed. Reddock and Sullivan both sick, the former with the chicken-pox. I have headache, sore throat, high fever and a severe cough. Am taking medicine.

18th. Felt better today. No drilling as Friday is wash day. Great electioneering going on, Capt. Easterling and Maj. Balfour, an outsider, are aspirants for lieutenant colonel and Capt. Jones for major. Some excitement in camp over the reported passage of a "Conscript Law" by the Congress of the Confederate States.[9] Saw a negro whipped for the first time in my life this afternoon. It was a painful sight. The negro had run away.

19th. No drilling today. The election came off at 10 o'clock a.m. J.W. Balfour was elected lieutenant colonel, and J.W. Jones of the "Jeff Davis Rebels" was elected major. Two of the companies present refused to go into the election. The new lieutenant colonel celebrated his election by "treating" the men of each company to a gallon or two of whiskey; consequently, there is considerable noise in the air.

Sergeant Duckworth and Howell of our mess start home tonight. B.F. Speed returned, bringing letters from home.

20th. Unwell again. Weather inclement. Kept my bed. Another Sunday is gone.

21st. Felt somewhat better. Three cases of measles have developed in camp. The patients were removed to an unoccupied house a few hundred yards away.

22nd. Still unwell. Have finished reading "Nelson on Infidelity" and find it a powerful argument in favor of revelation. Robertson returned this afternoon, bringing letters from home.

23rd. I had a letter this morning from Samuel Welch, a relative and a member of Company F, 27th Miss. Regt. at Pensacola, Fla.

Formed a battalion encampment on the ground occupied by the "Rankin Farmers." The makeup of our battalion is as follows:

> **Company A**, "Gaines Invincibles" – Capt. Angus Taylor, from Wayne County.
> **Company B**, "Covington Rebels" – Capt. T.D. Magee, from Covington County.
> **Company E**, "Jeff Davis Rebels" – Capt. J.B. Hart, from Yazoo and Warren counties.
> **Company C**, "Yazoo Pickets" – Capt. J.C. Clarke, from Yazoo County.
> **Company D**, "Rankin Farmers" – Capt. W.K. Easterling, from Rankin County.

By this arrangement we occupy the extreme left, Company E being our nearest neighbors. Col. Balfour is absent, Major Jones is in command and Lt. Sublett of Company C is acting adjutant.

24th. Camp guards were mounted for the first time today. I am still unfit for duty. The company has drilled some.

25th. Saw several pieces of artillery and large quantities of ammunition on the trains today; also a horse belonging to

Gen. Beauregard. The significance of this was made plain when, later in the day, it was rumored that New Orleans had fallen into the enemy's hands.[10]

A serious accident occurred on the M. and O. R.R. eight miles below here this morning, by which six soldiers were killed and about 15 others seriously injured.[11]

Am still unwell. Heavy rain in the afternoon. L. Sullivan returned today.

26th. Severe headache all day. No drilling since morning. Several of the company will start home tonight, among them Reddock and Powers of our mess. T.J.H. Sullivan is quite sick.

Another company, the "Raleigh Rangers" of Smith County, Capt. McAlpine in command, arrived today. They came here from Grenada, Miss., and we are told that other companies are coming.

27th. Some better. Attended preaching at the Methodist church, but did not learn the preacher's name. After reading the 24th chapter of Matthew, he preached from 1 Peter, 4:17 and 18. "For the time is come that Judgment must begin at the house of God; and if it begin at us, what shall the end be of them that obey not the Gospel of God? And if the righteous scarcely be saved, where shall the ungodly and the sinner appear?" It was a forceful discourse that drew tears from many eyes. Two or three other cases of measles in our company, and other sickness beside.

May 10th. Continued ill health and want of leisure must be my excuse for changing the plan of keeping this journal. Nearly two weeks have elapsed since I wrote here last.

Tuesday [April] 29th, G.W. Michel, a former schoolmate of mine, came into our tent. He is a member of Company F, 27th Miss. Regt., and in company with Lt. Baugh was on his way to his command. He stayed all day, and at night he, Robertson, Easterling and I had a long conversation in an empty coach. I predicted that we four would never meet again. Was quite unwell next day, but thanks to the skill of Dr. John Milloy (a private in our company), I soon became better.

On the 3rd inst., a member of McAlpine's company died of mumps after a few hours' illness. Next day another soldier, a member of the 36th Regt. who was left here sick, died of typhoid fever.

Monday, May 5th, our company sustained its first loss by death. W.W. Lee died of inflammation of the lungs, a result of measles. Our battalion accorded a soldier's funeral to the man who died Sunday and also to young Lee. I was too unwell to attend the burials. May the turf rest lightly on their graves. F.E. Collins has pneumonia, and Easterling has had a light attack of measles.

Have received and written numerous letters, among those received was one from Miss Collier. We will probably reënlist and reorganize in a few days. It is thought we will likely be sent to Vicksburg, Miss.

Last Sunday I attended preaching, morning and afternoon. W.C. Emerson, a Presbyterian, was the preacher. The afternoon discourse was against swearing.

Several companies have come in, and one from Jasper County has Joe Anderson, a cousin of mine, as a private, and my old school teacher J.F. Thompson as orderly sergeant. A new regiment will probably be formed. As several recruits are coming to our company, several of whom will wish to mess with us, we have secured another tent, and Robertson, Reddock, Easterling and I will leave our old quarters at No. 6 and set up a new mess.

During my illness (I am now on duty) I read Col. Claiborne's Life of Gen. Sam. Dale, who was buried at Daleville in this (Lauderdale) County. I also read many entertaining and instructive articles in the *Harper's* magazines. Thus I end this entry and weeks may elapse before I write again.

CHAPTER 2

Post of Honor, Post of Danger

June 1st. Well, here's a gap of three weeks to fill up. On Tuesday [May] 13th, Easterling started home on sick furlough. On Wednesday 14th we enlisted "for the war" and reëlected our officers, with the exception of Archy Fairley, who was supplanted by M.M. Lott.

As Dr. Crawford and Warren Blackwell, members of our company were going home, I resolved to go with them. Our train was due at midnight but did not arrive till about 6:30 o'clock the next morning. Soon after starting, I learned that Claiborne E. and Drury A. Bynum, cousins of mine, were on the train. Seeking them out I found that they, too, were soldiers and on their way to their father's home in Clarke County from their camp at Columbus.

Between Meridian and Desoto are three intervening stations: Oaktibbe [Okatibbee] in Lauderdale County, and Enterprise and Quitman in Clarke County. Enterprise was once the head of navigation on the Chickasawha River and is a beautiful town. The river, which is spanned by a covered wooden bridge, divides the town into two parts, the newer or the railroad town being on the eastern side. Quitman is the county seat, but the town is not visible from the station. My cousins left the train at this place.

We arrived at Desoto about 10 o'clock a.m., and having nearly sixty miles to walk we did not tarry long. We passed several nice country places, among them the residences of Mr. Eckford and Dr. Dixon. We stopped overnight three miles east of Claiborne with Mr. Morrison, who treated us very kindly. Williamson and Faler of the "Fencibles" were there, conveying home for burial the body of Williamson's brother who had lost his life in a railroad collision.

Long before daylight we were again on our way. Near Claiborne we met George, Franklin and John Robertson on their way to our company. From them I received a package of letters, and I arrived at my father's home about sunset on Friday, May 16th. Early on the following Thursday, May 22nd, I started on my return to camp, accompanied by James Maxey, who was to take my horse back after one day's travel. Dining with my sister, Mrs. Knight, we spent the night with Mr. J.S. Gandy near Claiborne, where we were kindly cared for.

At an early hour next morning I was on the road, "afoot and alone," and indulging (as I have an uncanny habit of doing) in a series of gloomy fancies. I soon passed the spot where it is said the first white man reposes that was ever buried in Jasper County. His name was Terrell, and many of his descendants sleep around him. By 12:30 I had covered 20 miles and was at Desoto.

It was 10 p.m. before I could get a train. There was nothing at Desoto to look at, and as I had eaten nothing since morning and could get nothing there, I soon became miserably tired of the place. I gladly accepted the invitation of a fellow soldier, Alexander Reid by name, to share his evening meal. When the train did arrive it was so crowded that I could get standing room only, and on the platform at that. Arriving at Meridian, I was informed that the battalion (which had been officially designated as the 6th Miss. Battalion) had gone to Vicksburg, but that a few men and tents had been left, and also that the train for Jackson would leave in half an hour. I purchased a ticket for Jackson and then double-quicked to the camp. There I learned nothing more than that my mess were all gone. Returning to the train I secured a seat, a whole coach in fact, for I was the only occupant. Just before starting, D.L. Wilkinson of our company came in. He was starting home on sick furlough and he said that two others of the company were on the train.

From Wilkinson I learned that on Sunday, May 18th, orders were received for all the armed troops to repair to Vicksburg at once. Our company was unarmed, but influenced by Lt. Lott, about 40 of them borrowed guns from other companies and left the next morning. The rest left the next Friday. [1]

Directly after the train started it began to rain and I went to sleep. We arrived at Brandon about 6 o'clock a.m. and a run of twelve miles further brought us to Jackson, where we made a stop of 30 minutes. Purchasing a ticket to Vicksburg I resumed my seat, and learned that Capt. Magee was on the train. I found him and Dr. Milloy in another coach. We soon started and the captain pointed out the Capitol as we passed.

At Jackson the railroad crosses Pearl River. From there to Vicksburg, a distance of 45 miles, it runs through a fertile section. The stations are Clinton, Bolton's, Edwards and Bovina, the latter being on Big Black River. Of these stations Clinton is of the most importance, as Mississippi College and also a Female Institute are located there. After crossing Big Black the country became much broken, and by the time the train had reached the city it was very hilly indeed. I saw for the first time the "Mighty Father of Waters," now on a big overflow. The rain was pouring down in torrents and the vicinity of the depot was desperately muddy.

I found most of the tents, clothing, bedding and so forth belonging to the company was at the depot in charge of Jno. Carr. After repeated failures, a wagon was procured and our equipage placed in it. Two members of another company and myself were sent with it to conduct it to our encampment. As none of us had the remotest idea of its whereabouts, we had a disagreeable time finding it, but at about 5 o'clock p.m. we found it. Wet, tired, hungry and sleepy, I did not fall in love with the place. It is on a narrow steep ridge covered with a swamp growth, and not a level place on it big enough to erect a tent.

After a slight supper our mess put up a tent and we tried to sleep. Next morning I walked out on the ridge in front of our encampment. There rolled the mighty Mississippi River, its whole valley seemingly inundated; and there some two miles from where I stood, riding gracefully on the bosom of the turbid stream, were four or five vessels of the Northern fleet. I am so woefully ignorant of naval affairs that I shall call them all gun-boats, whether "ships of the line" or "revenue cutters" or whatever else they may happen to be. Their dark hulls seemed resting on the water, their sides bristled with cannon and over each one proudly waved the Stars and Stripes, once the "Flag of the Free," now, to us, the banner of subjugation. For miles I could see, in the world of waters before me, the current of the mighty stream winding like a huge serpent, and seemingly higher and of a bluer color than the flood through which it ran. I am told the flood is forty miles in width at this place. Of course, widespread ruin has been wrought by the overflow, but it is less unpleasant to contemplate than the desolation around us wrought by the hand of man in prosecution of war.

I was detailed immediately after breakfast to occupy a post in a chain of pickets from the edge of the water to the regimental headquarters. Three others of the company were on the same post. Read some in "Ovid's Art of Love," a piece of licentious trash I bought at Desoto, knowing nothing of its character. Thus I spent Sunday, being relieved about 10 o'clock next day.

On the same day (Monday, 26th) at about 5 o'clock p.m. I heard the first cannon fired, about 20 shots being thrown from the gun-boats into and toward the city. On the next day in the afternoon the firing was resumed, and about 125 shells were thrown into the city. About 10 o'clock p.m. 65 more were thrown in. I understand, however, that no person was injured and only a few houses sustained any damage. Surely the protecting hand of the Lord has been over the people.

On Wednesday, the 28th, the enemy began to bombard our camp, and one shell exploded in close proximity to our quarters. I confess I was uneasy and nervous; in fact, was badly demoralized as I beheld the great puffs of smoke from the guns, heard the horrid screaming of the shells, their deafening detonations when they exploded, and beheld the havoc they wrought. One feels utterly defenseless unless there is a chance to strike back, which in this case is out of the question.

On Thursday, 29th, our company was detailed as pickets and we took our station at the water's edge about 4 o'clock p.m. Next day the bombardment was resumed, most of the shells falling in and near the camp and that of the 26th and 27th Louisiana Regts., whose camp was a few hundred yards above us on the main ridge. At 4 p.m. as we were being relieved by Company C, a shell exploded at one of the posts covering three of the company and the relieving detail in dirt, but fortunately injuring no one.

Yesterday (Saturday, 31st) I procured a pass and in company with J.S. Robertson visited the city. Our battalion is camped about four and a half miles below the city on a tongue of land known as "Smede's Point" (I believe it belongs to Hon. Wm. C. Smedes). On one side is the river and on the other a bayou, now a great lake of backwater. On this point is stationed a detachment of Wither's Light Artillery, and I suppose we are here to support it. It is thought the enemy designs landing a force below the city, and for topographical reasons, he is most likely to attempt on this point. Hence we occupy the post of honor, as well as the post of danger. There are troops at intervals all the way to Warrenton, 12 miles below Vicksburg, and near the city are some heavy guns in position while new batteries are being erected.[2]

A good story is told at the expense of Gov. Pettus. Learning that the Federal gun-boats were coming up the river, he hurried to Vicksburg and as soon as they came to anchor, five miles below the city, he sent a flag of truce demanding the *unconditional surrender* of the fleet. It is said that he received a politely worded response of "If you want them, come and get them." They are still there. But at this rate it will take me a long time to get to the city with my pass.[3]

To me there was much that was novel and interesting in this visit. The city itself is a study. It is built on a series of steep hills, the western base of which is washed by the great river. These hills, called the "Walnut Hills," are naturally very fertile, and I think are the most northerly highlands that touch the river in Mississippi. Along these declivities the streets are located and houses are built, the sidewalks of one street often being on a level with or above the roofs of the houses on the next street below. The most beautiful yards

and gardens I had ever seen were here, generally arranged in
terraces with stone stairways between, and I also saw finer
buildings than I had ever seen before.

The court house, on a bold eminence, is said to be the
finest in the state. It has a much more imposing appearance
than the Capitol at Jackson. I found it and the surrounding
square occupied by soldiers, who told me I could not go
upstairs. The Methodist church is another handsome building, but I did not go in it. A few squares more brought us to
the Catholic church, a costly pile of brick built on an eminence commanding a view of the river. [4]

Nearly all of our company are here but many of them are
already sick. Our mess consists of the four already named,
and George, Franklin and John S. Robertson. A brigade,
called the "3d Miss.," has been formed here and is commanded by Brig. Gen. M.L. Smith. There are said to be
about 6,000 troops here now. It is Sunday, and the rain is
falling steadily; and thus ends this entry. [5]

CHAPTER 3

'Rusting Out' at Vicksburg

July 3d. More than a month has elapsed since my last entry, and I must make the record more brief.

Our company was on picket June 4th and captured two deserters who were trying to reach the Federal gun-boats. Easterling came in on the 5th. Did picket duty again on the 10th. We are still without guns (those we brought from home and purchased by the state being unserviceable by reason of suitable cartridges), and some other companies are in the same predicament. Partly from this cause and partly from the increasing sickness in camp, no more whole companies are sent on picket but regular details were made each day from all the companies. This obviates the wholesale borrowing of guns heretofore practiced. I was on picket on the 12th and spent most of the day in reading.

On the 13th I took the fever, many were sick in camp and several had already gone to the hospitals, while others were applying for discharges. Franklin Robertson was also quite sick at this time. Reddock returned about that time and we received news of the death of M.J. Mitchell of the "Fencibles."

On Sunday the 15th I was very sick, and on the same day Stephen Robertson was also prostrated with fever. On Wednesday 18th, G.W. Atwood of our company died in camp of measles. On the same day Franklin R. having been discharged, started home. By him I sent letters and a part of the $50 bounty money I had drawn the day before. Sunday 22d, Rube, a negro belonging in our company, died of pneumonia.

Rev. A.R. Graves, chaplain of the 3d Miss. Regiment, preached in our camp on the 14th, 17th and 22d. Camp was shelled again on Saturday 21st, as had frequently been the case before.

On Wednesday 25th, some movement on the enemy's

caused several regiments to be sent to Warrenton before daylight. Though I was unfit for duty, hardly able to walk in fact, I followed on behind and joined the command in time to assist in being shelled out of a strip of timber along the river front. Immediately after this performance the two gun-boats, which had left their anchorage the night before, returned to their former stations and the troops went back to camp.

As I was a licensed straggler that day I did not reach the camp till night, but spent the afternoon at a farmhouse some three miles away where a Mr. Carter and his lovely young wife treated me very handsomely. For two or three nights past our camp has been shelled, making sleep somewhat uncertain.

On Thursday 26th, the enemy began a regular bombardment of the city, and with short intermissions during the night it was kept up till Saturday night. Our loss was only a few men killed and wounded. One lady, a Mrs. Gamble, was killed by one of the shells. Having reported for duty, I was on guard Thursday 26th and Saturday 28th. Sunday 29th a volunteer scouting party left our battalion early in the morning. We spent the day in tramping over recently submerged land and, cautiously approaching the edge of the water, were admonished to *halt* by a few discharges of grape and canister from the nearest gun-boat. *We halted.* [1]

The bombardment of the city was resumed. We have news of a great Confederate victory in Virginia.[2] Monday 30th, I was detailed to take charge of some sick men and see them safely aboard the train. Owing to a blockade of trains consequent upon the arrival of a large body of troops, this duty required two days for its performance. Meanwhile, our pickets had been skirmishing with a detachment of the enemy that had effected a landing. Five of the latter were killed, while our loss was one man accidentally killed.

Found W.R. Reddock (J.V.'s father) in camp on my return. Was detailed for picket duty next day (yesterday) and am writing this just as the relief detail is approaching. There was a false alarm yesterday morning followed by more

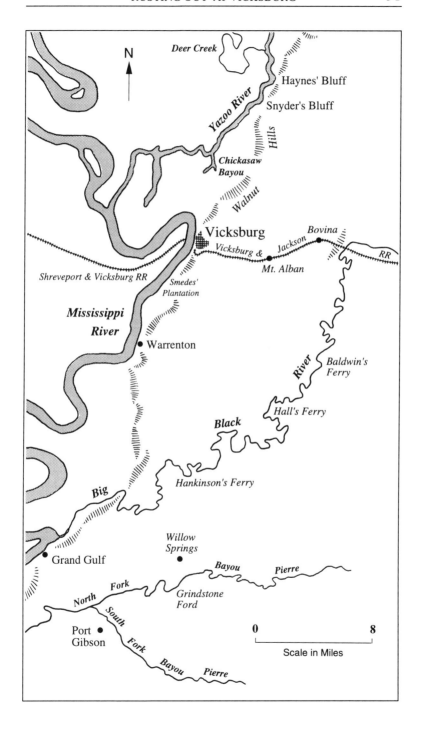

skirmishing in which one Federal was killed and three of our men are missing. Only two of our company were reported for duty this morning except those on the picket line. We were relieved tonight by a detail from the 28th Louisiana Regt. The bombardment of the city kept up every day.

July 4th. After a quiet forenoon the two Federal fleets (for several gun-boats have made their appearance and are at anchor a few miles above the city) fired about 150 shots in commemoration of Independence Day, I suppose. Alas! How it is perverted! I have just seen Gen. Smith (our brigadier general) and am not favorably impressed with his appearance. Maj. Gen. Earl Van Dorn arrived some days ago and assumed command. Gen. John C. Breckinridge is here with his brigade. Other troops, I know not who nor how many, are also here.[3]

Our battalion is having a hard time. We are at the same place and are positively suffering for drinking water, and our food is not suitable for sick men. We have done the police and picket duty of a full regiment since we came here. There are not enough well men in the battalion to man the picket line and relieve it. Four other companies were mustered into the battalion at Meridian, making nine in all. Of these, A, B, C, D and E came here at first. About May 31st Company F from Lauderdale County, Constantine Rea, captain, arrived in the vicinity of our camp, but has taken no part in the duties we have been performing. It is said that Company G from Smith County, Capt. Sheppard, is camped about a mile from us.

Our former adjutant, J.M. Sublett, was elected captain of Company C at Meridian, and G.W. Tiller of Company E served as adjutant for about a month, when Thos. E. Williams was appointed. Elisha Stuckey of our company died at Miss. Springs Hospital this morning. Easterling and John Robertson have the fever. George R. is very unwell.

About 9 o'clock p.m. there was a slight display of fire-works on board the Federal fleet.

July 6th. Sunday, but how unlike the Sundays at home! Am on picket again today, though quite unwell. Yesterday

[Mass. MOLLUS, USAMHI]

Gen. Martin Luther Smith

afternoon a few shots were fired from our batteries without eliciting any response. About 9:30 o'clock p.m., however, the enemy waked up and for about an hour he furiously bombarded our works, our guns, in turn remaining silent.

Another one of the company is dead. Addison Braddy died in camp this morning. I took him to the city hospital last Monday. His father came Friday to take him home, and they came to camp that the battalion surgeon might examine the young man. He rapidly grew worse and today he answered the roll call of eternity. I believe he leaves a family. His father intends taking the body home for burial. A few scattering shots today.

Easterling and John R. are better, but George R. is very sick with fever. Another one of our boys is going down into the dark valley. It is a wretched time. Fifty or sixty of our company are sick in hospitals. Some are sick at home. The rest are here and of the whole number less than 10 are reported for duty.

July 7th. Andrew J. Lott died in camp at 7 o'clock this morning. I am very, very sick. Stephen R. again has fever. They tell us we will certainly move tomorrow.

July 15th. Several things have occurred, but I cannot remember them distinctly for I have been sick unto death. On the morning of the 8th tents were struck for moving, and during the forenoon all that were considered fit for duty marched away. The rest of us lay there during the day around the unmoved baggage. About sunset the weakest ones were hauled away, and those that were able to walk at all were advised to make an early start next morning, afoot. Among this number were Stephen and I. Long before we reached our destination, which was two miles beyond the city, I became deathly sick, then delirious, and knew nothing of our arrival in camp, nor of what transpired during the next two or three days.

F.D. Turnage died in camp on Thursday 12th, and Capt. Magee has gone home sick. They moved us again on the 14th to this place, which is in the woods near a big spring called, I think, "The Four Mile Spring." Stephen is dangerously sick and I can barely walk. At six o'clock this morning Benj. Rodgers died at the place we left yesterday. Those who saw him die say he expressed a willingness to go, and died rejoicing in hope of Christ. This afternoon we learn that Dr. John Milloy, who started home with Capt. Magee, died at Brandon on the way. Only three of our company are at the last encampment now; they will be brought here

[Mass. MOLLUS, USAMHI]

Heavy Confederate guns overlooking the Mississippi River just south of Vicksburg.

as soon as they are able to be moved. Since sunrise the cannonade has been incessant.

July 22d. The cannonading last Tuesday 15th was occasioned by the passage of the Confederate ram *Arkansas* through the Federal fleet above the city. J.M. Speed and R.C. Hathorn, both of our community, reached camp on the 16th to see their sons who were both away at the hospital. They bring discouraging reports of the crops.[4]

On the 19th Stephen R. and Reddock, with several others, started to the hospital. In the afternoon of the same day my father came into camp with Reddock's father. Father had heard that I was dead. When I met him I was so weak that I wept. I had utterly despaired of ever seeing any of the home folks again, and even now I feel that these hills will be my burying place. We have learned that J.T. Howell is also dead, but that he breathed his last at home and his wife and babe received his dying caresses. I went with father to the city on the 20th, and then to the depot as he intended starting home. After bidding him farewell I returned to camp completely exhausted and utterly despondent. Sick yesterday and all the others of the mess are down. Only three in the company are reported for duty, and they are specially detailed to make beef soup for the rest of us. The stuff they call beef soup is only a nasty, sticky mush, and I hope I'll never see any more like it.

Some shells are thrown into the city every day, but this morning about daylight a furious firing began, which lasted about two hours. I have just learned that one of the Federal mortar boats ran our batteries and that another attempted it but had to turn back.

July 23d. Our battalion attempted some picket duty again today. A light rain this morning. At this time, sunset, there is heavy cannonading below the city. Weather warm. I think we sick men are slowly improving.

August 2d. The two fleets steamed up and down the river on the afternoon of the 24th and the morning of the 25th, and have not shown themselves since. It is probable no more attempts will be made to take this place till late autumn or winter. There are constant rumors of our removal to some other point, but nothing definite is known.

Troops are being concentrated at Tangipahoa, La., but for what purpose I do not know. I saw the 4th Louisiana Regt. last Monday and was well pleased with the men and especially with Col. H.W. Allen. A member of his regiment informed me that he left home as a private; eighteen months afterward he is acting brigadier general.[5]

Easterling left for Jackson Hospital last Monday. There is still a great deal of sickness, and our doctors have no medicines a part of the time. We skin willow and dogwood trees, boil the bark and drink the tea. I am having fever again every day.

There are rumors of a disorganization of the battalion based on these grounds: At the organization in April last, only five companies participated and we are now told that we were not entitled to a lieutenant colonel. On the 14th of May a new enlistment of the companies took place, also a new reorganization. No new election for field officers was held. In a few days we were ordered here, Balfour and Jones being recognized as lieutenant colonel and major, respectively. After some weeks Capt. Easterling of Company D addressed a communication to Gen. M.L. Smith setting forth the foregoing facts. For this he was, on the 28th of June, placed under arrest and is now being tried by a Court-Martial. He is charged with using disrespectful language toward a superior officer. It is said by some that Balfour may, in turn, be called to account. Dissatisfaction also exists in regard to non-payment of the men.

Added to the five companies originally composing the battalion are Company F, Capt. Con. Rea, Lauderdale County; Company G, Capt. Sheppard of Smith County; Company H, Capt. McAlpine of Smith County; and Company I, Capt. Pringle of Newton County. These last companies were quite full and some of them have but recently arrived; but the men are said to be falling sick very fast. D.R. McLane died at Clinton on the 26th ult.

August 11th. We have slightly moved our encampment, though we still use water from the same spring.

We are still in the dark in regard to the finding of the Court-Martial in Capt. Easterling's case. Balfour is gone and rumor now has it that he has been cashiered. Adjutant Williams is also away and First Sergeant Cole of Company F is acting in his place. Mr. James Pickering was in camp a few days since. His report, confirmed by late letters from home, considerably brightens the crop outlook. Capt. Magee returned on the 6th after an absence of several weeks. Most of the members of the company are still on the sick list. I am again having fever. George R. is still quite unwell, and John R. is in a deplorable condition, having many symptoms of dropsy. Numerous and conflicting reports have reached us for two or three days regarding the loss of the ram *Arkansas* and the reported capture of Baton Rouge, La.[6]

Sunday, August 17th. Attended preaching today. Mr. Weatherford from Lauderdale County preached. Irving Dykes died at Clinton on the 12th. Some of the men have returned from the various hospitals, though none of them seemed fully recovered.

August 31st. Sunday again. About the time of my last entry the Federal fleet again appeared in the river above the city, creating considerable commotion. The capture of our transport *Playfair* [*Fair Play*] with 2,000 stand of arms increased the consequent excitement. The ostensible object, however, is the exchange of prisoners, but our leaders have wisely thought best to be on the alert. Hence, on the 19th, we received orders to be ready to march at a moment's warning as the enemy were landing troops at Haynes' Bluff on the Yazoo River. After several hours of wearing suspense, which was occasionally aggravated by the reception of new orders setting a new hour for starting, or requiring us to be ready to move at the tap of the drum, the excitement gradually subsided and we again settled down to the "rusting out" process of inaction.[7]

Lt. Lott arrived on the 20th having been absent since June 15th. Blackwell was with him. I took John R. to the city hospital on the 23d. He is suffering a great deal. On my return I found Easterling in camp. He is still unwell. On the 25th, Richard Robertson (John R.'s father) arrived in camp accompanied by a Mr. Nichols, who brought us Leaf River boys a wagon load of provisions from our homes. I went with the old man to the hospital, where I left him.

I was reported for duty on the 28th for the first time since July 7th. George R. is also considerably improved, though Easterling is having fever again. We greatly enjoyed those home-raised provisions. We drew muskets on the 29th, having received knapsacks and haversacks a few days previously. Ex-Lt. Fairley paid us a visit yesterday. I was truly glad to greet him.

Two more of Company B have died since my last entry. Winston Morris died at home on the 23d inst., and J.R. McPhail at Clinton on the 25th. Two other deaths have not been noted in these pages. Marion Cook died at Miss. Springs on the 1st of August, and W.M. Pace at Monticello on the 7th. Thus we have lost by death 14 in all in a little over two months. Seventeen in all have died, including two who never left their homes. Almost as many have been discharged and our roll now carries 95 names exclusive of commissioned officers.

Capt. Easterling was released from arrest and his sword returned yesterday. Lt. Col. Balfour is still absent, leaving Major Jones in command.

Sept. 7th. On Friday the 5th inst., the Federal gun-boat *Essex* came in sight of the city. We fired two guns and she fired one.[8]

Stephen Robertson returned from the hospital Friday and Reddock on Saturday. Neither are well. George R. is on duty again and Easterling is improving. Orders have been received for a new election of field officers tomorrow. Great electioneering is going on.

Sept. 8th. After 24 hours of excitement, chagrin and disappointment to many of us, I will make a brief entry. All the forenoon was spent in the midst of the excitement that usually attends an election in which everyone feels a personal interest. Party lines were sharply drawn, two tickets were in the field and the adherents of each were manfully working for success. By 10 o'clock a.m. everything was in readiness for an election, every man having his ticket already written. Instead of ordering the election to proceed, Major Jones positively forbade it and threatened to arrest every company commander who should hold one or allow it to be held. Well, we are pretty mad, but there seems to be no help for it.

October 12th. A month has passed, and on one pretext or another the reorganization of our battalion is seemingly as far off as ever. We are now told that as soon as a special order is received from the War Department at Richmond directing it, an election will be held. Col. Balfour is still absent. It is said he is in Richmond and is endeavoring to have the command officially designated "Balfour's Battalion."

A few things occurring since my last entry demand a brief notice. We supposed that we had marching orders on Sept. 10th, but when the order was read on dress parade it was simply an assurance that we would receive such orders as soon as the brigade reported 2,000 effective men. Following the hopes aroused by this order, when *ten less* of effective men were reported by the adjutant next morning, we did not feel very sanguine of an early departure.

On Sunday, Sept. 15th, I went on the picket line for the first time since July. I was posted on the bank of the river about five miles above the city of Vicksburg, of which I had an unobstructed view. The mighty river with its long sweep, the dense forests, the distant village on the Louisiana side, and the "Hill City" combined to make a rather interesting view to which, when night came on, the stars and then a slightly waning moon added new and softened charms.

23rd. I was again on picket and got a thorough wetting in the rain. I was already unwell, but on my return to camp I found that Dr. McCormick (our regimental surgeon) had George R. apply for a discharge. I drew up all the necessary papers and had them signed by the company and battalion officers, and in doing so got wet again. I was very sick for a few days when my ailment developed into a pronounced case of jaundice.

About this time we drew four months' wages and twenty-five dollars, commutation money, making the exact amount received by each private $71.76. Those whose enlistment dated from May 3d received $41.56 each. We are beginning to need our winter clothing. Our company shipped some to Brandon last summer, and I have just written to know if it is still there.

November 24th. Another gap of more than a month. Sick and tired, I'll try to make a short entry.

Tuesday, October 14th, Dr. Crawford of our company was detailed to go home and secure winter clothing for our men. I went with him as far as Brandon. The officials who examined the passengers to intercept soldiers trying to leave the army were not very strict, I suppose, since by a madeup story I passed myself as a citizen returning home from a visit to relatives in camp. Arriving in Brandon I went to the "Shelton House" kept by Mr. Travers, where I remained till Thursday, 16th. I found our clothing all right. On Wednesday afternoon there was a militia drill in the city. In

[Mass. MOLLUS, USAMHI]

**Looking east across the Mississippi River at Vicksburg.
At center is the Warren County Courthouse.**

company with Lt. Clarke of Company D I returned to camp
on Thursday. On the train was the same officer who had
questioned me as I went out Tuesday. I told him the whole
story, which he evidently enjoyed, though I could see he
was a little vexed at the way he had been imposed on. The
interview ended by his asking me if there was anyone on the
train who could vouch for me. I referred him to Lt. Clarke.

About the 23d, Reddock started home on sick furlough.
He had been *very* sick, the doctor even expressing the opinion that he would die. I had written to his father. Stephen R.
is quite unwell.

On Monday, Oct. 17th, I was detailed to go to the city as
one of the patrol or police guard. The detail consisted of
about one hundred men from the brigade, of whom perhaps
75 were French Creoles but few of whom could speak or
understand a word of English. The army regulations were
read every morning in both French and English so far as
they related to our present duty. Our rations were scant and

we had to hire them cooked. Various duties fell to my lot while on this detail. Perhaps the most disagreeable was guarding a boat laden with coal at the water's edge on cold, dark, windy nights. Two others were with me, but neither of them could speak a word of English or understand a word I said, neither could I understand a word they said. The officer who posted us there probably informed my comrades for the night what they were required to do, but I was utterly in the dark as to my duty. I was glad when daylight came.

Another memorable duty was being placed as a "look out" just under the great bell of the city clock in the Court House tower. It was perhaps a hundred feet from the ground to this bell, and we had often counted its strokes at a distance of four or five miles. Sitting within a few feet of it and watching the ponderous hammer automatically striking the brazen sides, the din was almost overpowering. While occupying the position one day, I saw a herd of Texas cattle, five hundred in number, swim across the river. They were driven in apparently just opposite the city, but they were borne downward by the current until the landing on the eastward side was made about two miles below the city.

I returned to camp Friday, Nov. 7th. During my absence another company had been mustered into our battalion. It is the "Kemper Guards" from Kemper County, under the command of Capt. D.C. Durham, and will be known as Company K. These men are not raw recruits. They went out in July 1861, became incorporated in the 59th Virginia Regt., Wise's Legion, were captured at Roanoke Island in February last and paroled, were exchanged in September and ordered to join a Mississippi battalion.[9]

Crawford returned on Saturday, Nov. 8th. Through him we learn of the death of John and James Welch, and G.W. and Thos. J. Mitchell, all of the "Fencibles." In the death of the two last named young men, Cader and Sallie Mitchell have lost, inside of twelve months, 6 sons, 1 daughter and 1 grandchild. But the saddest message of all to us was the announcement that Stephen R.'s little boy was dead. May God comfort the hearts of the bereaved parents.

Saturday 8th, I went for the first time to brigade inspection. About 1,000 or 1,200 men out of the four Louisiana Regts. and our battalion were present. The next Saturday, November 15th, we were inspected again. This time about 2,000 men were in ranks and executed several maneuvers by order of Gen. M.L. Smith. I was sick again on Sunday 16th and am not fully recovered yet. Stephen R. is on duty. George R. has chills and fever. Easterling has been appointed company nurse and does no other duty now.

On Thursday 20th, a flutter of excitement was caused by the announcement that a man named Gerault had been assigned to the command of this battalion, and a few minutes later the officer himself came into camp. Next morning the drums beat as usual for regimental drill, but when line was formed an order was read to the effect that J.F. Gerault had been assigned to the command of the 6th Miss. Battalion, and that the company commanders should meet him at 10 o'clock a.m. with lists of all arms, equipments, etc., furnished by the Government. The officers met and drew up a protest against his assuming command to be handed to him as soon as he arrived. He failed to make his appearance and on Sunday 23d (yesterday) an order was read stating that he had been suspended.[10] Thus the matter stands at present. If Col. Gerault had not hailed from Louisiana, probably his appointment would have been less distasteful; but just now our officers entertain a sort of prejudice against those of the Louisiana Regts. Whether well founded or not, this prejudice is very real. There is also a matter of controversy in our battalion. Capts. Rea and Magee each claim to be a senior captain, the former having been commissioned as a staff officer.

A great deal of card playing is now going on in camp, the officers indulging in the greatest extent. So prone are we to follow the example of others that our mess secured a broken deck of cards and played till we became so ashamed of ourselves that we threw the old cards away.

Elder W.W. Keep, a Baptist preacher, has been appointed chaplain of our battalion. He is a good speaker and seems to be very zealous. He distributes tracts once a week, and I am always glad to see him coming.

Lt. Buchanan returned to camp a few days ago, having been home for two or three weeks. Lts. Lott and Graham are both absent and have been for months.

We are required to move inside the line of fortifications, and yesterday Lt. Buchanan was sent with a party of men to prepare the ground. Balfour has not yet returned. Harvey Freeman died at Hazelhurst August 29th. We have about 65 men in camp now, and the general health is decidedly improving. Duckworth has resumed the duties of orderly sergeant.

CHAPTER 4

Chickasaw Bayou

December 4th. We are in our new quarters in the mud and the weather is very cold. John S. Robertson died on the 23d of November. The doctor said he had pneumonia, and he and Howell were both messmates of mine. We moved to this place (which is not far from where we encamped last July) on the 27th and 28th of November. It is not a desirable place for a camp, both wood and water being scarce.

We have, I suppose, been placed with the 26th, 27th and 31st Louisiana Regts. in a new brigade. On Saturday the 29th we were minutely inspected by our new Brig. Gen. S.D. Lee. Gen. Smith has been promoted to major general. Our new general made a very favorable impression on the men.[1]

Orders from brigade headquarters read Saturday afternoon directed us to hold an election on Monday, Dec. 1st, for lieutenant colonel and major. Only 9 companies are included in the order. 1st Lt. Davenport of Company K, 26th Louisiana Regt., was designated to superintend the election. Electioneering began again. Sunday Nov. 30th I spent several hours in the city cemetery and saw many things that were of interest to me.

On Monday, Dec. 1st, we held the election about which we had talked so long and thought so much, and over which some had fretted themselves somewhat. Capt. W.K. Easterling of Company D was elected lieutenant colonel and Lt. W.H. Clarke of the same company was elected major. The vote was practically unanimous, Companies C and E declining to take any part in it.

Next morning a detail of 200 men was called for from the battalion. It took nearly every effective man but they went off like it was a frolic. They soon came back. That afternoon John W. Jones, our former major, quietly took his departure. He was a good man.

On dress parade an order was read designating our command as the "46th Miss. Regt."

(Author's note — For some months this will be more of a narrative than a journal).

Lt. Buchanan, having been temporarily assigned to duty as adjutant, took charge of the office on [Dec.] 12th. About the same time Companies C and E were detached and sent to a point a few miles north of the city on Chickasaw Bayou. From certain movements of the enemy it was thought he contemplated landing a force in that vicinity. A few days subsequently Company F was also detached and sent to join C and E.

An old neighbor, Richard Robertson, arrived in camp on the 13th. He came after receiving a notice from me that his son was dead. May God comfort those old men whose sons precede them to the grave.

Lt. Col. Easterling arrived in camp on the 14th, though he is unfit for duty. We constructed chimneys to our tents, which did good service in the cold wet weather that followed. For several days thereafter we essayed battalion drill under Maj. Clarke. We were also required to keep three days' rations prepared and to hold ourselves in readiness to march at a moment's warning.

December 19th another one of our company, John Braddy, died at Crystal Springs, Miss., after an illness of many months.

On Saturday Dec. 20th I was detailed to write for the adjutant, which relieved me of any other duty. On the same day we were notified that President Davis, who was in the city, would review us on the morrow.

At an early hour next morning the men were in line with clean clothes on and everything was in readiness for the review. It was till late in the afternoon, however, that the reviewing party arrived. The men had been in line six or seven hours without food, and did not feel as enthusiastic as they did in the early morning. Not being in the ranks myself I failed to get as good a view of Mr. Davis as I desired. He is a spare made man, and I should say a rather ugly one. His complexion is sallow and his face is on the "hatchet" order. He was attired in plain citizen's dress, and I should think there was little in his appearance to mark what he really is — one of the most noted men now living — and, as I think, posterity will regard as one of the greatest.[2]

Gen. Joseph E. Johnston and staff were also present. "Old Joe" looked the most perfect specimen of a soldier I ever saw. Rough and ready in exterior he impresses one at a glance that he is no ordinary man. He is past the meridian of life, but looks hale and hearty and bids fair to live many years longer. Gens. Smith and Lee with their respective staffs were also present.[3]

It was known that the Federals were probably landing troops on the Yazoo River, and Gen. Lee had promised Major Clarke that our Regt. should first engage them. Hence we were not surprised when at 3 o'clock a.m. on the 25th we were aroused by the "long roll" and ordered to proceed *at once* to man the fortifications above the city.[4]

One fact now transpired that did not speak well for the efficiency of our officers. There were not enough guns by fully one-third to arm the effectives in the regiment, and less than 30 rounds of ammunition for what guns there were. The ordnance was absent. I was called out of the ranks, required to make out a requisition for guns and ammunition, and proceed at once to the city to have it filled. I did so but the officials, through whose hands the paper had to go, were so tardy that it was 11 o'clock a.m. before I could return to camp. The Regt. had just come in without the loss of a man. In the afternoon we drew four months' wages, being the second payment since we entered the service. Thus ended our first Christmas in camp.

Our detached companies, however, were not faring so well. The enemy began to land troops on the eastern bank, and our companies engaged his pickets on the 25th. This was kept up through the 26th with two or three slight casualties on our side. On the same day, I made another requisition for ordnance stores, and while in the city I had a fair view of the Federal fleet as it was shelling the woods to

[Mass. MOLLUS, USAMHI]

Chickasaw Bayou, photographed in February 1864.

the north of us. At 3 o'clock a.m. Saturday 27th, we were ordered to proceed at once to the scene of action. It was bitterly cold, dark and raining, yet the men fell into line with
alacrity. To my utter disgust I was again called out of line
and ordered by Col. Easterling to remain in camp. The regiment filed off and I, feeling disgraced, waited for daylight.

A little after sunrise the faint rattle of distant musketry
was borne to our ears with the occasional boom of a cannon.
This continued all day, and I think these were the most rest-
less hours I ever experienced. Supposing my company to be
engaged, I could not reconcile myself to being absent from
it, though I was acting in obedience to positive orders. Feeling sure that some were being killed or wounded, and not
knowing who, mingled with the excitement one naturally
feels on hearing the din of battle, added to the feeling already mentioned and rendered my situation almost unen-
durable.

In the afternoon rumors from the field began to come in,

but they were extravagant and conflicting. Seemingly one of the most reliable (for it was from a man who said he was just out of the fight) was that "the 46th Regt. was cut all to pieces and *every one of Capt. Magee's company except seven* was killed."

The next day the suspense was equally great. It was Sunday but the deep thunder of the artillery and the incessant rattle of musketry indicated that the contest was assuming greater proportions, and was getting hotter every hour. In the evening, Ordnance Sergt. McLaurin arrived from home, so I lost no time in turning the ordnance business over to him and prepared to go to the front. About this time, however, Dr. McCormick came in and stated that at the time he left the field, Company B had not fired a gun, and that only one man in the regiment had been seriously hurt at all. This assurance, of course, relieved my mind to a considerable extent; but I had also received letters from home which brought one piece of information that made it important that I should see *one* of the company as soon as possible. George R.'s wife had borne him a son. By dawn Monday 29th, I was on my way to the firing line, "armed and equipped" with a haversack of bread and beef, and that letter to George.

Our brigade occupied the extreme right, and as the enemy held a portion (or at least commanded it) of the intervening road I was compelled to retrace a part of my steps and proceed by another route. The firing was hotter than ever that morning, and I learned before reaching my command that Adjt. Gen. Paul Hamilton had been killed.[5] I found our regiment posted on Blake's Levee and to the right of the bayou which has given a name to the battle. In a few minutes after I had reached my command the main assault on our position was made. It was on our left and almost entirely hidden by a fringe of willows.

Heavy, lead colored clouds covered the sky. The deep toned thunder of the artillery was almost drowned in the ominous roar of musketry, while enveloping the whole hung thick folds of smoke. But above the boom of cannon and bursting shell, above the din of small arms piercing the sky with its clear, shrill alto, came shout upon shout from the battling boats. How the nerves quivered and the heart wildly beat to join the fray! A staff officer galloped up and ordered Lt. Col. Easterling to form in line in the open field behind us. As we did so emerging from a fringe of timber, our own artillery at the base of the hills in our rear was turned upon us, but fortunately the mistake was rectified before any harm was done. Never have I longed more keenly in my life to hear an order than I then was to hear, "Forward, double-quick!" Gradually, as the assaulting columns were beaten back, the firing abated, while the shouts of victory along our lines swelled louder and louder. Resuming our position on the Levee (it was a mistaken order that caused us to leave it), we watched and waited.

The particulars of the battle were learned by degrees. I did nothing and saw nothing worthy of special note. A fringe of timber prevented our seeing the assault except through one small opening, but a dense pall of smoke hid everything; and after the smoke had lifted or been beaten down by the rain, the ground was too level to allow us to see any portion of the field whereon the dead lay. Those who saw the field said that our loss was very heavy, while that of the enemy was much greater. The loss of our popular Adjt. Gen. cast a gloom over the whole brigade.[6]

The clouds grew denser and soon the rain began to fall. An artillery duel was kept up till night with occasional volleys of small arms. Tuesday 30th and the night following the rain was almost incessant, rendering our position very unpleasant as the air was very cold and we were not allowed to kindle any fires. Very little firing that day.

Wednesday 31st, a flag of truce was sent in by the enemy asking permission to bury his dead. That night he began to reëmbark his forces. I was in front of our line on picket that night, and I came near freezing it seemed. It was New Year's eve, and we thought of home and its dear associations as we stood silent in the icy darkness.

1863

CHAPTER 5

A Cheerless Waste of Waters

Thursday and Friday, January 1st and 2d, slight skirmishing was kept up. On the latter date I was one of a reconnoitering party that approached near enough to the gun-boats to draw their fire. The timber around us was torn up considerably, but none of our party were hurt. That afternoon we were relieved (the 35th Miss. taking our place) and were ordered to return to our camp. It was raining again and the road was desperately muddy. The whole way was lined with newly arrived soldiers, who amused themselves near the *real* slippery places by calling to some imaginary person *up a tree* and seeing some fellow lose his footing as he looked upward while walking along. I did not get caught that way but I did slide down a steep hill in a sitting posture, with my haversack of cooked food and several shovels full of slush "boiling over" between my thighs. We reached camp about 7:30 o'clock p.m. The next day, Saturday 3d, the Federal fleet steamed up the river and the attempt to turn our right flank was abandoned.

Nothing of special importance occurred till Thursday, January 15th, at which time the Federal fleet again appeared in the river above the city, and there was no time after that the boats were all out of sight. From that time onward we were required to repair to the city at 2 o'clock every third or fourth morning. This was soon changed to every alternate morning. The object, we were told, was to guard against any surprise the enemy might attempt. The men were becoming dissatisfied, and some were threatening to desert. This threat was carried into execution on the night of the 24th by H. Hester, W.P. Dyes and W.R. Speed.

On the 28th, Capt. Magee started home on detail of one month to bring in deserters, stragglers and recruits. He returned on March 3d bringing with him many who had deserted from his and other companies.

Prior to Capt. Magee's departure it had become pretty well understood that a man named Sears had been appointed colonel of this regiment. On the 30th of January Col. C.W. Sears arrived in camp and assumed command on the 31st. As we learned him better he became a trusted and beloved officer. [1]

On the morning of Feb. 2d the Federal ram *Queen of the West* ran by our batteries, sustaining but slight damage in doing so. History has recorded her capture on Red River, her subsequent exploits and her final destruction. [2]

Stephen R.'s wife came into camp on the 12th and left on the 15th. She was accompanied by Messrs. Mitchell and Speed.

On the night of the 14th, the *Indianola* also ran by our batteries. She was sunk by the *Webb* and the *Queen of the West* on February 24th in shallow water and blown up on the 25th. [3]

On the 17th of February we were required to relieve the 17th Louisiana Regt. which was occupying some old tents near a steep ridge known as the "Backbone." Our duty consisted of manning some rifle pits contiguous to the river at 3 o'clock every morning and remaining in position till sunrise. Each regiment remains there one week, and hence we returned to the camp on the 24th.

Immediately after Col. Sears' arrival, Lt. Buchanan declined to serve as adjutant any longer. Lt. Stanford of Company C assumed the duties of that position until the 21st of February when ex-Lt. J.C. Porter was appointed adjutant and at once entered his duties. About this time Cols. W.E. Baldwin and W.S. Featherston were promoted to brigadier general and we were placed under the former. Our brigade at this time consisted of the 4th and 46th Miss., the 17th and 31st Louisiana Regts., Wofford's and Bowman's artillery, and Smith's and Haynes' cavalry. [4]

On the 19th of February the Federal fleet began to throw shells into the city again. On the second of March we again went to the "Backbone," returning on the 9th. Capt. Magee came in on the 3d as already noted.

On the 6th day of March we witnessed a military exe-

[Mass. MOLLUS, USAMHI]

Gen. William E. Baldwin

cution. The victim was a youth, almost a boy, who had deserted from a Tennessee Regt. and enlisted in the Federal
Army. He was captured at Chickasaw Bayou and tried by a
Court-Martial. He met his fate with fortitude. It was a solemn and impressive scene.[5]

Lt. James A. Graham having resigned on the 2d, we held

an election to fill the vacancy on the 13th of March. On the second ballot T.G. Crawford was elected.

Another member of Company B has answered the roll call of eternity. Evan G. Freeman, one of our most reliable men, died at the city hospital on the 19th after a long illness.

On the 23d we again went to the rifle pits. Just at daybreak on the 25th we heard the pickets firing up the river and we knew that some kind of craft was approaching. Soon they came in sight, two gun-boats, one some distance in advance of the other. Our batteries opened finely, the hills fairly trembling under the terrific roar. On sped the gallant barks, but the terrible storm of iron that was hurled against them proved too galling. One careened and then went under in front of the city. As she went down a mighty shout went up from the thousands of soldiers who were looking on. The other boat floated past our batteries, though in an apparently disabled condition.[6]

It was just a year that morning since we left home, and as I was reflecting on the changes twelve months had wrought we received orders to march at 3 o'clock p.m. For some time the enemy had been operating in the vicinity of Yazoo Pass, Cold Water and Deer Creek, and we naturally concluded that we would go to one of these places. We marched away at the designated time and bivouacked for the night about two miles above Chickasaw Bayou.[7] Started again at 3 o'clock a.m. and reached Haynes' Landing on the Yazoo River by daylight. Understanding that fighting was going on at Greenville, we felt sure that that was our destination. Evidently we would soon go somewhere, for the mail packet *Dew Drop* steamed up and we went on board and were under way by 10 o'clock a.m., leaving a wake of foam behind. Before I had got into position to my liking we left the main channel of the Yazoo River and proceeded up Deer Creek which, at this time, was running upstream. Its channel was crooked and narrow, and we frequently collided with overhanging trees. After a great deal of bumping and thumping to the imminent danger of our smoke stacks, scape pipes and jack-staff of the steamer, as well as the hats of those of us who were on the hurricane deck, we debarked

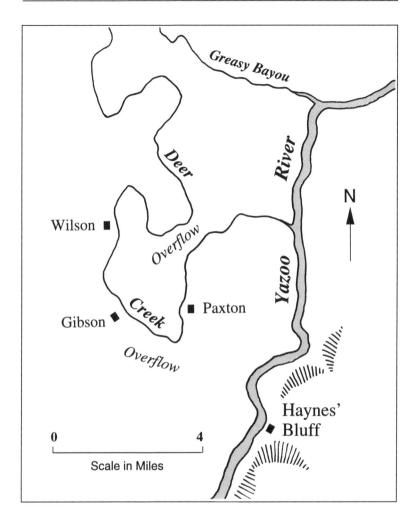

at the plantation of Mr. Paxton, about six miles above the mouth of Deer Creek. The shore on either side from Haynes' to this place was entirely submerged, though the marks on the trees indicated that the flood lacked several feet of being as high as it was the year before. This was the first vestige of farm we had seen, and surely the prospect here was cheerless enough. One ridge hardly large enough for a garden held a lot of negro cabins, while across a wide swift current of water was another knoll containing the barn, stables, etc. All else was a cheerless waste of waters.

The steamboat could go no further, and no other means
of transportation was in sight except a small scow which
was gracefully anchored by one end having drifted against
the bank and the other against a sapling. Said vessel was
manned by half a dozen men of the 26th Louisiana Regt.
Only half of our regiment could go at once and Company B
was in the first load. We soon learned that our progress was
slow, whether it was sure or not. Indeed, for a time it
seemed that it was *not* sure, for the wind blew us out of our
"reckoning" and deposited us on a partly submerged
"May-Haw Tree." By dint of hard work with Crawford for
pilot, steersman, boatswain, captain and admiral all rolled
into one, we succeeded in extricating ourselves and proceeded on our way. We each took practical lessons in
"working our passage" and at dark we reached Victor F.
Wilson's negro quarters, which was our destination. The distance from Paxton's was four or five miles and the only
intervening landing was about midway between the two,
and which consisted of another negro quarter also belonging
to Mr. Paxton. There was a foot of dry ground visible here.
The negroes were all in their cabins with a dug-out fastened
to each door post. Near the top of the doors was the water
line of the flood of the year before.

After debarking at Wilson's we marched about three-
fourths of a mile over fresh plowed land and bivouacked in
an old "deadening" already occupied by the 3d and 26th
Louisiana Regts. and 1st Miss. Battalion. Gen. S.D. Lee was
in command, and the enemy was reported about 10 miles
distant but falling back. The balance of the regiment came
up next day. [8]

During our stay at this place we had some new experiences. Our regiment and the 26th Louisiana being entirely without food, obtained permission from Gen. Lee to
shoot some wild ducks, an abundance of which were in
sight. Not confining themselves to feathered game, the boys
opened fire on a herd of cattle and for a time it sounded like
a sharp skirmish. An order to cease firing from headquarters
prevented a heavy loss to the owner of the cattle at least.
Perhaps he was revenged, for a portion of this very beef was

issued to us as rations, and as we did not have a grain of salt nor a sign of a cooking vessel, and as with the beef was issued some coarse, unsifted corn meal which when placed on a chip would get dry and crumble before it would cook, our meals were rather unsatisfactory.

Saturday morning, March 28th, the expedition commenced its return. An old flat boat having been added to our fleet, we were able to transfer a whole regiment at once. The 3d Louisiana and 1st Miss. Battalion both being small were taken the same trip. On Saturday night there was a violent storm of wind and rain. The ground we occupied was heavily timbered, and this timber had been deadened some years before and was ready to fall. Several large trees fell near us, two of them threw dirt on me as I sought a more open space. Providentially, no one was hurt with us, but we learned subsequently that several men were killed by falling timber on the east side of the Yazoo River.

Sunday 29th, the 26th Louisiana started down the creek, a detail from our regiment being aboard to take back the boats. I was one of that detail and I never engaged in much harder work than that return trip was. The wind was blowing a gale right against us, and we frequently had great difficulty in forcing our way through the drifts that obstructed the channel.

Next morning we started, a portion of our regiment being again left behind, as a detachment of artillery required half of our fleet. We stayed all night at Paxton's and the balance of the regiment came down next day just as the steamer *John M. Sharpe* came up. We went aboard leaving Company E as scouts. In a few hours we were landed at Haynes'.

Col. Sears had been ordered to report to Brig. Gen. Hébert, and taking a skiff at Paxton's he proceeded to Gen. Hébert's headquarters at Snyder's Bluff. Some two or three hours after our arrival at Haynes' he joined us, informing us that we would remain where we were until further orders. This was an unwelcome announcement.[9]

The next day, April 1st, a Federal gun-boat came up the Yazoo River and threw a few shells in the vicinity of our lower works. We were hurriedly marched to Snyder's Bluff, three miles, where we remained until the afternoon of the next day when we returned to Haynes'. I was appointed sergeant that day.

We remained at Haynes' until Thursday, April 16th, performing heavy guard and fatigue duty. During our stay at that place we learned that two others of our company had died. Wm. R. Speed was taken sick while we were on Deer Creek and sent to the camp at Vicksburg, where on the 10th he died of congestive chill. E.L.L. Speights died at Lauderdale Springs on the 14th.

CHAPTER 6

Port Gibson

We returned to Vicksburg on April 16th, when tents were
immediately struck and the regiment moved to a new
encampment on a hill further from the grave yard. Stephen
R., George R. and I, all being unwell, remained at the old
camp that night.

Between three and four o'clock next morning I witnessed
an impressive scene. Being aroused by the pickets firing I
knew another battery-running enterprise was afoot. Hastily
climbing a high hill I obtained a pretty fair view of the
splendid panorama. Across the river two or three buildings
were on fire, the flames leaping madly upward, lighting up
the sky and the dense curtain of smoke that swung over the
river with a livid glow. The whole surface of the stream was
lighted up and far out on its broad bosom was a fleet of five
or six steamers and two gun-boats. The latter were firing as
rapidly as their guns could be worked, while our batteries
were sending forth a stream of shot and shell. The dense
smoke that partially concealed the flashes of sulphurous
flame added to the wierdness of the scene.

One of the boats took fire. The flames carried upward,
losing themselves in a dense volume of smoke that shone
like a rosy sunset cloud. The air was full of bursting shells
and screaming shots, while through it all could be heard the
wild hurrahs of our men. It was a sight never to be forgotten, and while a sensation of awe came over me to behold such a display of man's destructive energy, it awoke the
savage in the heart and filled it with an enthusiastic desire to
be in the thick of the work of death. Another bark went
down, and the agonizing wails of the drowning wretches on
the water were faintly heard amid the exultant tones of the
victors' shouts.

The other boats ran past, the flames completed their work
of ruin, the cannons were hushed and the gray streaks of the

morning were stealing over the eastern hills. Quiet once
more reigned over the bosom of the "Father of Waters."
After this, five companies of our regiment were sent to Fort
Hill every morning at 3 o'clock.[1]

Drew two months' wages on the 21st. On the night of the
22d one gun-boat and five transports succeeded in running
past our batteries. Attended brigade drill on the 23d. About
this time our regiment was greatly excited over reports of a
Federal raid led by Col. Grierson, which passed nearly
through the entire state.[2]

Another gun-boat ran past our batteries on the morning of
the 26th. Stephen R. and I both went to the regimental
hospital. A little after noon a man named Walters of Company C was walking across the yard, fell and died in less
than one minute.

I remained only a day at the hospital. Easterling came in
from Canton about the same time, having been away since
February.

Tuesday 28th at 10 o'clock p.m. we were ordered to prepare two days' rations immediately. To carry out this order
required nearly all the rest of the night for some of us. I was
unable for duty but resolved to go with the command.
Receiving no orders to move as we expected, at seven
o'clock our company was sent on a fatigue detail. About
sunset we were notified that the regiment would move at
once.

We formed the brigade in the city and about dark started
on the Warrenton Road. We marched till 2 o'clock a.m.
when we bivouacked two miles below Warrenton (the scene
of our exploit last June). By sunrise on the 30th we were in
motion and reached Hankerson's [Hankinson's] Ferry on the
Big Black River about noon. The steamer *Charm* conveyed
us across the stream where we rested four or five hours.
About 5 o'clock p.m. we started southward again. The roads
were now more level, the air seemed purer and the spirits of
the men were wonderfully elated. Again and again we made
the "echoes" ring with our shouts. Jest and repartee were
heard on every side, and altogether "Baldwin's Cavalry" (as
someone dubbed us) enjoyed themselves better than on any

march they had ever made. But physical fatigue will dampen the ardor of the most elastic spirit, and as long hours dragged by, with no orders save "close up!" the enthusiasm seemed to die away and a great weariness of limb overtook us.

At 2:30 a.m. we reached Big Bayou Pierre [north fork of Bayou Pierre], where we rested until daylight. Big Bayou Pierre at this point is a beautiful stream, spanned by a new suspension bridge. It was now pretty well understood that our destination was Port Gibson, distant about 8 miles. We were in motion again at an early hour, the three left companies of our regiment (B, D and G) being sent forward under Major Clarke as a vanguard. Along the road we met both white men and negroes, who informed us that the fighting was near Port Gibson. Soon we heard the roar of artillery and then the sharper rattle of musketry. The command "Double-quick" was given and away we went.

In due time we crossed Little Bayou Pierre [south fork of Bayou Pierre], on the south bank of which stands Port Gibson on another new suspension bridge. Before we knew it we were falling down and against the railing because of the swing our footsteps gave it. From the hasty view obtained as we double-quicked through it I should say that Port Gibson is one of the wealthiest, as well as one of the most beautiful towns in the state. It stands on a level plain, the streets are broad and regularly laid out, and some of the buildings are handsome and costly. But I had no time to observe anything.[3]

It was an exciting time! The loud peals of artillery rent the sky and reverberated along the hills till their echoes blended with the sharp din of musketry that was rolling toward us from Grindstone Ford. In the streets all was confusion. Men with pale faces were running hither and thither, some with arms and seeking a command, women sobbing on every side, children in open-eyed wonder clinging to their weeping mothers, not understanding the meaning of it all, and negroes with eyes protruding like open cotton bolls were jostling each other and everybody else, continuously asking about "dem Yankees." The ladies cheered us through their tears and besought us to drive the invaders from their homes. One lady, while she prayed Heaven to protect us, said we felt as near to her as though we were her own sons going forth to battle. The wounded, too, were meeting us, some in vehicles and some in litters, and many a poor fellow with a shattered limb or a gaping wound would wildly hurrah for the "brave Mississippians."

We sped on. Louder roared the cannon. The din of the musketry grew more deafening. We met our flying squadrons, regiments cut to pieces till a remnant only was driven from its position by a force fivefold greater than its own. Already we were in advance of our new line and were going forward upon the run when we were ordered to "right about."

We rejoined the regiment and formed a new line of battle, our regiment occupying a small eminence to the left of the road with a small stream in our front. We had barely formed our line when the enemy opened fire on us with artillery and small arms. Just at this time a sad accident occurred. Easterling being weak from his recent illness, had been unable to keep up in our forced march. Coming up a little later utterly exhausted, he sat down by a tree. When the bullets began to whistle about us he took his gun by the muzzle to draw it to him. The hammer struck the tree, the cap exploded and the whole charge struck his right arm, literally tearing it to fragments from the wrist to above the elbow. Never will I forget the horror-stricken face as he cried, "Oh! Pitt, I have ruined my arm!" Seeing his clothes burning I called Crawford who stood near him to extinguish the flame. Asking for water, he fell fainting as I reached him, but revived as the water was placed to his lips. He was placed on a litter, borne to the rear and I never saw him again.

But the screaming and bursting of shells, the whistling of shot, the ping of bullets, the shrieks of the wounded and the groans of the dying were calculated to strike terror to hearts unused to such scenes. I frankly confess that I was badly demoralized.

Company C was deployed as skirmishers along the little

[Mass. MOLLUS, USAMHI]

Col. Claudius W. Sears, 46th Mississippi, was promoted brigadier general in 1864.

creek. The 4th Miss. on our left was soon hotly engaged, while further along the line the firing seemed to be heavier still. As we formed our line Col. Sears called out: "Fix bayonets, boys! And if they come, bleed 'em!" With fixed bayonets, expecting a charge every minute, we held our line till about one o'clock when we were ordered to cross the narrow creek, on the opposite heights of which the enemy was posted. We did so and were met by a terrible fire of grape, canister and musket shot. In a few minutes, however, we were ordered to resume our former position. We left our dead across the creek but brought most of the wounded away. Resuming our position in line, our skirmish line was reënforced and for the balance of the day the firing was mostly confined to the pickets with occasional artillery duels.

After our return from across the creek Capt. Magee asked Lt. Lott where his blanket was, and he replied that it was "over on the hill."

"You had better go and get it," said Capt. M., "ere you will lose it."

"By —, I reckon it's marked!" was the drawling reply.

About sundown we fell back half a mile and formed another line. The firing had ceased and the twilight was changing to deep dusk when suddenly, about two hundred yards to our right, a deafening volley of musketry pealed forth. It was the 31st Louisiana repelling a cavalry advance.

Taking the quick step, we marched back to town nearly three miles, having, as we supposed, entirely lost Company C. The retreat had now commenced in earnest and utter confusion was seen on every side, or rather heard for it was now dark. We had drawn no rations since leaving Vicksburg. That morning the town people received our rations and had them prepared for us; but we marched through town without making any halt. When we had gone a mile or two, the southwestern sky was aglow and we understood that the bridge across Little Bayou Pierre was in flames.[4]

Such confusion as the road presented! Whole families were flying they knew not where, while delicately nurtured ladies implored us by endearing epithets to save them from the hands of the foe. My eyes filled more than once as I marched by seemingly unheeding these tearful appeals. For I thought of the peaceful homes in Covington County and reflected that their inmates might one day be doomed to a fate like this. By a rapid march we reached Big Bayou Pierre about 12 o'clock midnight, where we halted to rest two and a half hours. As we passed out of Port Gibson I gave a negro a five dollar bill for three hens that he carried. Letting Capt. Magee and Major Clarke have one each, I undertook to fry the other during this halt. It was certainly the *toughest* chicken I ever tried to eat.

At 2:30 o'clock a.m. Saturday, May 2d, the bridge was fired and we started again. At Willow Springs (a deserted crossroads hamlet) we turned to the left toward Grand Gulf. As day was dawning, George R. and I "fell out" and slept for some hours under a tree. The brigade, or rather a few men from each regiment, formed a line of battle on the north bank of the Big Bayou Pierre about midway between Grand Gulf and Port Gibson. The two places are, I am told, only seven miles apart and are connected by a railroad, but as the enemy was in the way we had to march some twenty miles.

Troops had been coming in all day and I supposed the fight would be renewed next day. About midnight, however, Saturday May 2d, the retreat began. At daylight Sunday morning our brigade was put in motion. Our progress was slow at first, as the wagon trains were in front. A little after sunrise a series of explosions were heard behind us. It was the blowing up of the magazines at Grand Gulf.[5]

As the wagons moved we increased our pace, and the frequent boom of cannon close behind us convinced us that the enemy was moving too. This was one march in which the command "Close up!" was wholly unnecessary. We reached Hankerson's Ferry on Big Black River about 1 o'clock p.m. A brigade or two of fresh troops was sent to the rear, and by 3 o'clock all the wagons and most of the troops had crossed over. Our brigade was formed in line of battle on the northern bank. It was near sunset when the improvised pontoon bridge on which we had crossed was cut loose, and while this was being done the enemy's skirmishers began firing from the opposite bank. Being placed in line to move from the position we then occupied, a few small shells thrown across the river was an incentive to greater alacrity in obeying the command "Forward, march!"

After a march of two or three miles we came to the encampment of the main army. The brigade also halted here, but our regiment was sent out on a crossroad about two miles to do picket duty. Returning to the brigade next morning, we soon set out on the march to Vicksburg, the brigade being commanded by Col. Richardson of the 17th Louisiana.[6] I do not know why there was so much haste; but we made quick time all the way, resting about one hour on the spot where we bivouacked the first night. We reached camp about 4 o'clock p.m. on Monday 4th, the regiment having about fifty men in line and Company B being represented by four others and myself. My feet had blood blisters on the soles, and the others were no better off. We had marched about 150 miles in less than five days besides the fighting; and this was no trivial performance for troops unused to long marches.

During the night and till noon the next day, the stragglers kept coming in. Company C came in all right, having been at one time entirely surrounded by the enemy. They were extricated through an expedient of Capt. Sublett's as daring as it was successful. As they emerged from a wood they saw in front of them a Federal line of battle facing away from them. In ringing tones the captain gave the command, "Battalion, by column, forward, double-quick, *march!*" Into the woods on both sides the Federals dashed and Company C passed unmolested through the gap.

Altogether, "Baldwin's Cavalry" was worsted on the trip. Our company had two wounded and two missing, there being several killed and wounded in the regiment.[7] But that which depressed me more than anything else was the conduct of some of our officers. *And some men had already begun to suspect the motives as well as doubt the judgment of Gen. Pemberton.* [8]

CHAPTER 7

Debacle on the Big Black

On reaching camp we learned that J.H. Williamson of our company had died of typhoid fever at the regimental hospital on the first day of May.

Tuesday, May 5th, just 24 hours after reaching camp, our brigade was again put in motion. We moved out on the Baldwin's Ferry road and bivouacked near the Four Mile Bridge on the railroad, where we remained till the morning of the 8th. We then moved some ten or twelve miles and halted at a point said to be 10 miles from Hall's Ferry, 10 from Vicksburg and 9 from Warrenton.

On the afternoon of the 7th, Private S.H.P. Wilkes and I were sent back to the camp to prepare muster and pay rolls for Company B. Completing the task in the forenoon of the 8th we invested our "change" in a bag of cakes and started to the command. Reaching the point where we left it, there were no soldiers there nor could we meet or find anyone that had the least idea as to what direction the brigade had gone. We found other troops encamped along the roads, but "Baldwin's Brigade" was an absolutely unknown quantity so far as they were concerned. Night overtook us, and we had to make our supper, breakfast and dinner off our cakes so that when we overtook the command in the afternoon our stock in trade was so diminished that we barely realized our original investment.

On the 10th the 31st Louisiana was sent about six miles on the Hankerson's Ferry road to do picket duty, and the next day Companies B and G of the 46th Miss. were detailed to occupy a point on the road from Hall's Ferry to Warrenton, some three miles south of where the brigade was encamped, where we did heavy picket duty. We were at this time receiving only about one-third of a full ration, and considerable "foraging" was indulged in by our boys. In one of the few expeditions of that nature I undertook, I came

upon the pleasant home of a Mr. Petty. It is quite an imposing looking place but pervaded by a home-like atmosphere that was truly restful. A school for girls was being
taught there and before the war a successful male academy
had existed at the same place. The local name is "Mt.
Magnolia," and after a pleasant visit of some hours I left,
deeply conscious of the fact that the owner impressed me as
being *a Christian.*

On the 12th we were relieved from picket duty and, returning to the crossroads, we found the brigade had again
moved. Following it up we found it about two miles east
near Antioch Church. Next morning our regiment was sent
forward on the Hall's Ferry road to do picket duty again.

It should be borne in mind that the army of Gen. Pemberton was maneuvering along the northwestern side of Big
Black River, and that in changing our positions we frequently encountered other portions of the army, and that
other commands frequently marched past us. The Federal
army was on the other side of the river.

We were relieved on the 15th and returned to the brigade
which was set in motion at once, and at dark we reached the
railroad at Mt. Alban, a way station some six miles east of
Vicksburg. We halted till morning. At 10 o'clock a.m. the
4th Miss. was detached and sent off toward Bovina some
four miles distant. In the afternoon the rest of the brigade
moved in the same direction, our regiment and the 17th
Louisiana being posted about two miles north of Bovina on
the Bridgeport road. Before reaching Bovina the roar of
artillery could be heard distinctly on the eastern side of the
river. It was the bloody engagement at Baker's Creek, or
Champion Hill, as the Federals call it.[1]

It may not be amiss to state that after landing his forces
at Rodney [on the Mississippi River, about 18 miles southwest of Port Gibson], the Federal Gen. U.S. Grant moved to
the eastern side of the Big Black River and succeeded in
placing himself between the wings of Gen. J.E. Johnston's
forces. On Friday 15th, Stevenson's division encountered
the enemy near Edward's [Station on the Vicksburg & Jackson Railroad]; on Saturday 16th was fought the battle of Ba-

ker's Creek, as already noted; and on Sunday 17th occurred the short by sanguinary struggle at Big Black Bridge. Brig. Gen. Tilghman was killed Saturday and his body was taken to Vicksburg for burial.[2]

When we halted Saturday night the roar of the guns at Baker's Creek was still borne to our ears. Pretty soon several wounded men came into our camp, relating some of the particulars of the struggle and stating that our forces were falling back.

Soon after sunrise Sunday morning 17th, sharp volleys of musketry announced that the enemy was advancing on the railroad bridge. We had some earthworks there, but I do not think a single man who participated in Saturday's engagement believed we could check the enemy's progress. While I make no pretensions to military science, it seems to me that a blunder was made, *if these works were intended to guard the approaches to Vicksburg.* At this point, at least, the western bank of the river is elevated and precipitous while the eastern side is flat and level. These earthworks were on the eastern side and *below the enemy,* while the river cut off the retreat in the rear if our forces were driven from their position by superior numbers.

I will not attempt to analyze my feelings on this occasion. I dreaded the battle as never before. It seemed to be impressed on me that I should be killed in the fight, and the thought of meeting my God unprepared never seemed half so appalling before. I communicated some of my apprehensions to Stephen and George R. The latter admitted that he shared my feelings to some extent, but said that the thought of the judgment of God was not a terrible thing to him.

I employed myself in making several lists of the men present, which I handed to the different company officers that we might be able to ascertain our exact losses should one or more lists be lost. The firing seemed to be growing hotter, and presently some cannon shots were heard.

At 9:30 o'clock a.m. we were ordered to the railroad bridge.[3] It was about three miles and we went at a double-quick most of the way. Reaching the spot one glance was enough to show that all was lost. The bridge with a trestle three-fourths of a mile in length was in flames, a few yards below in midstream was a burning steamboat, and some of our men were climbing the steep banks without arms and dripping with wet, having swam the stream. Our regiment took position at the western bank to cover the retreat, and though for a time subjected to a galling fire we did not lose a man. The 4th Miss., however, had fared badly. They had crossed the river early in the morning and taken position in the rifle pits; when these were carried all were captured save those who swam across the stream.[4]

By 12 o'clock we were in full retreat. Our brigade brought up the rear, and so far as I could see was the only one that preserved any resemblance of discipline. Had the enemy closely followed us that day he could probably have entered the city without serious opposition. The spirit of our troops had undergone a great change. Instead of the high hopes that animated us last week, a feeling of demoralization seemed to permeate the rank and file, and none of us were hopeful as to the results of the campaign.

On Saturday as we passed one fine residence, a number of young ladies stood near the road. With tears and smiles they greeted us and spoke words of cheer; and as our regiment filed by one sweet young voice said, "Remember, Mississippians never surrender!" We saw no smiling faces as we marched toward the doomed city. It was all deserted. I passed the same spot again after the siege was ended and found a woeful change. The mansion had been sacked, the fine grove destroyed, the shrubbery and the crops all trampled down and the last vestige of fencing burned away. It had been occupied by the enemy as headquarters, perhaps for some general.

Our brigade was halted below the city but was not placed in the trenches. We remained there all night. Next morning the 17th Louisiana and the remnant of the 4th Miss. were sent to the camp above the city for the purpose, it was said, of washing, changing clothing, etc., and it was further said that our regiment and the 31st Louisiana would go for the same purpose as soon as they returned. About one o'clock p.m., however, we were ordered to proceed to our camp. As we leisurely wended our way we suddenly heard musket firing on the Milldale road, and a few minutes later the boom of a cannon. It was the pickets of Shoup's brigade skirmishing with the enemy.[5]

About this time a staff officer met us and ordered us to occupy the same position we did last Christmas. Passing by our camp in obedience to the order, we found the 17th Louisiana already deployed and our regiment was moved up to the picket line. While deploying we suddenly encountered a Federal regiment executing a similar maneuver. In a few minutes the firing became general along the line of the 17th, the 4th and the right of our regiment. Our left companies were occupying some rifle pits and supporting a battery that had been brought up. The enemy also had placed some light artillery and began playing upon our lines. This fire was kept up till night, and in front of Shoup's brigade and the 17th Louisiana there was a continual fusillade all night. We lost several men.

Just at daybreak Tuesday morning, May 19th, we fell back to our main line of works. There had been a line of earthworks constructed some time before extending from Haynes' Landing on the Yazoo River to Warrenton, but these fronted the river and were useless since our position had been turned. Hence no effort was made to hold them. It is proper to state that all the outposts such as Snyder's, Milldale, etc., had been abandoned, and large quantities of commissary and quartermaster stores had been destroyed, and several large guns along the upper defenses had been spiked and dismounted.

CHAPTER 8

Dreary Days Under Siege

It is no part of my design to attempt a general sketch of the siege of Vicksburg. I can only relate a few that I saw. Common history will preserve its most important events, and those who were eye witnesses of its most bloody details will transmit to posterity an outline of what they saw. But after all histories are written and the tongue of the last survivor is stilled in death, the Recording Angel will have sealed a heavy volume and labeled it "The Untold Sufferings of Vicksburg's Siege." When I look back now, after the lapse of weeks, to that long, bloody and horrible battle, it seems more like a fearful dream than an actual experience.

It is well, perhaps, just here to give some idea of our position. The Mississippi River at this place runs nearly due south, and was denominated our "rear." Our right rested on the river some two miles below the city, while our left also rested on it about as far above. Our front, which described the arc of a circle, was about six miles in length, the center of which was perhaps three miles from the river. Thus our line, including the river, was about ten miles long.

Our forces, I think, were placed as follows: On the right was Stevenson's division, in the center was Forney's, and on the left was Smith's – the whole commanded by Lt. Gen. John C. Pemberton. I do not know what brigades composed the two first-named divisions.[1] The last was composed of Shoup's, Baldwin's and Vaughn's brigades and a battalion of State troops (militia). Next to Forney's division, on our [Smith's] right, were Shoup's Louisianans, then Baldwin's 31st Louisiana, then the Mississippians, then the State troops, and then Vaughn's Tennesseeans.

Immediately in front of our brigade and continuing to the river was a deep valley some two or three hundred yards in width, which was a cultivated field last year. It was so free from any object affording shelter that it saved our lines from any serious assaults, and afforded no protection for the sappers and miners to begin operations. On our extreme right, however, a narrow ridge extended from the line of the 31st Louisiana to the center of the valley. Availing himself of the opportunity afforded by this ridge, the enemy tunneled it, and I suppose had a mine ready to spring at the time of the capitulation.[2]

Having made these explanations I will proceed to note an event here and there, feeling my utter inadequacy to convey a correct impression of what the reality was.

We had barely got in position on the morning of the 19th when a few volleys of musketry were heard near the position we held overnight, then a cannon shot or two, and then *a charge.* The enemy had assaulted and doubtless carried our deserted works. Elated with success, he came nearer and we were soon under a brisk skirmish fire. This was kept up all day, the enemy gradually establishing his lines. In the afternoon a charge was made on our center, but it was repulsed. Company B lost one of its best men in this day's fight. John Williams, a litter bearer, was shot through the abdomen with a minié ball and died a few hours afterward.[3]

Wednesday 20th, Thursday 21st and Friday 22d there was desperate fighting on most parts of our line. Column after column was hurled against our works, only to be driven back in confusion and leaving the ground in front of our lines literally blue with dead and wounded Federals. Never before had the idea I once entertained of what a battle was like been so nearly realized as now. The spectacle of perhaps sixty or seventy thousand men *all fighting at once,* with upward of three hundred cannon belching forth their thunder, is a scene I cannot attempt to describe. In these charges the enemy reached our trenches in many places and desperate hand-to-hand conflicts occurred. A few prisoners were taken; it was those whose intrepidity carried them into our works where they were made captive.

On one of these days, I think it was Wednesday, a line of the enemy advanced to the center of the valley in our front,

[Mass. MOLLUS, USAMHI]

Gen. John C. Pemberton

but was compelled to retreat in utter confusion. Beyond them to our right it appeared as though whole regiments went down at once, so terribly withering was the Confederate fire. James Maxey of our company was shot through the arm this day, and Gen. Baldwin was seriously wounded in the shoulder about the same time.[4]

On Friday 22d, however, the fighting was heavier and more stubborn than on any previous day, and I have heard the statement that the Federal loss on that day was greater than in the whole siege. Ours, up to this time, had been comparatively light, our regiment having had five or six killed and something over twice as many wounded. After the 22d there was only one more general charge. A brisk fire of pickets and sharpshooters was kept up day and night with but few intermissions till the end of the siege.[5]

On the afternoon of Monday, May 25th, a truce of two or three hours was arranged in order to bury the dead who lay between the lines. These bodies had become so offensive that our troops could hardly remain in the trenches along those points where the slaughter had been greatest. Hence our men gladly assisted in the burial of their fallen foes. And among them were found living men who had fallen, perhaps on Wednesday and certainly not later than Friday before, who had lain there without a drop of water or a particle of shade. When the gruesome task was completed we, the common soldiers of both armies, met on halfway ground and had a friendly chat. Old acquaintances were hunted up and the broken ties of friendship and consanguinity were reunited. Although our foes were elated over their recent victories and the success of their armies in other fields, and though they knew that famine would ultimately compel us to surrender, yet I found *not a man* who was willing to go home and leave the South alone!

When the bugles gave the signal that the truce was ended, I saw *two* pairs of brothers clasp hands in farewell and go in opposite directions. After such a meeting it was with seeming reluctance that the firing was resumed, and even next day it seemed less vicious than before.[6]

The policy of the enemy had shown itself to be a close

and vigorous siege. He had become satisfied that he could not carry our works by storm. Hence he began to fortify his position, keeping up a heavy cannonade from the land while his mortar fleet threw shells into the city. A steady fire of sharpshooting was one of his most annoying as well as most destructive proceedings. Day or night there was little variation and almost no cessation.

On Thursday 28th, the Federal ironclad *Cincinnati* came down the river below the bend and engaged our batteries along the shore. The contest was soon decided. Her crew could only run her to the opposite bank and save themselves when she went to the bottom in shallow water, however. No other gun-boat or ironclad attempted to cope with our shore batteries after that, though the mortar boats above the bend continued to throw shells into the city.[7]

On Friday 29th about 5 o'clock p.m., the enemy opened the most furious fire of artillery on our lines and in the city that I had ever heard. This continued for about an hour. On Saturday afternoon the performance was repeated, and at 3 o'clock a.m. on Sunday 31st it was resumed and continued till daylight.

We fired not a shot in reply! In the trenches we had orders to fire no gun unless the enemy came within 200 yards of our works. Hence along our front there was seldom a gun fired (after the first week), even in response to the sharpshooters. To attempt an artillery duel was madness. Every gun we had in position was commanded by several heavier and better pieces. Any gun we could place was speedily dismounted and every earthwork we could construct was promptly battered down. At many points, too, our lines were exposed to an enfilading fire.

Just here it may be well to glance at our condition from another standpoint. On the evening of the 18th of May we were exhorted to hold the place for only twelve hours longer, being assured that Gen. Johnston would join us, by that time, at the head of a heavy force. We were repeatedly informed that he was coming, that dispatches had been received from him stating that he had gained important victories, and that the siege would surely be raised in two or three days at farthest. This was repeated so often and the men were so often disappointed that they naturally became skeptical and despondent. In our regiment (I knew nothing of the sentiment prevailing in any other) a willingness to capitulate soon became quite prevalent. They realized that they were starving; they saw themselves surrounded by a force five times greater than their own; they beheld the enemy entrench himself and build stronger and better forts than ours; and they saw their comrades being shot down every day *while they were not permitted to fire a gun!* They were worked all night building a parapet or mounting a gun that dared not fire a shot, only to see their work demolished before the day was an hour old. They had experienced all this, and had no confidence in the assurances of their officers. They saw nothing before them but death or a prison after weeks of gnawing, debilitating hunger, while all the glory of their achievements, and all the praise of their fortitude, and all the honors of their unavailing heroism and devotion to duty would be heaped upon the heads of those who *never saw the foe.* [8]

Who shall blame them if brave spirits did despond? Who shall wonder if, at times, the *man* triumphed over the *soldier,* and he longed in his heart to give up the doomed city and go home for a while and rest? And yet, if he expresses such a thought, away he must go to jail! If he grumbles at his fare he must be reprimanded! If he ventures to reply he must be punished! All this and more have I seen. Without boasting, I can say that I did not entirely despond during all those dreary days.

The enemy in building his forts had constructed embrasures to protect his cannoneers, while we had nothing on the whole line except loose earth and bags of dirt thrown up during the night to be scattered before they were half completed. Already his sappers and miners were at work. One of his heavy guns enfiladed the right of our regiment and we had already lost several men. [9]

On the night of Monday, June 1st, the city was set on fire by the enemy's shells and one square was burned. It was a magnificent spectacle from our lines, but a sad one. Frequently in the night we watched these mortar shells. From the flash of the [muzzle blasts we] beheld them rise, go streaming across the sky like a flying meteor, describe a great curve and pitch headlong to the earth, gathering momentum as they fell. Sometimes they bursted high in midair with a detonation like thunder, sometimes exploding near the ground, and they buried themselves in the earth and tore out great holes when the explosion came.[10]

W.J. Manning of our company was shot through the chest by a minié ball on Wednesday, June 3d. He was a litter bearer and was passing in the rear of his own company when he was shot. I distinctly heard the ball strike the ground after passing through his body, when it ricochetted and went whizzing onward as though it had met no obstruction. I helped to carry Manning to the rear. At a little spring we rested him a little. He requested someone to pray for him. One of the little group at the spring, a stranger to me, responded. A few of us knelt down with bursting shells and whistling bullets above our heads, and the stranger earnestly plead for mercy for the dying man before us. Realizing that his wound was mortal, he entreated me to take a last message to the dear ones at home: "Tell my old father, Pitt, when you see him that I died at my post. Tell my mother that I loved her to the last. And my dear wife and children, Pitt, remember me to them and tell them how gladly I would have seen them before I died. Take a husband's and a father's blessing, it is all I have to leave them."

We bore him away and placed him in the surgeon's care, and I never saw him more. He lingered two or three days before he died.

On the afternoon of the same day, June 3d, about sunset, we distinctly heard heavy firing in an easterly direction and conjectured at once that Gen. Johnston was coming at last. *How high rose the hopes of our men!* And how eagerly we listened for a renewal of the fight on the morrow. But we heard it no more, and in a day or two the men were as despondent as ever.

Between midnight and daylight on the 5th and 6th of June, our right was furiously bombarded for an hour or two each morning. It was also a favorite, or at least a common performance of the enemy at this time, to shell the pickets during the night. It was annoying, but our regiment had no one killed on the picket line by these shells. Capt. Wm. H. Adair of Company E, 4th Miss. Regt., was killed at one of our picket posts at daybreak on the 5th. He was the field officer of the night and was making his last round when he was struck. His was a choice spirit, and at the surrender a neat monument erected by his company marked his grave in the city cemetery. Sleep on, gallant soldier, till the archangel's trumpet shall summon thee to leave thy dreamless bed!

On the same morning our regiment was called on to give up one of its bravest men. Adjutant James C. Porter was shot through the head by a minié ball. He never spoke again, though he lingered many hours ere he died. Few men seemed more reckless of danger on the battlefield than he, and few seemed cooler or more self-possessed. When the shot flew thickest and the din of battle rose highest, when the air was heavy with the odor of smoke and blood, his eyes would dilate and his bosom heave as though he gloried in the carnage. He is dead.

The 31st Louisiana Regt. had a picket fight on the night of the 8th. Our picket lines were often only a few feet from those of the enemy, and at this point they were close together. The Federals had dug some pits for their own protection. On the night in question our pickets, being first on the ground, took possession of these pits and held them till about 10 o'clock p.m. when they were finally driven out after fighting a whole regiment for half an hour.

Another one of Company B died that day at the regimental hospital. Wm. Erasmus Carter, after a long illness, passed away. In the *unwritten* records of the Confederate armies are few records cleaner than his. No boy (for he was only a boy) more cheerfully assumed a task or faced a peril than he. Both he and Manning were sons of Baptist preachers.

Immediately to the left of our company was a redoubt where we had a 32-pound Parrott gun when the siege began.

This gun after four or five days was bursted into fragments. I was looking on when the lanyard was pulled. The concussion was terrific, and as the smoke lifted I expected to see dead men all around, but strange to say not a man was hurt. A sixty-four pound Columbiad was then mounted in its place, which did little service, however. Two or three carriages were shot to pieces and had to be replaced, and though we worked at it every night it was fired less than once a day. Our whole night's work was often destroyed by sunrise next morning. The Federals had a ten-inch rifled gun trained directly upon this redoubt, and as we worked at night we kept one man watching for the flash. At the signal, all lay down. This gun was also frequently fired against the bank behind which we fought. The size and momentum of the ball was such as to drive it through several feet of earth and burst in our midst. A fragment of one of these shells wounded Lotan Sullivan in the thigh on the 11th. He was also a litter bearer.[11]

On another occasion a shot from this gun proved very annoying to some of us. It was dusk, our stint of food had been distributed, and we were in the act of eating. Perhaps two spoonfuls of molasses had been issued to each man, and George and Stephen R. and I had ours together on a plate. Just then a shot from this heavy gun was fired. It struck our works about a foot from the top, came through, scattered a few boards we were using for a shade, and covered us completely in dirt. When we scratched our food, our molasses and our shreds of fresh beef were entirely ruined. Our "pea-bread" was intact, however, barring the grit that adhered to it.

On Sunday June 14th, there was rapid firing at some point on our right. We were informed subsequently that a mine had been sprung under our lines, and that the enemy endeavored to force his way into the breach caused by the explosion. He was repulsed, however.[12]

And so the days wore on – each one almost a repetition of the one that preceded it. The long, hot, dreary days and nights of toil and danger were telling on the men. Emaciated by hunger, worn out by constant watching and utterly skeptical as to any promised hopes of relief, their despondency deepened, and they felt more keenly than ever how useless it was to prolong the struggle. They heard no sound from one sunrise till the next save the crack of the rifle, the boom of the cannon, the screech of the shells and the "whizz" of bullets. Our world lay inside those beleaguered lines, and a dreary world it was! How often, when on the silent picket line, the thoughts would revert to the homes we had left in that other world outside, and an intense yearning for those peaceful scenes would come over us. And yet, amid it all, there dwelt in my heart a feeling that it was good to die for freedom.

How anxiously we listened, how fervently we wished for some token of relief, but we listened and wished in vain. None save those who were there will ever fully comprehend our experience during those monotonous days. There was an unrest, *a fever of the mind,* intensified by the pangs of hunger that utterly baffles my poor powers of description and makes the whole seem unreal. Was it any wonder that the heart grew callous as to the things of eternity? And yet I did not feel condemned in the sight of God, and in order to turn away His wrath I strove to lead a better life. I read the New Testament a great deal, but its gracious promises were not for me and the condemnation still remained.

But to resume my meager record. Shortly after midnight on the morning of Saturday June 20th, there was heard an unusal bustle around the enemy's lines. Wagon trains were moving, drums and fifes were heard and there seemed to be a sound of the tramping of many feet. About 3 o'clock a.m. a furious bombardment was opened all around the lines which was kept up for about six hours.

During these days I read Marion Harland's "Moss Side," having read "Nemesi's" a week or two previously. I had also quite recently read "Zanoni" by Bulwer Lytton. Comment on these books is useless. I was best pleased with "Zanoni." I had also read "Great Expectations" by Charles Dickens since the siege began.

On Sunday morning June 21st, two men in Company G immediately on the right of our company were struck by the same minié ball. It passed entirely through one's loins and entered the abdomen of the other, inflicting a fatal wound in each. The men were brothers-in-law.

CHAPTER 9

Vicksburg's Last Hours

Thursday June 24th in the afternoon, the enemy began to show himself in great numbers all along our front as though he intended an assault, and in a few minutes there was a tremendous explosion to our right followed by a desperate charge. A mine had been sprung, and from where we were we could see the dust mingled with timbers and the bodies of men. The charge was beaten back with great loss to the assailants, greater by far than ours by the explosion. Two or three other mines were subsequently sprung, but no serious assault was made.[1]

About this time a personal incident occurred that I venture to relate. On the left of our regiment was a small detachment of the 12th Louisiana Regt. They were required to maintain one picket post after night. One night after I had placed our regimental pickets I desired to ascertain if those of the 12th Louisiana were in line with ours. Not finding anyone I gradually made my way toward our breastworks, and at the base of the hill less than thirty feet of our main line I found them, a lieutenant and three or four men. The first intimation I had of their proximity (for it was a dark night) was the click of the hammers as they cocked their guns. I made no halt, and a moment later two men jumped on me and ordered me to surrender. It required considerable "talk" to convince them that I was not a Yankee. After I had proven my identity the lieutenant began to reprimand me for my rashness in passing in front of the pickets. I silenced him by the assurance that I should report the fact that he had not placed his pickets on a line with the others. I did report the matter, and when the pickets were sent out next evening there was a special order requiring the pickets of the 12th Louisiana to be posted in line with the others.

It was now a common topic of conversation that the garrison was to cut its way out of Vicksburg. From certain indi-

cations I feel convinced that some of our leaders did seriously contemplate such an undertaking. In view of the condition of the men, such an attempt would have been utter
madness. We were wholly unfitted for such exploits because
of the weakness from hunger and the stiffness of limb [en-
gendered] by weeks of crouching behind our works.

When the siege began we were receiving one-third of a
ration of meat and about two-thirds of a ration of meal. This
was soon greatly reduced. In lieu of the cornmeal we had
cow peas ground and made into bread. This bread after
being baked was about the color of an Indian, and a few
hours after being baked would, on being broken, show a
substance resembling spider webs which would stretch a
foot or more before finally breaking. For a time we had
fresh beef instead of bacon, and for a few days at one time
we had rice bread issued to us. Then the bread ceased altogether. Our ration then consisted of about one teacup-full
of boiled peas and a small bit, perhaps about two ounces, of
bacon. For several days before the capitulation we had,
instead of the bacon, about 3 or 4 ounces of *mule meat.*

Curl the lip in derision if ye will, ye dainty epicures, but
I ween ye never tasted a morsel more sweet than *"mule
meat and peas"* was to us! The flesh of the mule seemed of
coarser grain, but more tender than that of the ox, and had a
decidedly "horsey" flavor. To starving men, however, it was
very good. I have strong reason to believe that a dog had
been eaten in a Louisiana regiment a long time before any
mule beef was issued to us, and I know that a mule killed
near our line the first week of the siege was partly cut up
and presumably eaten by some of our men. And as to the
peas! I have wondered while eating them if I would ever
again find anything else that tasted so well.

Each regiment, or each company in fact, had its detail of
cooks who received the rations, cooked them and distributed
them to the men, bringing them up to the lines about dusk.
Often have I seen men so hungry that when the rations
came, they would eat the last morsel allotted them at once,
and not leave even a crust to stay the pangs of hunger till
another twenty-four hours had passed. Norvell Rodgers and

J.H. Ware were the cooks for our company and well did they perform the duty assigned to them.

On Friday July 3d, about 8 o'clock a.m., a flag of truce was sent out and by 10 o'clock the firing around the line had principally ceased. It was renewed about 3 o'clock p.m. and continued for about an hour, when it ceased altogther. Numberless conjectures were indulged in as to what was afoot. I felt assured that negotiations for a surrender were in progress, but when I expressed such a conviction I was hooted at by the regimental and company officers. Some of them even went so far as to state in detail the object of the truce and the result of the negotiations. It would be a-musing, if not so repugnant to candor, to witness the sub-terfuges resorted to to keep the men in ignorance of things of an unpleasant nature. The policy may be a wise one, but my experience has never demonstrated its wisdom.[2] That night while on the picket line, I endeavored to look the whole matter calmly in the face. I realized more forcibly than I had ever done before the strategic importance of the position we held, and the magnitude of its loss to the Con-federacy. But the more I reflected on the matter the firmer grew the conviction that we were prisoners, that perhaps we would be paroled and could go home.

The morning of the 4th dawned clear and serene. The cannon's roar and rifle's crack were hushed, the pall of smoke was lifted and the sun rose up in a cloudless sky. Even then the memories of the day could stir the despondent heart, and the blood ran quickly at the thought of what the day meant to the American people. But, oh, how burned the haggard cheek with shame and indignation to realize that on that day of all others Vicksburg should be surrendered! Why could not the deed have been consummated yesterday or tomorrow?

At an early hour we were informed that terms of ca-pitulation had been agreed upon, and about ten o'clock a.m. we performed the humiliating task of marching in front of our works and stacking arms in full view of the enemy, and under the direction of a Federal officer. Some of us wept as we did this, for we realized that this was the end of all our sacrifices. For this ignoble ending we had fought, had watched, had hungered and shed our blood, and many a brave comrade had gone to an untimely grave. Thus perished the glory we had so dearly won – thus had fallen the confederate Saragossa. To intensify the humiliation of the men was the suspicion, to many it was a conviction if they expressed themselves correctly, that Pemberton, our commanding general, had been false to the flag under which he fought.[3]

I need not dwell upon the time intervening between our surrender and the reception of our paroles. The terms of the capitulation were briefly these: all the officers to keep their sidearms and the field officers to retain their horses.

Shortly after the stacking of our arms the Federals marched into the city. It was gratifying to listen to the encomiums upon the endurance and bravery of the surrendered garrison that fell from the lips of the Federal soldiers. Not one time did I hear a soldier say, "We have *taken* Vicksburg!" Often did I hear such expressions as, "We thought you had three, or at least two, strong lines of works and men enough to occupy them. We find only one slender line manned by skirmishers. You have made a wonderfully brave defense."

On the 5th bountiful rations were issued to us, and on the 6th the paroling commenced. Our regiment was paroled on Friday 10th, and Saturday 11th Smith's division marched outside the lines. Our baggage was inspected before we passed the lines.

Belonging to Capt. Magee was a negro man who was as desirous of going home as any of us. He had asked for a parole every day since the surrender, had been put off on one pretext or another, and he was at the lines with the rest of us but without any written permission to pass them. We formed in a mass around him as we passed between the sentinels, but before we were entirely clear of them one of them saw the negro, and elbowing his way among us seized the negro by the collar and led him out of the ranks. Lt. Chamberlain, acting asst. quartermaster, brought his negro through the lines by having him lie down on the bottom of a

Mississippi Department of Archives and History

Copy of the author's Vicksburg parole, signed July 10, 1863.

wagon bed and piling boxes of crackers around him. It is not amiss to state just here that our regimental flag was also brought away. It was a silken flag and was presented to Company A when it first went into the field. It was now a mass of shreds and rags. In fact, most of it had been shot away but Capt. Sublett took the tattered thing from its staff, wrapped it around his body under his shirt and thus brought it away.

As soon as we had passed the sentinels, the Louisiana regiments of our brigade, disregarding the commands and expostulations of their officers, set their faces homeward and filed to the right. The officers appealed to the Federal guard and were laughed at in reply.

For 14 months we had been defending the Hill City, but now we were leaving it in the hands of the foe.

I will briefly notice our trip homeward. On Saturday night we bivouacked near Mt. Alban. Sunday morning we found that all of Company B had "straggled forward" during the night, except Capt. Magee, Lt. Lott, Stephen and George R. and myself. Norvell R. was also with us. We had been ordered to report at Raymond, and the fear of being sent to parole camp from that place under guard was the cause of the great stampede. Some of the company who had fallen out of line the previous afternoon soon came up. Continuing with the "rabble" (for no order was attempted), we crossed the Big Black River on a pontoon bridge where we encountered the last Federal guards. Some four or five miles the three Robertsons and I left the main road, turning to the right. During the afternoon we passed the fine country place of John T. Watson. It was now deserted, the Federals having been there that day. We also passed the plantation of Dr. Phillips. That night we slept under an oak near where Loring's division had a skirmish with the enemy in May.

Leaving Raymond to one side we steered for Crystal Springs. That day (Monday 13th) we passed the hamlet of Dry Grove and slept in an outhouse belonging to Mrs. Wade, about 8 miles west of Crystal Springs. Tuesday 14th we passed the last named place on the N.O.&J. R.R.[4] This seemed to be a business place and surrounded by well situated clay soil. That night we stopped with a Mr. Catchings whose unfeigned and unstinted hospitality was touching to us. It was also a house of mourning. Two noble boys had gone forth at the call of duty, and both had fallen in the Sunday's fight at Shiloh. May God bless both the father and the mother.

Mr. Catchings sent negroes and horses to convey us to Georgetown on the Pearl River. This was a place of some importance before the railroad was built, as it was a shipping point for a great deal of cotton by way of the river. After we had crossed the river it was decided that Stephen and I should go on ahead of the other two, reach home one day sooner, and send horses back to meet them. So we parted company about 10 o'clock a.m. on Wednesday 15th.

Passing Westville in Simpson County we spent the night with Mr. McCollum, father-in-law of Lt. Buchanan. We were well entertained here. Next morning Lt. B. (for we had already passed most of our company) procured a carriage and taking us in it, put us down at his place about 10 o'clock a.m. After forming the acquaintance of his lovely wife and dining with the family, we were sent ten miles further on horseback. Just at nightfall I reached my father's door after an absence of fourteen months. S. and G. reached their homes the next day.

After resting a few days we four, in accordance with a plan formed after we left Mr. Catchings (in fact, he suggested it), made a horseback trip to the crossing of Rocky Creek some four miles from Ellisville, Miss. A Federal raid had been stopped at that point and Mr. Catchings in telling us about it stated that it was commonly reported that all the pistols of the party had been thrown into a pond by the road side before they surrendered. We found plenty of signs of a fight and saw the grave of the killed, into which the hogs had rooted until a human foot and leg were exposed to view; but though we waded across the pond time after time touching every square foot of the bottom, we found no pistols.

In August beginning Saturday 8th, there was a series of meetings at Leaf River Church. W.E. Sheppard was pastor and did most of the preaching, though E.L. Carter preached two or three times. The meeting was continued till Wednesday 12th. The second day of the meeting I became much interested in my soul's welfare, but it was only during the last public service that I was enabled to lay hold on Christ as my Savior.

After reaching home in July we learned that the Vicksburg garrison had been granted a furlough of forty days by a presidential proclamation. In the latter part of August another proclamation was published, declaring all paroles given to the two places as null and void, and commanding the garrisons of Vicksburg and Port Hudson to repair to parole camp at once. I shall leave for camp again in a few days, reporting, I suppose, at Demopolis, Ala.

CHAPTER 10

Parole

Enterprise, Miss. Sept. 5. Last Wednesday, Sept. 2nd, I left home again. During the day I passed the spot where I taught school in 1860. I stopped a while and let memory dwell on things of the past, and those thoughts held more of pain than of pleasure. I arrived at this place yesterday afternoon, having learned before my arrival that a parole camp for Mississippi troops was located here. None of my regiment has reported yet, and being directed to go to the 4th Mississippi Regt. I found a partial acquaintance in the person of Jas. Barnes, who has a brother in our company. With him I am messing.

At home, Oct. 4. As several pages of my journal are lost covering the events of September, I can but briefly notice what has taken place.

On Sept. 9th I obtained a pass to visit an uncle, the Hon. Drury Bynum, who lives some twelve miles from Enterprise. I went by rail to Quitman, however. The time spent with him and his pleasant family passed quickly and I returned to camp on the 13th. Some of the regiment had come in by this time, and in a few days F.E. Collins and John Barnes of our company arrived. Our mess was getting so large that a division was necessary, and as Barnes and Collins preferred to remain with the former's brother I went to some members of Company I of our regiment. Cooking utensils were too scarce to mess alone.

I made application for the payment of some wages due me, and after several annoying delays I finally drew four months' pay. Major Clarke reported for duty about the 16th of the month and for a day or two commanded the brigade. On Saturday 17th the 46th Regt. was officially recognized as a separate organization, and on Monday 19th I was appointed commissary sergeant. Not liking the position, I resigned after a service of two days. Lt. Buchanan came in on the 20th. Gen. Baldwin arrived about the same time and stated that he would petition for our immediate exchange.

A new brigade has been formed consisting of the 4th, 35th, 37th, 40th and 46th Miss. Regts. For the next few days we were much interested in the news from the bloody field of Chickamauga.[1]

Sunday 27th I attended preaching at the Presbyterian church. Mr. Rutherford preached from Isaiah LV: 10-11. I am ashamed to say that I slept most of the time. On the 29th I applied for a five days' furlough and asked God to move the hearts of the officers to approve the application. I attended preaching that night, and as it was threatening rain I remained all night in the Methodist house of worship. Next morning I received my furlough *approved.* God had heard and answered my prayer. That night I went to Uncle Drury Bynum's. He kindly loaned me a horse and next day I reached another uncle, Jonathan Anderson, from whose house I arrived at home on Friday afternoon. This is Sunday and I expect to start on my return to camp on Tuesday next.

In camp, Oct. 15th. But little of interest has occurred since my last entry. On Monday Oct. 5th, I attended a gubernatorial election at Ochoha and cast my first vote. I left home again next morning. That night I stopped at the residence of J.L. Gandy in Jasper County. Mr. G. was not at home but I was well cared for. I reached Uncle Bynum's by noon and found my cousin, Dr. J.M. Bynum, just arrived from Gainesville, Ala., and much afflicted with rheumatism. Remaining with them overnight I came on here Wednesday 7th, and found that another member of Company B, Jasper Bond, had come in. They had formed a separate mess and I, of course, went with them. Lt. Crawford had been here, and both he and Lt. Buchanan had gone home.

At Uncle Bynum's I saw a list of the killed and wounded in the 7th Miss. Regt. at Chickamauga. Among the killed were the names of two men with whom I had gone to school. They were Capt. G.A. Robertson of Company G and John H. Copeland of Company I.[2]

Next day I went to the conscript camp to deliver some letters and expected to find Franklin R., but he was not in camp. Called at Mrs. W.P. Carter's and found that she was ill with typhoid fever. J.M. McRaney of our company came in on the 11th. We are required to move our camps and place ourselves in regimental order.

I have attended preaching nearly every night of late. Mr. Rutherford is generally the preacher. He is preaching in the Baptist meeting house. His sermons are full of the fat of the Gospel, and are calculated to build up the Lord's "little ones" as well as to awaken sinners. I was much interested in two sermons, one on "Predestination" and one on "Free A-gency," and with his statement that no finite man could reconcile the two doctrines, but that God could.

Oct. 21st. On Friday 16th we moved to our new camping place. The next day was the monthly preaching service at the Baptist house of worship. When I went in Mr. Ruth-erford was just closing his "Inquiry Meeting." He intro-duced me to Dr. William Howard, the Baptist pastor. At 11 o'clock the latter preached from II Chronicles XXVI: 5, "As long as he sought the Lord, God caused him to prosper." Dr. Howard is not a brilliant man, nor an eloquent one, but he seems to have deeply drunk of the waters of salvation.

In the afternoon a large crowd assembled on the left bank of the Chickasahay River, just above the bridge, to witness the ordinance of baptism. There were nine of us to be baptized, and while the people sang "Am I a Soldier of the Cross?" one by one we went down into the water and were baptized in the "name of the Father, Son and Holy Ghost." At night there was preaching again, at the conclusion of which the Lord's Supper was administered. Thus in one day I have participated in both the ordinances of the church of Christ.

On Thursday last we were reviewed by President Davis, accompanied by Gen. J.E. Johnston, Lt. Gen. Hardee, Maj. Gen. Forney and Brig. Gens. Hébert and Baldwin. It was a grand and imposing display of the pomp of war and the glory of the world. Mr. Davis made a speech in town after the review, though I failed to hear him.[3] S.J. Eaton of our company reported today. There is some dissatisfaction in camp because of rumors of exchange, and I understand several have gone home without leave.

Nov. 4th. On the morning of Oct. 24th we were officially notified that the 4th and 46th Miss. Regts. had been exchanged with Gen. Pemberton and staff. I asked Col. Sears to detail me to go home and notify the officers and men of the company. The request was granted and I started about noon. Reaching Uncle Bynum's I found his eldest son, Lt. J.H. Bynum, at home on furlough, and spent the night very agreeably. Next morning was Sunday. My uncle sent me a few miles on horseback, after which I proceeded on foot. Just at sunset I reached Tallahala Creek, and going a few miles further supped with a Mr. Frank Ulmer, after which I again set forward. The night was pleasant, the road dry and I made good time. By midnight I was in the neighborhood of my old school house. Seeing some camp fires off the road and feeling sure that it was an encampment of cavalry or of deserters, I resolved to investigate. I soon saw that it was cavalry and approached the nearest camp fire where I saw a sentinel on duty. He did not see me till I came up close and spoke to him. After some moments' conversation I made a movement to go on, when I was informed that I would have to stay there till morning. I soon had every officer on the ground (two lieutenants) aroused, and after considerable talk and some "bluffing" on my part they allowed me to proceed, seemingly apprehensive that they had incurred some dire penalty by detaining a soldier in the execution of a duty for which he had been specially detailed.

I reached my father's in the forenoon, and as soon as I had dined I mounted a horse and rode 20 miles to Capt. Magee's. We wrote orders till after midnight. Next morning I rode to Lt. Buchanan's, a distance of 20 miles, where I ate dinner and started for home, making a detour through the "Sullivan Hollow" neighborhood in Smith County, arriving at father's a little after dark. We were soon startled by a meteoric explosion which sounded like the bursting of a heavy shell, and an hour afterward a valuable dog belonging to my father was shot near the house, presumably by some deserter.

On Saturday 31st I started back to camp. At sunset I passed my old school house, and going some four or five miles further I lay down in the woods and slept. An hour before day I was again on the march. Reaching Oak Bowery Church in Jasper County a little before 11 o'clock, and learning that it was preaching day, I waited for the service. H.T. Jones (Congregational Methodist) was the preacher.

I reached Paulding that night and was kindly cared for by a Mr. and Mrs. J.M. Bradley, the latter of whom is my cousin. On the afternoon of the next day (Monday 2nd) I reached camp and found that three others of the company had come in.

The Baptist meeting is still in progress. Dr. Howard has returned to his home in Gainesville, Ala., but Elder N.C. Clarke, a missionary of the General Association, is here preaching. I heard him last night and considered it a helpful sermon. Alfred Prine and Jasper Bond of our company were baptized today. This morning for the first time in my life I attempted to lead in public prayer. Brother J.L. Lattimore, who is an ordained minister living in this town and who is a sergeant in the 37th Miss. Regt., was conducting a prayer meeting and called on me to lead. *I tried!* with fear and trembling.

November 6th. Night before last I again heard Bro. Clarke preach from the words "Lord, revive thy work." It was good to be there. Yesterday was a rainy day. I read some, slept some, wrote some and spent a lot of precious time in idle dreaming. They have just come in, a part of my company. Lts. Buchanan and Crawford, Stephen and George and about eight others arrived this afternoon. I am disappointed that so few have come.

Nov. 19th. Before and after my last entry we were busy constructing cabins and making preparations for cold weather. On Monday 9th we received orders to be ready to march at a moment's warning. All building was suspended, the companies were "ranked and sized" immediately, the ordnance sergeant was forthwith dispatched for arms and accouterments and the men were set to drilling. Altogether the camp presented a scene of great activity and real military bustle. Of course, rumors as to our destination were rife and, as usual, were all wrong.

Four or five more of Company B came in that day, Mr. Wm. Howell accompanying them. Through him I sent letters home. Next day, the 10th, just at nightfall, Capt. Magee, Lt. Lott and some others came in. The usual greetings incident to such an arrival were passed, and I had just "turned in" for the night when my father rode into camp. He had undertaken to bring the luggage of two members of Company B to camp. He had left them a few miles back since it was necessary that he start on his return next morning. I went with him till I met four of the company, among them the orderly sergeant.

Our marching orders had been countermanded, building was resumed and drilling was kept up. On the 11th we were armed with Austrian rifles.[4]

On Sunday 15th, Bro. Lattimore preached in our camp. He has made application to be appointed chaplain of our regiment, and as a recommendation by the officers is necessary this service was to afford them an opportunity of hearing him. Everyone affixed his name to a paper I drew up, and when I last saw Bro. L. he informed me that everything was moving along all right.

We have brigade drill every afternoon, which is to keep up until further orders. I am acting sergeant major and do not know when I can return to the company. Capt. Magee is acting lieutenant colonel and Capt. Heslip, major. About 35 of Company B exclusive of officers are in camp.

CHAPTER 11

Return to Duty

Near Resaca, Ga. Nov. 30th. This cold morning I am seated near a big fire with the sun shining in my face to bring up my journal. On Sunday 22d, Brother Lattimore preached in our regiment at 10 o'clock a.m. and at 2 o'clock p.m. Bro. E.L. Carter preached. I think I never heard a better sermon in my life than the one in the afternoon.

That night we had orders to march next day. Considerable dissatisfaction was developed at this order, and several deserted from the different regiments. About dark we marched to the depot and at ten o'clock we started. We had lost five men by desertion during the day and George was sent to the hospital sick. At Shubuta some four or five others got off, among them Lt. Crawford and Stephen R. I knew nothing of it till we reached Mobile as I had secured the *whole top* of a box car about the middle of the 4th Miss. Regt. I slept but little during the night as my position was an unsafe one in which to court the drowsy god.

Between Waynesboro and Winchester occurred one of those strange phenomena that baffles all attempts at solution. I was idly observing the objects as I passed them as well as the darkness would allow. Suddenly I became conscious that the scene was a familiar one. Surely I had seen it before, that southeastern slope, those few stunted short-leafed pines, the sparse undergrowth of oak and sumac and above all, an old field on my right. Each feature seemed as familiar to me as the premises at home. There, on that very spot, I once saw a *house on fire!* It was an old building, but I surely saw it burning. I vainly strove to remember when or how. It might have been a dream, but when or where I dreamed it I could not recall. I looked for the bare spot where the house had stood but could not see it. Yet everything else, even to a small brier patch near where the building burned, was vividly, even painfully real. The more I strove to solve the problem the more puzzled I became, and at last I gave it up as a hopeless task.

About 9 o'clock next morning we reached Citronelle, Ala., a celebrated summer resort for the people of Mobile and about thirty-three miles from that city. It is a pleasant looking place on a ridge of high pine hills. It was about noon when we landed in the Gulf City, as Mobile was often called. From the depot we were marched directly to the wharf where, at about 2:30 o'clock, we went on board a steamer. I saw but little of Mobile. Near the wharf were a couple of floating batteries and an uncompleted structure which I was told was a "monitor." Some fortifications below the city were visible and away down the bay arose a column of black smoke as from a steamer. There was also a line of obstructions across the bay not far below the city.

I hoped we would get out of sight of land but in this I was disappointed. Soon after we started I observed a low-lying mass of rather dark looking cloud in the northwest which seemed to be moving in our direction, and pretty soon the wind, which was blowing gently from the south, suddenly changed and a much colder and stronger wind came down from the north. The bay now presented a beautiful spectacle, its surface being covered with white-capped dancing waves, which on striking the steamer threw their silvery spray over the lower deck.

It was about sunset when we debarked at Tensaw Landing on the east bank of the Tensaw River and some thirty miles from Mobile. A train of cars was in waiting for us and we were soon in the box cars, ready for transportation to any point in the Confederacy. Having slept but little the night before all hands went to sleep as soon as we started which was about dark. At daylight we were at Pollard, Ala., some fifty miles from Tensaw. We had been there since one o'clock a.m.

Starting at daylight we ran for several miles through a poor pine woods composed of low ridges between which "bays" and gall-berry flats were greatly in evidence. Thirty miles from Pollard is Evergreen, a nice village and the county seat of Conecuh County. Here some of our boys (a part of the 40th Miss. was on the train with us) became reckless and "charged" every pie-vendor and cake basket they got sight of, besides being guilty of some other boisterous conduct. After a stay of half an hour we pulled out and made a run of forty miles to Greenville, the county seat of Butler County, where we made another half hour stop and where the scenes of the morning were reenacted. Greenville is a nice looking town and the first place of any size we had reached.

At 1 o'clock p.m. we left Greenville and about ten miles further came to Fort Deposit, a town of some importance and is, I think, in Lowndes County. No other place of importance was passed till we reached Montgomery, thirty miles further.[1] It was dark when we reached the capital city of Alabama. I was detailed at once as a patrol guard where I remained till midnight when I was relieved. I made my headquarters at the Exchange Hotel, where I had a barber to shave me. He cleaned only the "high places" of my face, and when he was done I was most frightfully "ring-eyed." A man is liable to get smoked who rides 200 miles or more on top of a box car.

From what I saw of Montgomery I should pronounce it one of the wealthiest and cleanest cities in the South. The Legislature was in session, I think. After being relieved from guard duty I found my regiment at the West Point depot in the eastern part of the city.

About 8:30 o'clock next morning we pulled out for West Point, distant about 90 miles.[2] It was a monotonous run that day. The first place of any importance we saw was Auburn, more than sixty miles from Atlanta. The next place of any importance is Opelika, which is rather a nice looking place. A branch road to Columbus, Ga., interesects the Montgomery and West Point road at this place. From some cause we stopped here some two hours, during which time three or four fat shoats were killed by the train which kept moving back and forth on the track. In every case, however, a soldier had hold of the animal's hind legs when the accident occurred.

It was dark when we reached West Point so I did not see

the town at all. From this point to the Florida line the
Chattahoochee River is the boundary between Alabama and
Georgia, and I think the town is mostly on the eastern side
of the stream. Because of a difference in the gauge we
changed cars here and soon started again. Everybody went
to sleep and I saw nothing of importance till we reached
Atlanta about 8 o'clock next morning.

It is said that we had orders to proceed no further than
Atlanta, but through somebody's blunder we started toward
Chattanooga about 11 o'clock a.m. – no one, not even the
conductor, seeming to know where we were going or by
whose orders we were being moved. During our short stay
in Atlanta I remained at the depot and saw but little of the
city. It does not seem so nice a place as Mobile or Montgomery, yet I think it is more of a *business* place than either.
There are some extensive fortifications here, some of the
formidable looking being along the Chattahoochee River
which runs a few miles north and west of the city.

Twenty-two miles after leaving Atlanta we came to
Marietta. I really think there are more beautiful girls in this
town than in any other of its size in the Confederacy. And
they seemed more patriotic, too, for the road was lined on
both sides with them, and they cheered us as we passed. We
had our old bullet-tattered flag on a new staff, and it was
carried by Tom Malone, a big Irishman in Company H, who
waved it faithfully all the trip. At Marietta a beautiful young
lady held a silken Confederate flag and when our gallant
Hibernian saluted her flag and she returned the salute, our
boys fairly made the "welkin ring" with their shouts.

Ten miles further we reached Big Shanty where we were
delayed some two hours by passing trains. These trains, laden with wounded soldiers, were running without any
schedule and were so close together that it was dangerous to
make a start. We did start, however, and after proceeding
about three miles came so near colliding with a southbound
train that the two engines were only a few feet apart when
brought to a stand still. We had to run backward to Big
Shanty.[3]

By 8 o'clock a.m. we reached Dalton, Ga., about 97

miles from Atlanta. But long before this point was reached we had seen thousands of stragglers from Bragg's army, which had been driven from before Chattanooga. Long trains of wagons were seen moving to the rear. At Dalton the scene presented all the confusion incident to a retrograde movement of an army. There were hundreds of men without arms separated from their commands, wagon trains with no one to direct them and women and children with no one to protect them. All sorts of people were running hither and thither, *and it was a great place to hear the news.* There was not a cartridge in that portion of our brigade that was here, yet we were within a few miles of the enemy and expected to be rushed to the front. At this juncture, Cols. Barry (of the 35th Miss.) and Sears came up and the former assumed command of the brigade. After some two hours' delay it was arranged to return to this place. We accordingly did so, arriving here at 4 o'clock p.m. on Saturday 28th.[4]

Resaca is about 85 miles from Atlanta and is in Gordon County. It stands on the right bank of the Oostanaula River in a mountainous region. There is no town here. Large numbers of government wagons are in sight, though yesterday and today they are moving toward Dalton and this morning I saw several pieces of artillery moving toward the front, and it is probable that Gen. Bragg will not retreat any further. All the regiments of the brigade are here now, also Gen. Baldwin.[5]

The weather is bitterly cold and the men seem to be low spirited. This feeling is said to pervade the entire Army of Tennessee. I do not know exactly what has happened at the front. That our army was driven away from Chattanooga is very evident, and from the confusion we witnessed I infer it sustained a very severe repulse. I learn that our friends in Company I, 7th Regt., are all safe. If we remain here long I will try to visit them. We are now supplied with ammunition and may be sent to the front.[6]

Dec. 4th. A rainy cold day. We have stretched a blanket and have a tolerable shelter from the rain. I have seen many a soldier entirely barefoot and thinly clad since I came here. To such, this is indeed bitter weather. We have organized a prayer meeting in the regiment. May God help us to be useful.

Dec. 6th. Sunday. Last evening in company with four others I walked out a few miles from camp and ate supper at a farm house, where we had an abundance of substantial fare. It is said this morning that we will move to the front at once.

Dec. 9th. We are still here, doing nothing. We have been informed many times that we would go to the front or back to Mississippi right away, but so far all such rumors have proved groundless.

Before we left Enterprise an examining board, with Col. Sears as president, was appointed to examine all officers in the brigade entitled to promotion by election or seniority. The elections resulted as follows: Company B, J.T. Duckworth; Company F, R.N. Rea (son of the captain) and Aaron Roberts; Company G, J.H. Linbough; Company H, Rufus White; and Company I, Jefferson Bell and S.S. Turner. Rainy and cold yesterday and last night. Today the sun is shining and it is the mildest day we have experienced since coming here.

I have been reading in "Acts" and wished to converse on many points, but there has been no one present who feels enough interest in matters to converse about them. Since leaving Enterprise I have been messing with Lt. Buchanan, Sergts. McLaurin and Pickering, Wilkinson and J.T. and Z.F. Duckworth. An order from Gen. Hardee directs that two men from each company be detailed as company cooks. For some reason the measure is regarded with disfavor.

Dec. 11th. Nothing of interest to record. Our prayer meeting last night was a precious time. Threatening rain today.

Dec. 14th. Today I am twenty-four years old. What a multitude of emotions are evoked by the thought! What an eventful year it has been to me! Above all others is the thought "I am born again." The family record gives Dec. 14th, 1839, as my natal day; in the record of my soul it is Aug. 12, 1863.

[Vann R. Martin Collection]

Lt. Col. William K. Easterling, 46th Mississippi, resigned his commission in December 1863.

Heavy rains last night and a cold north wind today.

Dec. 16th. Our regiment worked on a road yesterday leading toward Dalton. We have been ordered to have company drill, but cannot find a level place big enough for a drill ground.

Dec. 20th. It is night. Another Sunday is gone! We are in the woods and the tumult of the camp is hushed in sleep. Late in the afternoon of my last entry it began to rain, and about midnight we had a storm of wind that made a plaything of our frail shelter, accompanied by a perfect deluge of rain. In a moment we were soaked, and as we could have no fire we had to stand or sit or lie in the water and mud till daylight, and the rain was still pouring down. It was truly a disagreeable time. As Lt. Buchanan, some others and I were huddled around the place where our fire had been, and Lt. B. was grumbling at our case, Sergt. McLaurin (who had covered his face with something and was still lying down) called out, "Yes, that's what you get by voting for 'peaceable secession'!"

"Yes, by George! And I'd do it again!" replied Buchanan as quick as a flash, and he grumbled not another word that night.

Friday, the 40th Regt. was sent to this place as pickets. Yesterday (Saturday) we worked the road again and at night received orders to come here this morning. We did so and are now in the woods. It is a pretty location for a camp as there is plenty of wood and water. We will erect cabins at once, though our officers still think we will return to Mississippi. We are five or six miles from Resaca and not far from some high mountain peaks. This place seems to have two local names, to wit, "Snake Gap" and "Sugar Valley." As we have seen neither snakes nor sugar today, the proper name is still a matter of uncertainty.

The distance to Resaca, the nearest station, and the desperate condition of the roads over which rations are to be hauled is the greatest objection to the encampment. Some changes have occurred in our regiment. Lt. Col. Easterling has resigned; Clarke will be promoted. Rea will become major, and Magee senior captain. This entitles our company to the right of the regiment and we are in our new position. My fire is burned out, the moon is going down in the west, and with regret I close my book to seek a soldier's bed and dream a soldier's dreams.[7]

Dec. 25th. Christmas again. It is a cloudy day and the wind is wailing through the valley like a spirit of unrest. We have completed our cabin except the chimney. It seems we came to this place to keep the roads in order, rather than to do picket duty. Our regiment and the 40th [are] working on alternate days. This is *our* day to work, but we have a holiday. I will also state that this is not "Snake Gap" at all. At one time a railroad was graded through this valley, but there is no evidence that a track was ever laid. I think it leads from Rome to Dalton.

Yesterday I climbed the rocky heights northwest of us and beheld some grand scenery; but, on the whole, I was disappointed. After a walk of three miles with considerable climbing, I reached the highest point of land within several miles perhaps. To the north, east and south were valleys with miles of alternate woodland and farms. I could see the villages of Resaca and Tilton, could catch glimpses of the Oostanaula, and away down the railroad I saw a train of cars and its engine. How it seemed to creep along! Its rush and roar did not reach my ears at all. Westward was a wild succession of peaks and rocks, but not one vestige of the presence of man.

Dec. 27th. Sunday and raining again. A dreary, dreary day and, as usual, I have indulged in such dreams as fancy chose to paint. We are snugly sheltered, and we ought to feel thankful to God that we are not like thousands of others who today are exposed to all this inclement weather. Yesterday on dress parade an order was read that one man in every 30 would be furloughed home. The fortunate one in our company will probably be selected by lot.

Col. Sears has directed that all non-commissioned officers be examined as to their qualification for the places they fill. Major Rea, Capts. Magee and Burgess, and Lt. Wiles constitute the examining board. An effort has also set on foot by Col. Sears to send the commanding officer of every company home as a recruiting officer. I hope he may succeed.

Dec. 28th. Gen. Baldwin inspected us today. We drew for a furlough yesterday afternoon and Sergt. H.H. Bass was the lucky man. Rained heavily last night. Becoming cold.

Dec. 29th. Just twelve months ago today was fought the battle of Chickasaw Bayou. We held an election today to fill the vacancy occasioned by Lt. Lott's removal. Sergt. A.H. McLaurin was elected.

1864

Mississippi Sojourn

We remained at "Sugar Valley" till the 16th of January. We were comfortably situated and our duties were not extra heavy. During our stay there I secured a pass to visit the 7th Miss. Regt. at Dalton. In company with Sergt. Pickering I started during the afternoon of the 13th. Night overtook us and we had to stop with some Tennesseeans. Next morning we found the regiment we sought and spent the day with them very pleasantly.

I was also much gratified to have placed in my hands one day the commission of John Lee Lattimore as chaplain of the 46th Miss. Regt. I lost no time in forwarding it to his address.

On Saturday January 16th, we left our camp and proceeded to Resaca. On Sunday 17th we boarded the train for Atlanta. From there to West Point, thence to Montgomery by rail and from that place to Mobile by steamboat followed without any breaks or stopovers, but in a leisurely manner. We reached Mobile Tuesday 26th, and marched out to Dog River Factory where we erected some temporary cabins. Sometime either before or after we left Georgia, Lts. Duckworth and McLaurin were examined and assigned to duty as second lieutenant and junior second lieutenant of Company B, 46th Miss. Regt. F.E. Collins was made orderly sergeant.

Feb. 4th. I will briefly note one or two events. Yesterday morning in compliance with orders, we proceeded to man the fortifications below the city. Our brigade occupied the extreme left of the line and was therefore immediately on the bay. When placed in position, the right companies of each regiment were deployed as skirmishers. While we were deploying, many of the ignorant people on the outskirts of the city thought that fighting was about to begin. Seeing how badly frightened they were, some of the boys said and did things to add to their dismay. It was *funny* but it was not *right* to cause so much disquietude. We returned to camp about 2 o'clock p.m. Afterward, when the drum beat for dress parade, a part of the regiment, that is, nearly all of Companies H and K, stacked arms and refused to perform any more duty until they were paid some, at least, of the wages due them. About 35 men were placed under guard and taken to brigade headquarters. They are still in custody. We will have prayer meeting again tonight.

Feb. 12th. I am on guard duty today. On Thursday 4th inst., we received orders to be ready to move at 4 o'clock next morning. Owing to lack of transportation facilities we did not leave our encampment till noon. Saturday 6th about 4:30 o'clock p.m. we started up the M.&O. R.R., our destination being understood to be Meridian, Miss.

There are no towns of importance on the railroad between the two places, except Enterprise and Shubuta. I will name some of the stations. First is Whistler, a suburb of Mobile. The next place is Citronelle in the hills thirty-three miles north of the city. Many of the wealthy families of Mobile have summer residences here and there are some fine cottages to be seen. The next station is Deer Park. I understand the principal business here is shipping venison. There is no town. The next station is Escatawpa, then State Line, about sixty-five miles from Mobile. Then comes Buckatunna, Winchester (the county seat of Wayne County, Miss.), then Waynesboro and Red Bluff. All these are on the eastern side of the Chickasahay River. The next is Shubuta, the only town west of the river. This place has done a great deal of business, having shipped more produce than any other point on the road between 1856 and 1860. Next above Shubuta is Desoto, then Quitman and then Enterprise. It was with feelings of real pleasure that I approached the latter place. True it was night and I did not expect to see a single face that I knew, yet there are pleasant associations connected with my stay there. My church membership is there – it was there God's people first welcomed me as one of them and there I was baptized. It is fifteen miles from Enterprise to Meridian and there is a little station called Oakatibee in between.

We arrived at Meridian about 4 o'clock Sunday 7th. We had been so crowded in the cars and it had been so cold that we slept but little, and in a few minutes after stopping we had plenty of fires burning. The vicinity of the depot was thronged with soldiers awaiting transportation westward. As soon as it was daylight I walked over the place, visiting our old encampment and other familiar spots. Some houses, generally of a shabby sort, had been erected since I was there before.

Ascertaining that we could not leave in several hours, I took occasion to visit Mr. McLemore who lives some two and a half miles east of town. With Mrs. McLemore I left some clothing and about 175 MS. pages of this journal. After partaking of a nice dinner I returned to my command.

(Author's note — It is proper to state here that Mrs. McLemore placed the MS. in one of her trunks, and on the approach of the Federals sent her trunks away. They were captured by the enemy and rifled of their contents. Some days afterward, a gentleman named Pickering, or Pickard, found a roll of MS. with my name on it where a Federal detachment had spent the night. He kept it. The next May a soldier named Creel, who had just reached camp, informed me of its whereabouts. I wrote to Mrs. Pickering and after a delay of some months, I received it in a mutilated condition. The entries for September 1863 and January 1864 were entirely lost).

That night Judge Harper of Covington County came to us. By him I sent letters home, which are perhaps the last I shall be able to send for some time hence. On Monday 8th all the brigade except our regiment was sent toward the front.

I have omitted to state that a large force under Gen. Sherman had marched eastward from Vicksburg, devastating the country through which he passed, and was at that time some 20 or 25 miles west of Meridian and moving in that direction.[1]

We were ordered to be at the depot at daylight next

morning. We were there on time but there was no train there to haul us. We were then ordered to be ready to move at 12:30 o'clock p.m. Long before the designated hour arrived we learned that we would return to Mobile. As Mississippians, we were greatly hurt at this announcement. We had come home, as it were, to check the progress of the invader who was marching through the center of the state. With indignant hearts we learned of his advance and the wholesale destruction that attended it. We knew that our forces in his front were steadily falling back, but now the whole state was to be abandoned without a single blow. No wonder the hearts of her sons burned within them; and no wonder if they learned to distrust the policy that gave up their homes to the torch and their families to the tender mercies of the foe. And all this time it was stoutly maintained that our force was greatly superior to that of the enemy.

Another feature we did not like was this: A large portion, perhaps all, of Loring's division was composed of the Vicksburg garrison, and we knew that these troops had been sent to the rear. At the time we understood that to mean that our leaders doubted the validity of the recent exchange.

All these things tended to demoralize us, and in the first heat of my indignation at the entire abandonment of my own state I resolved to leave the regular service, help organize an independent command and fight the enemy nearest my own home. I found that nearly the entire regiment, officers and all, viewed the matter as I did. After reflection, however, when I had grown more cool, I could not obtain my consent to abandon the Government in its dark hour. It is true I believed that incapacity, if not worse, characterized the [War] Department at Richmond and many of the minor departments, that the Government as at present organized will fail to establish itself, and that if the war is continued a great while longer, it will be by small independent organizations in which each man will feel personally responsible for the success of every undertaking. Yet I felt under such obligations to the "powers that be" that I could not turn my back on them yet. Heart and soul, as well as physically, I had enlisted in the Confederate service, my sympathies had been with the Government so unfalteringly, and I had desired its success above any earthly thing so long and so ardently that I felt it my duty to follow its standard to the bitter end. In such a frame of mind we waited around the depot. By noon the rest of our brigade had returned, having been only a few miles out, and the long afternoon dragged by.

About 10 o'clock p.m. we started on our return, but so many had left the regiment that some companies were slimly represented. I knew that many of my own company would leave the train at Shubuta, so I remained awake till we had passed that point. It was about 2:30 o'clock a.m. on the 10th when they left. I bade them farewell and to the very last they begged me to go with them, promising to make me their leader, to make no stop at home, and not to go there if I would lead them against the foe. I doubt if I'll ever see one of them again, but these men *are neither traitors nor deserters.*

It was about 3 o'clock p.m. when we reached Mobile. The same afternoon we marched out to our former encampment. There are only about one hundred and fifty enlisted men in the regiment – so many have gone. Company B numbers nine officers and all. The rest of the brigade came in yesterday. All the regiments have suffered more or less by desertion, if it may be called that.

Yesterday I went to the city. I saw much that interested me, yet I cannot undertake a description thereof. Some of the streets have splendid buildings on them. I suppose Government Street is the handsomest thoroughfare in the city. One of the imposing buildings on that street is used as a Female College now. I noticed several nice churches, though I went inside none of them. Perhaps I was most interested in the "Soldiers Library" on Water Street. There is a large assortment of reading matter, books, pamphlets, magazines and newspapers all conveniently arranged, and seats and tables for writing. I was informed that it was fitted up at the personal expense of Rev. F.B. Miller, post chaplain, by whose exertions it is still kept open.

On my return in the afternoon I visited two cemeteries, in both of which I saw fine tombstones and costly shafts. Perhaps the most suggestive of any I saw was a white polished shaft standing on a grayish colored pedestal. There was no carving of any sort to mar the polished stone. On one side was chiseled the name "Bessie," on the opposite side "Eighteen." As I walked among these stately shafts, all commemorating the virtues of those who slept beneath, I asked myself if they slept any more sweetly than the uncoffined dead on half a thousand battlefields. It was with pensive feelings I left those cities of the dead.

Brother Lattimore, our chaplain, about the last of January, having started to Georgia about the time we left, missed us on the way. We left him at Enterprise. He wishes to move his family to a safer place.

Feb. 15th. Nothing of special interest since my last entry. Several more of the regiment have come in, amongst them one more of Company B. The regiment now numbers about 225, including officers. But those who are here are dispirited and cannot fight; they, as well as those who left us, would have made a splendid fight in Mississippi, but since the whole state was given up without striking a single blow the men have lost confidence in the Government, and especially in its representatives. Most of those who have left us have left the service for good, so far as the regular army is concerned.

It is said that Mobile is to be evacuated. Such a step would, perhaps, be a wise one, for what benefit it would be to the Confederacy, after all the railroads in Mississippi are in the hands of the enemy, is more than I am able to see. It is urged that it is the key to the Alabama River. This is true, but if the Federal column now at Meridian is so minded it can push on to Selma and control the river there. We may allow ourselves to be besieged and have the Vicksburg tragedy enacted over again, but viewed from my standpoint it will not pay to do this. Besides, we can be starved out here though the enemy never comes in sight of the city.[2]

The enemy has Meridian. It is reported that a heavy force is moving from Huntsville, Ala., to form a junction with

Sherman at Selma or Montgomery. If this be so, and another column should move from Pensacola to Pollard, we would be entirely cut off from all sources of supplies. It is plainly in evidence that the region contiguous to Mobile is not capable of sustaining an army. It is a shame, a stigma on the fair fame of the Confederacy that thirty-five thousand hostile men should march entirely through Mississippi and Alabama, and no obstacle be placed in the way to impede their progress. We are told that the country is devastated where they go — that their trail is marked by the smouldering ruins of burned dwellings, that crops are destroyed, and that everything that ministers to the necessities of life is laid waste by a remorseless foe. Never did I once think that such degradation could come upon my beloved native state, so long as she had *one* son left whose heart beat true to freedom, home and God! An apathy seems to have fallen on our armies and stilled the energies of our people. We are lying still till the chains of slavery are forged and the manacles fastened to our wrists!

Sometimes I wonder what posterity will think of this war after the last spark of Southern resistance is extinguished in blood. Why such wholesale destruction of life and property? Why such rivers of undying hatred? What induced thirty millions of the human race living under the same government, all speaking the same language and having a common origin, to engage in such an unholy strife? Already three quarters of a million of the best and bravest of the land have given up their lives. A hundred thousand widows and nearly half a million orphans fill the land with lamentations. With us in the South, the wheels of social progress are stopped, religion is retarded and the arts and sciences are laid away and covered with dust; forgotten are the amenities and all that elevates, ennobles and adorns. And for what? Nominal freedom will come to some four or five millions on an inferior race, who will probably be invested with the right of suffrage without intelligence to use it, thus affording to the world the most conspicuous example in all its history — that republican governments are a failure.

I may be wrong in these predictions. It is not given to

man to pierce the veil that shrouds the future. God can yet open a way for our deliverance and make us a prosperous and a mighty people, but *is* such his purpose? We have written, spoken, preached and prayed as though we knew that God purposed the achievement of our independence. It is a sweet sentence which says "God loveth whom he chasteneth." No worldly prosperity and no national success should make us for one moment willing to forego the love of the eternal Father.

The members of Companies H and K who stacked arms before we went to Meridian have been sent to Montgomery. It will go hard with them, I fear. Raining today.

Feb. 17th. Wednesday. Am here in camp all alone today. On Monday last, about dark, we received orders to prepare five days' rations and be ready to move at daylight. It was the sharpshooters alone, the right and left companies of each regiment, that had such orders. I was not well, being nearly sick, and crippled by a severe boil. It was thought best that someone should remain with the company baggage. Lt. Buchanan required that duty of me, so here I am. I can have roll call and company inspection as many times a day as I see proper, or I can dispense with them altogether.

The sharpshooters left at daylight Tuesday morning under Major Rea.[3] They were ordered to report to Col. Maury of the 15th Confederate Cavalry at Hall's Mills, said to be some six or eight miles from this place. I have heard nothing from them since. I would rather be with them, of course, but then I have much more leisure for reading here than if with them. Bro. Lattimore came in Monday and has a number of books to which I can have access at any time. I find that I can be edified and spiritually strengthened by conversing with him.

The 36th and 39th Miss. Regts. and the 7th Miss. Battalion have been attached to our brigade. There are still some desertions among the Mississippi troops, it being reported that about forty have left in the last two nights. It is further reported that the 35th Miss. Regt. will be dismissed from this brigade as soon as paid off.

Feb. 20th. Since the date of my last entry the weather

has been very cold. On Thursday morning the sky was overcast with clouds and a strong north wind was blowing. About 3 o'clock p.m. snow began to fall, which continued till after dark. I do not know how the others of my company stood the cold. I have not heard from them yet, but I knew they were not as well furnished with extra blankets as I was.

There is a gloom over our camp today. *Gen. Baldwin is dead!* That proud dashing form is cold and stiff in death, the light in those eagle eyes is gone out, and the splendid mind has ceased to exist so far as we are concerned. A few hours since, Brig. Gen. Wm. E. Baldwin seemed a favorite of fortune. He was in the prime of life, blessed with health, riches and honor, respected by his soldiers and confided in by his superiors. The path of preferment seemed to be already open before him.[4]

Feb. 22d. Two years ago today we were mustered into service as soldiers. The whole scene rises before me and I can recall some of the emotions I felt that day. I can feel again the thrill of pride that swelled my heart as I was the first one to step to the designated line. Of the number who followed me only two or three are in the field. Some are dead while many more have abandoned the cause and gone to their homes. I vividly recall the speech of Lieut. Fairley, the election of company officers and then the naming of the company. This latter subject was one of great importance, and many names were suggested. I proposed a very *bloody* one, one that seemed almost terrible enough to frighten the Yankees into making overtures of peace, and which was not adopted and therefore the war is not yet ended.

And I remember the "drill" we had after the meeting adjourned. I've drilled considerably since then, but I doubt if I ever felt any more interest in it than I did that day. And I guess that Gen. Hardee himself would have been puzzled to explain some of the maneuvers we executed there on the streets of Williamsburg.[5] The war was a popular thing then.

Gen. Baldwin's remains were buried yesterday. I think nearly the entire brigade attended the funeral, only one regiment bearing arms. The funeral procession of the General of Brigade is one regiment of infantry, a company of cavalry and two pieces of artillery, though as many others as wish to can join the procession, carrying only sidearms. I did not leave the camp. Have had no word from the company yet.

Feb. 24th. On the date of my last entry Lt. McLaurin came in at nightfall, and remained until this morning. He was detailed to return to camp and forward cooking utensils, ammunition, etc., to the battalion. From him I learned some facts connected with their locality, duties, etc. They are bivouacked on a stream called Bayou Batre, not far from the hamlet of Bayou Le Batre. It is about 27 miles from Mobile and hence about 22 from here. They are within a few miles of Pascagoula Bay. They marched the whole distance the day they left here. The men are said to be in good spirits, their duties are light and the locality is splendid foraging ground, the price of vegetables, milk, poultry, etc., being very low when compared with prices here. The forces there consist of the 15th Confederate Cavalry, two field pieces and three battalions of sharpshooters. The village is peopled entirely by "dagoes," and I suppose the name is true of most of the surrounding country.

They will likely remain where they are until some movement on the enemy's part necessitates a different disposition of our forces. That will be in the near future, however. Ever since yesterday morning there has been a heavy bombardment somewhere down the bay – at Fort Powell, I understand. I know nothing of its importance as a means of defense. The newspapers speak confidently of our ability to hold this place, but their confidence is almost enough to make one doubt it.[6]

Brother Lattimore preached Monday night. Text: "And as Moses lifted up the serpent in the wilderness, even so must the Son of man be lifted up; that whosoever believeth in him should not perish but have eternal life." The sermon was, upon the whole, a very instructive and impressive one.

Sergt. B.F. Devlin of Company G died suddenly yesterday afternoon. He was for several months commissary sergeant for the regiment. He attended the funeral Sunday, and yesterday when the company marched out to dress parade they left him sitting in his cabin. When they returned he was dead. His remains were buried this afternoon. I have been quite unwell for some days and am still afflicted with some severe boils. I am low spirited, too, and feel quite lonesome at times. Col. W.S. Barry of the 35th Miss. Regt. is commanding the brigade.

Feb. 29th. I am still alone, but am improving some physically, mentally and spiritually. I have been reading "Ripley's Notes" on Acts. I find it an interesting and instructive work.

We are informed that the Federal column which reached Meridian has gone back toward Vicksburg. If such is the fact I shall expect some of the company to return with Capt. Magee who, with the other company commanders, was detailed as a recruiting officer in January and is expected back in a day or two. At least, I can hope for a letter. The bombardment at Fort Powell continues.

March 3d. "Rejoicing" in a new pen, also a new bottle of ink for which I paid $2.00 a spoonful, I sit down to my journal. Capt. Magee returned March 1st. Not a man came with him. I am ashamed of my company. I was so proud of its record and of the reputation of the regiment that the disgrace that has come to both humiliates me. But if I was disappointed in the failure of the men to report for duty, I was even more disappointed in not receiving any letters from home. I had only a brief verbal message from father. Things at home are in an unsatisfactory shape. The "deserters" are causing a great deal of trouble and are cruelly harassing those who disapprove of their course. Father is getting his full share of their vindictiveness.

Another "match drill" came off yesterday at Camp Cummings – McNair's, Quarles' and our brigade being the contestants. I was unable to attend. I don't think our brigade made a very creditable showing.[7]

I suppose our sharpshooters will return from Bayou Le Batre tomorrow as the 35th Regiment has been dispatched to relieve them. The weather has been quite cold for a day or two. I attended prayer meeting last night. Am feeling less downcast than I did. I had a long talk with Bro. Lattimore last night. It was some comfort to know that his spiritual conflicts had been similar to my own.

March 4th. An incident occurred yesterday afternoon that to some extent, at least, varied the monotony of camp life and that deeply enlisted my sympathies. It was the "losing and finding again" of a little boy. He was about two years of age and could walk about the yard. His mother and little sisters thought he was asleep. Presently they missed him and began to search about the premises. Failing to find him they became alarmed and called in some of the neighbors. The mother came into our camp begging for help to find her lost baby. It was pitiful to watch her distress. The child was found about two hours afterward in the woods a mile from home. He was still walking steadily away from home. A negro boy was the first one to discover him. The little fellow said he was going to "see his papa," who I understand is somewhere in the army. I did not learn the family's name. It gladdened our hearts when the wanderer was found, but our gladness was tame compared to the *mother's joy.* And if her joy was so great we are told that the Father's rejoicing over the return of one of the lost children of men is even greater than hers.

March 8th. Nothing of special importance has transpired. The company returned Saturday 5th. On Sunday we had two sermons in the regiment. That in the morning was on the "Great Supper" and in the afternoon on the "Goodness and Severity of God." An interesting Bible class at night. Lesson text: first chapter of Acts of the Apostles.

Yesterday we were paid up wages to Jany. 1, 1864, and commutation for clothing for the year ending Oct. 8, 1863. As the "old issue" of Confederate notes will soon be worthless, it seems the Treasury department is very anxious to get rid of it, hence the large installment of wages we received. All the officers who were detailed to secure recruits have returned, and there has not been half a dozen brought into camp.

March 11th. Agreeably to orders received we will be "on the wing" again in less than twenty-four hours, so I will devote a little time to these pages. There has been some excitement among the officers this week in consequence of a rumor that Col. O.S. Holland of the 37th Miss. Regt. had been promoted to brigadier general and assigned to the command of this brigade. A protest against such assignment was drawn up, but I do not know the precise grounds of opposition. I suppose, however, they are not wholly *disinterested* ones. There seems to be a general desire, in the regiment at least, that Col. Sears should receive the coveted promotion. Such a promotion would enable several others to take one more upward step on the ladder of distinction.

On Wednesday last I was sent to the Government distillery near this place, in command of a corporal and nine privates to guard the premises. Large quantities of whiskey are manufactured here, and some of the men soon drank enough to render them boisterous and afterward utterly useless as guards. It was a dark gloomy day with a copious downpour of rain, accompanied by lightning and thunder. Supposing that I had an opportunity of sending letters by hand, I wrote to the home folks.

We are under orders to march at 12 o'clock tomorrow. It is said that we will go to Pollard where the 37th Miss. Regt. already is, and that "Holland's Brigade" will likely be organized there. As it now stands the brigade is composed as follows: 4th, 35th, 36th and 46th Miss. Regts., and the 7th Miss. Battalion. The 40th Regt. has been transferred to another department and has gone. The 35th is at Bayou Le Batre and Col. Barry is reported as saying that his regiment *shall not go* into a brigade under Holland. The reason for this is, probably, the fact that Barry is Holland's senior and hence cannot brook the latter's promotion in preference to himself.

Pollard, Ala. March 14th. The regiment left the encampment at Dog River Factory about 1 o'clock Saturday. Being hardly fit for duty I was left in camp to superintend the removal of the baggage. Before relating my own experiences I will say that the regiment went aboard the steamer at 4 o'clock p.m. and arrived at Tensaw in due time. After a detention of some hours they left there at 1 o'clock a.m. Sunday, and arrived at Pollard about 8 o'clock a.m.

It was the understanding that the regimental baggage

would be hauled away Saturday afternoon. About dusk e-
nough wagons came to take on half of it. It was said the
wagons would certainly return before daylight, and as it was
necessary to keep a guard anyhow I made no preparation for
sleep. Company K's baggage being placed with ours, and
one of that company being left as a guard, I found an
agreeable companion for the night in Private Jacob Moors.
About 8 o'clock Sunday morning the wagons came for the
residue of the baggage and we proceeded to the city. At 2
o'clock p.m. we embarked on board the steamer *Senator,*
McNair's Arkansas brigade occupying almost the entire
boat. The wind was blowing strongly from the northwest,
and I suppose this was the reason we did not follow the
usual route. Steaming up the Mobile River some ten or
fifteen miles we entered a pass connecting with the Tensaw,
which stream we reached some distance below the landing.

In steaming through this pass, which was quite narrow in
some places with very low banks, the Arkansas troops had
much sport in shooting alligators. The air was cool but the
sun shone brightly, and we frequently came in sight of rusty
looking monsters lying stretched on the bank in the sunshine. The eagerness of the sportsmen generally prevented
their getting near enough to put in telling shots. From the
blood-tinged water, however, I judged that all the bullets did
not miss the mark. Every Saurian, however, was able to take
the water and pass out of sight.

It was about 5 o'clock p.m. when we arrived at Tensaw
and a train was being made ready for us. As all could not go
on one train another was gotten ready as soon as possible,
and we started on the last one about 8 o'clock p.m. and
arrived at Pollard about 1 o'clock next morning. As I was
perched on top of a loaded wagon and sleep was not to be
thought of, I observed the country along the railroad as well
as the light of the moon near its first quarter would allow.
There is little to be seen. For the most part it is low, flat pine
woods, too sterile to ever be brought into a state of cul-
tivation. Williams Station is, I think, the most important
stopping place.

We are now occupying some cabins that other troops

have built, though we will probably move tomorrow. Mc-Nair's brigade is here and we are commanded by Gen. Cantey. [8] This is a pretty encampment. It is dry and level, and has good wells of water and plenty of fuel. I think "old Pollard" is some distance from the depot. The town strangely reminds me of Meridian as I first saw the latter. It is, I understand, between forty and fifty miles from Pensacola and is in Conecuh County, Alabama. Some four or five miles west of this point is the Escambia River. Nearer still on the other side is the Conecuh River and the two form a junction some miles south of here.

March 23d. Camp Lee, 4 miles northeast of Pollard. One week ago today the regiment marched from its old encampment, I being again left in charge of the baggage. I came on next morning and found the whole brigade encamped in close order; not only the brigade but the whole division is here. It consists of McNair's brigade, commanded by Col. Coleman, on the right; ours in the center, and Cantey's Alabama brigade, commanded by Lt. Col. Holcomb, on the left. Brig. Gen. Cantey commands the division. The rumored promotion of Col. Holland is still an unknown quantity. Our brigade is encamped as follows, beginning on the right: 4th, 7th (Battalion), 46th, 39th and 36th. There is room between the 7th Battalion and 46th for another regiment. The 35th is still at Bayou Le Batre and the 37th is somewhere in the direction of Pensacola. This is a poor, thinly settled region. We are encamped near one of the finest springs I ever saw. It affords an abundance of water for two brigades. We have erected good cabins for the sixth time this winter and are well prepared to "settle down" till time to move. Pollard is one of the points where the Government issues rations to those civilians who are dependent upon it for support. It is said that more than 900 women and children draw rations here on the 1st, 11th and 21st of each month.

On Friday last, Lts. Buchanan and Duckworth started home on "unlimited detail" to collect the company. Of course, I sent letters by them. Have received letters from W.C.R. of the 7th Miss. Regt. and Miss Northcutt. It is only about 20 miles to where the latter lives.

The event of most importance to us as a regiment is this: Last Sunday Col. C.W. Sears was commissioned as brigadier general and assigned to the command of this brigade. The promotion was wholly unexpected, although he had been recommended to the Richmond authorities. He assumed command on Monday 21st. Col. Barry left as soon as he was notified of Sears' promotion. William H. Clarke will become our colonel, Constantine Rea our lieutenant colonel and T.D. Magee our major, if he can pass the examining board.[9]

March 25th. Just two years ago today since I left my home. Memory has been with me all day.

Wednesday night was the time for our prayer meeting. Two other preachers were present beside our chaplain – Gardner from Smith County, who has a son in Company G, and Rev. A.G. Bakewell, chaplain of the 7th Miss. Battalion. The latter is an Episcopalian and hails, I think, from New Orleans. Both made talks on Isaiah 55th, dwelling mostly upon the words "Seek ye the Lord while He may be found; call ye upon Him while He is near." The same night the band of the 36th Regt. serenaded Gen. Sears at his headquarters. I think he responded in a few "happy remarks." After the completion of this performance the splendid band of the 17th Alabama tendered a similar compliment to the new general. Col. Sears was a splendid regimental commander, and for his many high qualities I respect and esteem him.

The scramble for office and general placehunting has perhaps already lost us more than one battle and may lose us many more. Too many officers have seemingly forgotten the common good and seek only their own aggrandizement and the gratification of their personal ends. But all the corruption and all the indifference to the distress of our people is not confined to the army. All over the land, if we may believe common reports, balls, soirées and revelings are the order of the day. It is said that Nero fiddled while Rome was burning. We, to say the least, are aping his follies. Surely *now* is *not* a "time to dance."

March 31st. On the night of the 25th a meeting of the officers and men of the regiment was called to consider the subject of reënlisting for the war. We reënlisted, however, by adopting some very bold resolutions of the original fire-eating sort (but which I endorse) and were "mustered in for the war," be it long or short, on Sunday by Capt. I.V. Enochs of the 36th Miss. Regt. and acting inspector general of Sears' brigade. But I am compelled to say that it was the immediate prospect of obtaining furloughs that induced many of the men to reënlist.

A liberal system of furloughs has been promised and I trust it may be carried out. Furloughs are to be given to one officer, a non-commissioned officer and three privates in every company. Of course, applications were forwarded right away. Most of those who are left have families at home who would be very materially aided by a week or two of help from the head of the family, just at this time. I will not grumble, however. If I get to go home at all it will be so much more than I have expected that I will be grateful indeed. I have learned that my friend W.C.R. of the 7th Regt. passed this place on the night of the 28th, going home on furlough.

A meeting, or a series of meetings, is going on in the brigade. Elder Williams, an army missionary, is the moving spirit in the meeting. He is a Baptist, is quite a young man and I think his home is in Mobile. For the past two nights he has given us earnest, practical and pointed discourses. Last night his sermon was based on that passage in Romans (X:41), "For Christ is the end of the law for righteousness to every one that believeth." Much interest was manifested and several asked for special prayer.

We are under orders to be ready to march at a moment's notice. Col. Holland is in the direction of Pensacola and we may go where he is. We are also ordered to turn over all surplus baggage. This would seem to indicate that "active service" for the summer is in contemplation, at least.

Since we left Mobile the weather has been rather cool and disagreeable. The breath of spring is in the air, however.

April 7th. It is raining today. No events of special importance have transpired since my last entry. On Saturday, 2nd inst., the 35th Regt. arrived and took the position between us and the 7th Battalion. The ordinance of baptism was administered on Sunday afternoon, a man in Company G named Chambers being the candidate.

At dress parade on Monday, April 4th, an order was read making some changes in the regimental staff. The office of Ensign having been created by the last Congress, Sergt. Major R.H. Wildy was promoted to that position, and I was appointed sergeant major to be obeyed and respected accordingly. Quartermaster Sergt. Warren Cowan having been transferred to the artillery service, James Deer of Company D was appointed to fill his place. S.S. Griffin of Company C was made ordnance sergeant.[10]

So I am no longer a member of Company B. It cost me a struggle to sever my relation to it, though we are still together. I feel, however, that my presence in the company had some influence in inducing others to be more faithful in the discharge of their duties. On the other hand, I will be thrown with the chaplain more and will have opportunities for reading and study that I would not have in the company.

The meetings for preaching still continue. Tomorrow has been set apart as a day of fasting and prayer. Service will be held in camp and the ordinance of baptism will be administered.

Another order relative to furloughs has been promulgated and it is thought the pending applications will all be disapproved. There is on this account considerable grumbling. The numerical strength of the regiment is being considerably augmented by the return of absentees.

April 16th. Three miles west of Selma. I will attempt a brief summary of events since I wrote here last. At that time about a week had elapsed since any reference had been made to our marching orders, and we had come to regard them as an "April Fool."

On Friday 8th there was preaching in our regiment (the "chapel" of the brigade). Bro. C.M. Gordon, chaplain of the 36th Miss. Regt., preached. Christians in the brigade generally observed the fast. All duties were suspended and those who were not religiously inclined enjoyed a holiday. Having been required to assist Adjutant John McRae in the preparation of an important document, I was prevented from attending the ordinance of baptism in the afternoon. On Saturday 9th the Young Men's Christian Association of the brigade met. The whole session was consumed in reading and revising the Constitution.

That night we had orders to prepare three days' rations at once. Next day, Sunday 10th, we left Camp Lee about 4 o'clock p.m. We bivouacked near the depot that night and next morning the 4th, 35th and 36th left on the trains for Montgomery. Owing to lack of transportation facilities, the rest of us had to wait until Wednesday 13th. On that day we left Pollard at 8 o'clock a.m. and arrived at Montgomery at 5 o'clock p.m. On a former occasion I noted the principal points of interest on this road. Nothing of interest occurred on the trip, if we except one shameful practice that some of our soldiers indulged in, and that was the shooting of stock along the road as we passed. I never saw such lawlessness, such wanton destruction of property before. And the perpetrators of this outrage were Confederate soldiers and their victims were citizens of the Confederate States. We profess to be fighting for the "rights of property," among other principles involved, and here were men acting as hardly a savage would act. I felt hurt at what my fellow soldiers did and I wondered why Col. Clarke, who was in command, did not have it stopped. Such disgraceful conduct has led many citizens to look upon our own soldiers as ruffians and thieves. Many a well meaning soldier is too short-sighted to understand that our own conduct has caused this odium to attach to our names, and he is therefore resentful and ready to indulge in a course that only serves to widen the breach.

There are doubtless mean men all over our land who *ought* to lose their ill-gotten wealth; but let not him who wears a soldier's uniform lift a finger against such a man. Our cause has been already injured by our soldiers in this way. Some will say that the enemy can do no worse than our own men are doing, and if their sympathies are still with the

South they are compelled to withhold material support because of the lack of means. It may be urged that the man
who is influenced by such mercenary motives is not a true
patriot. Perhaps not, but observation has taught me that the
man whose patriotism is wholly unmixed with something
lower is exceedingly rare. But this is being brief with a
vengeance!

After leaving the train at Montgomery we marched to the
boat landing rather above the city, where we remained all
night. Quite early on Thursday the boat that was to convey
us down the river was moored to the bank, and as it began
raining in a few minutes after its arrival most of the men
went on board at once. It was a disagreeable day and we did
not start till about 4 o'clock p.m. As usual the boat was
crowded far beyond its capacity, the weather was quite cool
and we were quite uncomfortable on the trip. We arrived at
Selma about midnight, debarked and endeavored to get a
little sleep. A cold rain was still falling and we could get
nothing to make fires with. Sleep, therefore, was a failure
and we had to shiver in the mud and darkness till daylight.

About 9 o'clock a.m. Friday 15th, we started to find a
camping place. We are here in the woods some three miles
west of the city on a sandy ridge and near a large creek.
Wood and water are both plentiful and convenient, and I see
no reason why the location should not be a healthy one.
There is considerable wealth about this place, and as it appears no troops have ever been encamped here we will
probably fare pretty well – if the soldiers will respect the
rights of the citizens. It is uncertain how long we will
remain here. It was the impression before we reached this
point that we would make no stop here, but would proceed
at once to Montevallo.

About the time we left Pollard, Adjutant McRae started
home on a short furlough. Since that time I have been attending to his duties as well as my own, and find it a
considerable burden. Hope he will return soon. Have had no
opportunity yet of visiting the city.

April 25th. I have this day received a letter from Mrs.
McLemore of Meridian, Miss., informing me that the MS.

pages of this journal left in her care fell into the hands of the enemy and were consequently lost. I feel somewhat cast down at this news, but will endeavor to supply the main facts from memory.

(Author's note — In the proper place I have noted the loss and subsequent recovery of the MS.).

Nothing of great importance has occurred since I wrote here before. We are still at the same place and the regiment is recruiting quite rapidly. The adjutant has returned and things are moving on as usual. We have battalion drill in the forenoon and brigade drill in the afternoon. Yesterday we were reviewed by Brig. Gen. Hodge, special inspector general from Richmond. The parade was witnessed by a great many ladies. And in fact, the maneuvers of the troops, especially in the brigade line, are nearly always performed under the eyes of many of the fair sex.[11]

In the afternoon of Saturday last, the students of the Female Seminary at Summerfield (some six miles distant) came in a body to "see the soldiers." It was a charming sight to see so many lovely girls just budding into a lovelier womanhood all dressed in uniform, their hands filled with flowers, their faces wreathed in smiles, their eyes sparkling with girlish gaiety, and yet with sweet, womanly sympathy turned upon the weather-beaten Mississippi boys, while their lips gave utterances to many of a hopeful, helpful word. Many a rough, rugged nature felt softened and uplifted after meeting these purehearted girls. Not being over gallant by nature, and less so by practice, I failed to receive any of the bouquets that were so lavishly dispensed, often accompanied by dainty little scraps of paper on which a tender thought or fervent wish was traced.

Affairs are in a bad way at home. Col. Robert Lowry with his command, the 6th Miss. Regt., is in that section hunting down deserters.[12] Many have already been hung and killed otherwise, and altogether it seems that those peaceful hills and vales are to be reddened with blood, though no vast armies meet thereon. G.G.R. was intercepted on his return to the army and is still detained somewhere on the way.

I have had no chance yet to visit the city of Selma. I think it is more a city of homes than of business, at least that was my impression as we marched from the boat landing here. It stands on the right bank of the Alabama River and is something over a hundred miles, by way of the river, below Montgomery.

(Author's note — After another interval of months I must again depart from the usual mode of journal-keeping and resume the narrative form. And circumstances must render my narrative very brief. My notes taken on the ground were copious enough for all practical purposes, but I can do little more than transcribe them. Some day I may attempt a more elaborate account of the campaign in Georgia than I can give in these pages. It has been truly said that in keeping a journal the more one sees, the less he writes. It requires leisure to write up the daily events. This has been denied me. Sometimes for weeks I have been barely able to note the rapidly shifting scenes that passed before me like the passing of a panorama. Home, Nov. 15th 1864).

On Saturday April 30th, a general review and drill was ordered to give the citizens of the vicinity, and especially the students of the school at Summerfield, an opportunity of witnessing the exercises. The day was beautiful and clear, and everything passed off most agreeably. Not being required to take my place in line, Chaplain Gordon (of the 36th) introduced me to some young ladies. In the Misses Richardson of Summerfield I found two very agreeable and fascinating companions. Later in the day I formed the acquaintance of Miss McIlwain, who I found to be very entertaining indeed, as well as beautiful in figure and face.

Before the exercises were concluded it was generally understood that the brigade (the only troops there) had received marching orders. Adieus were said, sighs were breathed, tears were shed and vows were softly spoken that in some cases death has left unfulfilled.

Never have I seen a better state of feeling between the

soldier and the citizen than during our stay at Selma, and never have I seen soldiers deport themselves so well. Not a single jar occurred so far as I know; on the contrary, the utmost harmony prevailed and, without exception, we look upon our brief stay at Selma as the most pleasant experience of life in camp. Hence, there were heavy hearts when those orders came.

.

CHAPTER 13

The Georgia Campaign

All of the brigade except our regiment left the camp on Sunday, May 1st. It was understood that we were to go to Tuscaloosa, Ala. At sunrise next morning our regiment took up the line of march. After traveling six or seven miles we reached Craigs Ferry on the Cahaba River. After crossing, a march of seven miles further took us to Bethel Church where we stopped for the night. Tuesday 3d we marched about fifteen miles, our route leading us some two miles to the south of Marion, the home of Howard College and the Judson Female Institute, and the seat of Perry County. Wednesday morning we were fourteen miles from Greensboro, Ala., where we expected to overtake the rest of the brigade. Reaching the town an hour before sunset we learned that the other regiments were some four miles further.

As we passed through the town Sergeant Henderson of Company K met a friend who invited him to spend the night with him, and requested him to bring a soldier friend. This honor was conferred on me. I was the more ready to accept the invitation as I was informed that there would be a concert in town that night.

At the home of our host we were well entertained. At the supper table, however, my natural awkwardness, which had been aggravated by several months of life in camp, caused me to drop the syrup-pitcher in my lap. I also formed the acquaintance of Miss Annie Rowlandson, a very pretty girl and an agreeable companion.

After supper we attended the concert, the proceeds of which were to be devoted to some benevolent object. I would like to give a detailed description of the exercises, but have not time to do so. After some singing, which was probably pretty good, though to my uneducated ear it seemed very affected, there was a series of tableaux which were really fine, especially one, "Comin' Through the Rye."

The principal entertainment, however, was the performance of a lengthy so-called charade, the name of which I have forgotten. "Cousin Frank" who was dreadfully lovesick, said and wrote a great many silly things, and "Cousin Margaret" in a spirit of mischief said many more that were downright provoking. "Aunt Patty's" cap and "Daddy Hogan's" long-tailed, claw-hammer coat were very amusing, and the whole rendition was creditable to the amateur performers. With a comic speech that fairly brought down the house, the affair came to an end.

Greensboro is a beautiful town. There were on every hand evidences of wealth and refinement. A fine building just south of town is used by the Methodists as a college for young men. The town enjoys no railroad facilities, but there is more life and animation there than in any other town I know of. When the concert was over, Sergt. H. and I went out to where the regiment was bivouacked. During the night orders were received from Maj. Gen. French to proceed to Montevallo with the least possible delay. This made it necessary to retrace our steps for about ten miles.[1]

We took up the new line of march on Friday morning and traveled about 25 miles through the dust and heat, and many of the men gave out. Saturday, we marched only about -- miles, leaving Marion on our right again. Making an early start on Sunday 8th about sunrise, we passed through the village of Centerville, the seat of Bibb County. About noon we passed another hamlet called Six Mile. By 2 o'clock p.m. we had marched about eighteen miles and stopped for the night at a point some five and a half miles west of Montevallo. Monday, May 9th, we reached Montevallo and some two or three miles beyond it, and went into a regular camp near a magnificent spring.

Montevallo is in Shelby County and is fifty-four miles from Selma (by R.R. still less), yet we had marched one hundred and twenty-five miles to reach it. It is not a large town at all. Iron is found in the vicinity and there is a foundry here, where rough castings are made.[2]

Tuesday 10th we received orders to move again, and on the morning of the 11th we repaired to the depot after a night of drizzling rain. As usual, we had to wait for trains and it was two o'clock p.m. Thursday when we started.

It is eighty miles from Montevallo to Blue Mountain, but there are not many points of interest on the route. Shelby Springs, ten miles from Montevallo, is a beautifully situated place. There are extensive hospitals here and I think some furnaces for reducing iron ore. The place had some interest for our company because one of our members had been there for months as a hospital nurse, and rumor said he had been married there, having a wife already at home. About thirty-five miles beyond Shelby Springs we came to Talladega, the seat of the county of the same name. This is a thriving looking place. I think we crossed the Coosa River twice, perhaps oftener. From some cause we lay over all night at "Memford's" [Munford], some fifteen miles south of Blue Mountain, and it was 9 o'clock a.m. Friday 13th when we reached the latter place.

Blue Mountain is no town at all. It is simply the northern terminus of the unfinished Alabama & Tennessee R.R. It is in Calhoun County and would make a handsome site for a city. At 1 o'clock p.m. Saturday 14th, we again took up the line of march and spent the night near Jacksonville, [then] the seat of Calhoun County and some 16 miles from our starting place. Next day we marched some eighteen miles through a fine farming region watered by magnificent springs and mountain streams. During the forenoon we passed the village of Cross Plains, so named I think because the mountain valleys here cross each other at right angles. This is a pretty place. A few miles further we reached the village of Ladiga and near it a broad, swift stream called by the same name. It was necessary to wade this stream. The further bank was lined with ladies, many of whom wept in pity for the "poor soldiers" as we waded across.

On Monday 16th we passed the beautiful town of Cave Springs, Ga., about sixteen miles from Rome. This is one of the nicest places I ever saw and one of the most beautifully situated. It is in a vale surrounded almost entirely by mountains whose green sides shut in the view. Nowhere have I ever seen a spot more sequestered than this; and when the inhabitants turned out *en masse* to greet us, I fancied they had felt the horrors of war less keenly than others had done.

There is a natural curiosity here, which I visited after I was wounded. It is a grotto or cave in the hill side directly overlooking the small brick church which stands at the base of the hill a few paces from the finest spring I ever saw. I explored this cave for about fifty feet, but having no light and only one arm I was afraid to go any further lest I should break my neck. I don't know if it contains anything of interest or not.

Prior to our arrival at Cave Springs, quite early in the forenoon in fact, a white object was observed in the sky to the southeast, apparently about half a mile high and moving rapidly toward the south. We decided that it was a balloon, and that the enemy was endeavoring by that means to ascertain the strength of the reinforcements that were coming to Gen. Johnston.[3] The attack on Rome the next day, and the palpable attempt to cut off Ector's and Cockrell's brigades which were behind us, seemed to confirm this opinion.

At Cave Springs we were met by about thirty wagons belonging to the citizens of the vicinity, in readiness to haul the footsore and the sick to Rome, which place we reached about 8 o'clock p.m., having marched since morning about twenty-eight miles. I did not see the town of Rome at all. It is situated at the junction of, and between the Oostanaula and Etowah Rivers, which at this place unite and form the Coosa. Immediately on our arrival at Rome we went on board the train, and I went to sleep. I do not know how far it is from Rome to Kingston, the point where the Rome road intersects the road from Atlanta to Chattanooga. It is probably twenty or twenty-five miles, and a portion of the way the road bed seems to be on the bank of the Etowah River.[4]

We arrived at Adairsville about 2 o'clock a.m. Tuesday, May 17th, and about 10 o'clock a.m. we formed a line of battle through the town. During the day a man named B.W. Creel hunted me up and informed me that my lost journal had been found. The man had just enlisted in Company I

[Mass. MOLLUS, USAMHI]

Gen. Joseph E. Johnston

and was wounded a few days afterward.

We remained in line till about midnight, when we fell back some twelve miles to Cassville. Arriving at the latter place about 8 o'clock a.m. and bivouacking in a field, I obtained permission to visit the 7th Miss. Regt. and spent most of the day with my friends in that regiment. I learned many things about the home folks, also the particulars of the death of J.N. Easterling, who was killed at Resaca a few days previous. At dark we formed a line of battle and remained in position all night.[5]

Next morning the whole army formed in battle array and awaited the advance of the enemy. It was evidently Gen. Johnston's design to fight on this ground. A stirring battle order was read to the men and Lt. Gen. Polk made a brief talk to each regiment along the line.[6] Our brigade was on the reserve line and we were not brought under fire till about 3 o'clock p.m. It was the first time we had heard the *zip* of hostile bullets since leaving Vicksburg, and to me it was my first experience of danger after learning to trust it all to Jesus. Our regiment had five men wounded that afternoon, though we did not fire a gun. Gen. Sears, who was under fire for the first time after his promotion, was struck on the foot by the fragment of a shell. I, in passing, was within a few feet of him at the time and asked, "General, are you hurt?"

"I believe not," he replied as he coolly surveyed the damage. "I wouldn't mind it if it hadn't spoiled my new boot!"

As we were moving from one part of the field to another we passed the 27th Miss. Regt. (also in reserve).[7] At the head of the remnant of the "Fencibles," with his Bible in his hand, was the youthful captain Joel R. Baugh. He was reading aloud to his men. There was only time for a hurried hand clasp as we marched by and I saw them no more.

The enemy, however, did not make any serious attack but began to flank our position, a maneuver that became a familiar one before the campaign ended. About one o'clock a.m. Friday 20th, we began falling back. At daylight we passed through the town of Cartersville without making any halt. Nor did we stop till we had crossed the Etowah River, some twelve miles from where we started. After resting three or four hours we moved some three miles to the left, and about noon bivouacked near an old glass factory where we remained till Monday 23d. On Sunday Lt. Gen. Polk, who was a bishop in the M.E.C. South (I believe), attended religious services in our brigade. Chaplain Bakewell of the 7th Battalion preached, after which Gen. Polk offered some well-timed remarks. Through these remarks, for the first time I learned that Gen. Sears was a professor of religion.

The enemy having crossed the river with a portion of his forces at a point opposite Dallas, a countermove on our part became necessary. Hence about 1 o'clock p.m. on Monday 23d our corps began moving to the left. We marched twelve miles and bivouacked for the night. Started at daylight next morning. About 10 o'clock a.m. we passed through the little village of Lost Mountain, and after going a few miles further halted for the night about 1 o'clock p.m. The whole afternoon and night it was raining, and Chaplain Lattimore and I, having a hole to sleep in, were pretty well soaked before morning. Starting at daylight, Wednesday 25th, we marched about three miles and halted till 1 o'clock. While there, George R. came to us. I was glad to see him after his long detention on the way, and was more than glad to receive the letters he brought.

About 1 o'clock p.m. we were again put in motion and marched some three miles further. Stopping for half an hour, we could plainly hear the roar of artillery and rattle of musketry beyond New Hope Church, where the battle was then raging. Starting again at a "double-quick," we went across fields and woods, and after a march of some five miles (much of it over fresh plowed fields and all of it through mud) we halted for the night on the edge of the battlefield and lay in the road till morning. Being the recipient of a new shirt brought from home by George R., that night I parted with large numbers of companions who had gone with me on many a march. I left them hanging on a bush.[8]

On this march I first saw Maj. Gen. French, our division commander. His division consists of Cockrell's, Ector's and Sears' brigades. The first named are from Missouri, the second from Texas and North Carolina, and the last from Mississippi. Walthall's, Loring's and French's divisions make up Polk's corps.[9] Some rain fell that night. Next morning, Thursday 26th, we took position some three-fourths of a mile to the west of New Hope Church, our brigade being in the rear of Ector's and Cockrell's. Lts. Buchanan and Duckworth, Stephen R. and about twenty others of Company B

Gen. Samuel G. French

came to us while here. Once more the company presented
respectable proportions. We remained at this spot all day,
while on our right there was a brisk skirmish fire. On Friday
27th we moved about a half mile to the left, and forming a

line, threw forward skirmishers. About 1 o'clock these engaged the enemy and the firing was continued all the afternoon.

We commenced strengthening our position by trenches and breastworks. This work was nearly completed at one o'clock p.m. Saturday 28th, when we moved by the right flank to a point about one-fourth of a mile east of or to the right of New Hope Church. We there relieved a portion of Hood's corps, who moved still further to the right. We remained in these trenches till Saturday, June 4th, occasionally changing position as exigencies required.[10]

Companies B, E and G were detached on Friday 27th and did not rejoin the regiment till Tuesday 31st. Sergt. E.W. White of Company H was killed on Saturday 28th. During the entire time of our stay here the pickets were constantly fighting and there were occasional artillery duels.

About 12 o'clock Sunday night there was a false alarm. Not only the pickets on our front but the front line of battle, and especially the 35th Miss. Regt. which was in our front, fired volley after volley as rapidly as possible. The artillery on both sides became engaged and it sounded like a desperate battle. It was seemingly one of the darkest nights I ever saw. I had lain down without removing even my blanket or sword. At the first volley I sprang to my feet, but a little excited at the din. A moment later Col. Clarke jumped up, exclaiming, "Chambers! Chambers! Sergeant Major! Sergeant Major!" in such rapid succession that he failed to hear me till I had answered him the third time. When at last I made him comprehend that I was awake and up, he directed me to form the regiment while he danced around in the dark trying to find his boots, his sword and his hat. The regiment was soon in line, but the firing ceased after a few minutes. The pickets who came in after daylight informed us that while the excitement lasted they found it safest on the sides of the trees next to the Yankees.

Yielding to the repeated solicitations of Ordnance Sergt. S.S. Griffin, I prevailed on Col. Clarke to allow us to exchange places, which we did on Wednesday, June 1st, and I immediately entered upon my new duties. Josiah Rodgers of

Company B received a wound that day of which he subsequently died. There were other casualties. On Saturday
4th the enemy made several demonstrations, though no
serious assault was attempted. After night fall we fell back
to Lost Mountain, a distance of about six miles. The night
was very dark and the roads extremely wet and muddy.

On Sunday 5th I petitioned Col. Clarke to relieve me of
the duties I was then discharging and allow me to return to
my company. Several reasons induced me to take this step.
It was the earnest wish of Lt. Buchanan that I should do so,
but the most potent with me was the belief that my presence
in the company would make others more reconciled to the
hardships, dangers and privations of a soldier's lot. As ordnance sergeant I was not only exempt from most of the
hardships incident to camp life, but its dangers as well; and
I was necessarily separated from the company during active
service. The ordnance officer demurred to the proposition
and refused to give his consent for some time to any change.
Col. Clarke also dissuaded me but at last yielded the point,
and I gave up my sword and resumed a gun, feeling much
better equipped for killing Yankees. I chose to return as a
private, but without my knowledge my name was entered on
the roll as second sergeant.

CHAPTER 14

Kennesaw Mountain

We "lay around loose" at this place until Friday 7th, when we moved by the right flank to a point a few miles west of Marietta. We did picket duty that night, though we were not in contact with the enemy. Next morning we began to strengthen our line by throwing up breastworks. This position was known by various names such as the "Lattimore Line," "Pine Mountain" and "Moonshine Creek." On Thursday 9th we again moved to the right about one-half mile and continued the work of strengthening our position. Saturday 11th, the regiment again went on picket and remained till the afternoon of Monday 13th, during which time there was almost incessant rain. Fortunately for us, there was no picket fighting on our part of the line.

About noon on Tuesday 14th, Lt. Gen. Polk was killed by a cannon ball. He was on the line of Gen. Loring's division and was a mile or two to our right. He was a brave man and a Christian gentleman.[1]

The lines were gradually closed from the left, and on Friday 17th our pickets became engaged. Two men of our regiment, detailed as sharpshooters, were mortally wounded on the picket line that day. Heavy rains were still falling.

About daylight, Saturday 18th, we were aroused by heavy firing on our left and in a few minutes afterward our pickets came running in, and reported that the enemy were advancing. Our regiment was placed in reserve, where we were exposed to an enfilading fire of musketry and artillery all day, but with no serious casualties. Col. Clarke received a very slight wound. Ector's and Cockrell's brigades were more hotly engaged than ours, and the losses in the division during the day were said to be about two hundred men. Our brigade sustained a serious loss in the person of Lt. Col. Pardue of the 7th Battalion. He was a brave man, a good officer and a courtly gentleman.[2]

Darkness put an end to the conflict, though a desultory fire was kept up. About 9 o'clock p.m. our regiment was deployed and relieved Cockrell's brigade. We had one man for every forty feet. We kept up skirmish firing and occasionally added fuel to the fires in rear of the works. At 11 o'clock p.m. we were silently withdrawn and followed the command in another retrograde movement. Great quantities of rain had fallen during the past twenty-four hours, and everything was covered with mud.[3]

On this retreat it will be understood that the main portion of our line was not disturbed at all, only the center falling back some two or three miles. On Kennesaw Mountain was our next position where we remained just two weeks. I think I never experienced more that was unpleasant in the same length of time. Our brigade was on Little Kennesaw, and we had to do picket duty at its base. The pickets were changed after nightfall, and it was no pleasant thing to clamber up and down almost perpendicular cliffs for nearly half a mile. The first week of our stay was one of almost continuous raining. We had no fuel and consequently our clothing was wet all the time. Then the rains ceased, the weather became hot and our supply of water rapidly failed. Added to these unpleasant features was the fact that the enemy had perhaps fifty pieces of artillery bearing upon the mountain and that almost every part of its top and sides was exposed to the fire of these pieces. For days we had seen the huge bulk of Kennesaw in our rear, and as we marched in that direction on that Saturday night, the wish was frequently expressed that our brigade might be posted on its summit, and sure enough, we were.

It was a dreary prospect on which we opened our eyes on Sunday morning, June 19th. In fact, we were literally enveloped in the clouds. Nothing could be seen save a lead-colored mist that saturated one's clothing almost as quickly as a rain. Presently the mist began to gather into vast billows, between which rifts appeared. As these rifts grew wider we caught glimpses of the country below. Gradually as the sun arose, the clouds were lifted higher and I could soon distinguish the position we had occupied the previous day.

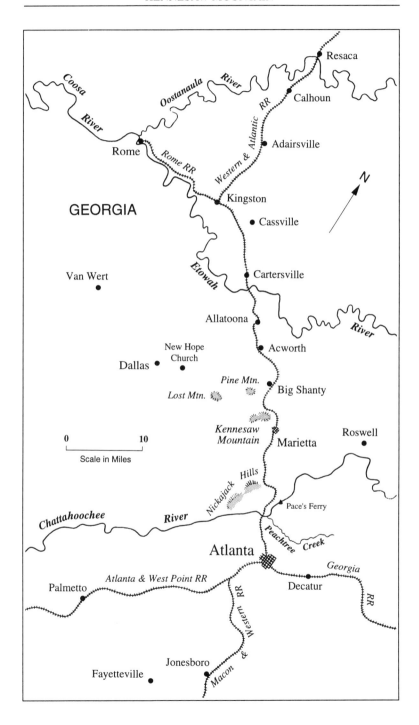

I saw the enemy make a gallant charge upon our deserted works and he doubtless carried them without the loss of a man. I saw his brigades and divisions debouching on the great plain below. First came a line of skirmishers to be closely followed by heavy lines of infantry and sections of artillery. A small detachment of our cavalry was in the enemy's front. Frequently they halted, where I suppose the ground was favorable, and as the Federal skirmishers came in sight they would fire a volley at them. This would always cause confusion, but quickly rallying they would boldly advance to find our troops had retreated to another position. This was so often repeated that it became a source of diversion to us who were merely lookers-on.

For miles in the enemy's rear the country was spread out like a map. His wagon trains were parked on a hundred open fields, and thousands of tents that sheltered his soldiers were visible from where we stood. By 10 o'clock a.m. his skirmishers had approached near enough to engage ours. Close behind them came his artillery. One reason why we had desired to be posted on the mountain was because we thought the position too elevated for cannon shot to reach us. We saw directly in front of us a battery placed in position in an open field. We had formed our line across the side of the mountain some fifty feet below its crest, feeling perfectly secure without any breastworks at all.

The first shot from the battery in our front fell at the base of the mountain, and we cheered derisively. The next shot came half way up the side, and the cheering was much fainter than before. The third shot struck the rocky cliff above our heads and instead of cheers, there was anxious looking for spots that would afford some protection. The third shot was instantly followed by a fourth, which cut a member of Company A in two. Our line was then placed on the crest of the ridge, where in some places ledges of rock formed a safe retreat from a direct fire.

During the afternoon a very heavy shower came up, and as I stood partially protected by my dripping blanket I had a worse fit of the "blues" – felt more despondent, in fact, than at any other time during the whole campaign. Stephen R.

who had been sent to the hospital from Lost Mountain, came to us during the rain.

Monday 20th our regiment was on the picket line. Sergt. Laird of Company D was killed and Reddock of our company was slightly wounded in the foot. By this time we had several guns in position on the mountain and frequent artillery duels occurred. As the shells from both sides passed over the pickets' heads, frequently exploding prematurely and scattering the fragments promiscuously, these duels were not calculated to soothe the nerves of the men on the picket line. Our guns were generally silenced after a few rounds, after which the enemy would proceed to "shell the woods" at a furious rate. This, or a somewhat similar performance, was of almost daily occurrance as long as we remained on that line.

Thursday 23d was the first clear day we had had in about two weeks. On that day there was heavy firing on our left, and as we knew that a part or all of Hood's corps had moved from the right the day previous we supposed a regular battle was coming on.[4]

About this time a strange incident is said to have occurred. Lt. Col. W.E. Ross of the 39th Miss. Regt., feeling indisposed, went to the surgeon and asked for a stimulant. By some mistake, chloroform instead of whiskey was handed him. He swallowed the draught and fell like a dead man. An incision was made in the trachea and an air pump was inserted, by which life was preserved till the effects of the drug could be counteracted. He is still in a helpless condition, and some express the conviction that he will never leave his bed again. While his home is in Mississippi, his family are said to be near Selma, Ala.

Saturday 25th our regiment went on picket again. From some cause a portion of Company B was not relieved on Sunday. I happened to be one of the unfortunates, and that Sunday was spent disagreeably enough. The only man near enough to converse with was a member of the 35th Miss. Regt. named Warbington, who hailed from Choctaw County, Miss.

We were relieved Monday morning, June 27th, and soon

after we had rejoined the regiment the enemy made the most serious assault on our lines that he had made since leaving Resaca. Our corps and Hardee's met the assault and the Federals were repulsed with great loss. The right of our brigade, where we were, was not engaged, but the picket fighting was more stubborn, the artillery firing was hotter and more incessant all day, and we stood in readiness to meet an assault which we momentarily expected. Late in the afternoon one of the Federal batteries began throwing shells directly at the frail breastwork behind which, at the time, our company was crouched. One of these shells penetrated the earth at the base of the works with the fuse still burning. In a spirit of rashness I leaped upon the breastwork, ran and stood directly over where it was, believing that when it exploded the fragments would all go to the rear. Another shell from the same gun, elevated a little, came whizzing through the air, barely missing my feet as it exploded. Sergt. Jonathan H. Bass of our company had at that moment stood up in the trench directly in front of the exploding shell. I never saw a human body more horribly mutilated than his was. He was a prompt and reliable soldier. [5]

Still later in the afternoon I had another narrow escape. The chaplain generally sent all the religious papers that came into his hands to me, to distribute to the different companies. Receiving a bundle of papers at this time, I proceeded to distribute them, and while I was at the extreme left of the regiment a vigorous artillery fire on our regimental line began. I was advised by the officers not to return to my company, but as I usually did, I disregarded the admonition and started back. Something like fifty yards of the distance was simply a naked rock, and as I was passing over this I heard a shell approaching, which by its peculiar noise I knew was about to explode. Dropping to the ground I crouched down with my face only a few inches from the rock. When the explosion occurred a large fragment of the shell struck the rock immediately under my face with great force and glanced off with a loud whizzing sound.

One other man mortally wounded and some four or five others with slighter wounds made up the regimental losses for the day.

We went on picket again Wednesday 29th. No event of special importance occurred after this time, except that we were exposed to a furious artillery fire on the afternoon of Friday, July 1st, and Saturday morning 2d, during which our regiment lost five or six men. Our losses at this place were light, however, in view of the fact that we were subjected to heavy firing nearly every day. Many of the solid cannon balls that were fired at us struck the rocky crest of the mountain and *ricocheted,* falling in and around Marietta which was some four miles in our rear.[6]

CHAPTER 15

With Backs to the Wall

On Saturday night, July 2d, we abandoned our position on Kennesaw Mountain and fell back beyond Marietta, passing that place about 2 o'clock Sunday morning. Going some five miles further we formed a new line on a series of low, flat ridges known locally as the "Nickajack Hills." We were placed in position about 8 o'clock a.m., our regiment being on the picket line. About 2 o'clock p.m. the Federal skirmishers came in sight and we kept up a spirited fight till after dark. About 10 o'clock p.m. our regiment was relieved by some of Ector's brigade and we "hunted" for our position in the line till midnight. Failing to find the rest of the brigade we slept by the roadside till daylight.

Monday morning, the 4th, we moved about a half mile to the rear and were placed in reserve. It seemed we were in direct range of one of the Federal batteries, and though a large number of balls fell among us only one man in the regiment was seriously wounded all day. That night we fell back to the Chattahoochee River and formed a line of battle next morning. By noon our pickets and those of the enemy were engaged. On Friday 8th our regiment was on the picket line. Though we fought all day no losses were reported. The 4th Miss. was on the picket line next day. About 10 o'clock in the forenoon the enemy charged our picket line and drove in our men. The 36th Regt. and Companies B and K of our regiment were sent out to retake the lost line. The 36th, supported by our two companies, charged in gallant style and retook the lost ground with some ten or twelve prisoners, the enemy leaving his dead and a few wounded men on the field. Our brigade losses for the day were about forty killed and wounded. Companies G and E were detached that day and sent to the left to strengthen Major Rea's battalion of sharpshooters. Two men of Company G were killed, and the gallant major himself received the wound that subsequently caused his death.[1]

That night, Saturday 9th, we crossed the Chattahoochee River and stopped about midway between the river and the city of Atlanta, where we remained until Monday 18th, except for one tour of picket duty which commenced on Sunday 10th and ended Wednesday 13th. This picketing was done along the river bank, one brigade going at a time. Our regiment lost three men wounded on Tuesday 12th.

Being relieved Wednesday 13th, we returned to the halfway ground where we bivouacked in order and enjoyed the first "rest" we had had since the campaign opened. Friday, Saturday and Sunday we had very interesting meetings for religious worship, during which nineteen members of the brigade were baptized, two of whom belonged to our company. There were several others who professed conversion. Saturday night, W.C. Robertson and C.M. Reddock of Company I, 7th Miss. Regt., were with us.

On Monday 18th we again formed a line of battle along the hills said to be on the south side of Peach Tree Creek. We had barely got in position when the rumor came flying like wildfire down the line that Gen. Johnston had been superseded as chief commander of the Army of Tennessee by Lt. Gen. John B. Hood. There was great indignation among the rank and file, and there were open threats of insubordination. For nearly three months we had been retreating, but the *morale* of the army was better than when the campaign opened. We knew that while we were losing ground the enemy was losing men much more rapidly than we were, and that after a few weeks more his available force would be no greater than our own. We had seen the retreat conducted without the loss of even a broken wagon wheel, and we had unlimited faith in the generalship of "Old Joe," as we liked to call him. We were willing to fight at any time and place he said so, believing that he would not ask us to fight unless the advantages were clearly on our side. Of Gen. Hood we knew but little; only the impression prevailed that he was rash to a criminal extent. We knew him to be a splendid corps commander, brave and reliable, but somehow we judged him to be lacking in those higher qualities

[Cumberland Gallery Collection]

Gen. John Bell Hood

that fit one for handling an independent army.[2] Nor did the first order that was promulgated tend to reassure the men or reconcile them to the change of commanders; for it was to the effect that no more picks and shovels would be allowed the men, that we would henceforth fight no more from breastworks and rifle pits.

This order, however, was not adhered to, as the very next day picks and shovels were distributed along the line and we were ordered to construct breastworks, which we accordingly did. The Federal army had crossed the Chattahoochee River near Roswell and was moving down upon us from the north. Wednesday 20th, went on picket again. There was a fight on Peach Tree Creek that day in which our forces were driven back. We abandoned the picket line along the river that night, and the next day, Thursday 21st, our regiment did picket duty in front of our recently constructed line of breastworks.[3]

That night we fell back to Atlanta. Gen. A.P. Stewart had been placed in command of Polk's corps and Stephen D. Lee had succeeded to the command of Hood's corps. These two corps occupied the works around the city while Gen. Hardee with his corps was hovering on the left wing of the enemy. About noon on Friday 22d, Gen. Hardee attacked the enemy's left. A general, hard-fought battle ensued. Hardee's, Lee's and a part of Stewart's corps were engaged. The fight resulted in a Confederate victory, but it was purchased at a fearful sacrifice of men and we failed to utilize the advantage gained.[4]

I can only briefly note the events subsequently occurring on this line. We remained there till Sept. 1st, and there was continuous fighting on the picket line and occasional discharges of artillery. Sometimes the latter was as furious as anything of the sort I had heard all summer. On *our* part of the line the Confederate artillery had the advantage of position and caliber, and hence we suffered less annoyance from the enemy's cannon than the troops on the other parts of the line. During our stay at Kennesaw Mountain I became somewhat indisposed and did not recover till September, yet I remained at the front all the time and nearly always took my turn of duty.

On Wednesday July 27th, Brig. Gen. Ector was severely wounded – had his leg shot off, in fact.[5] It was rumored that promotion awaited him. All that day and the night following our troops were moving to the left, and on Thursday 28th was fought the most disastrous engagement of the whole

[Mass. MOLLUS, USAMHI]

Gen. Matthew D. Ector

campaign, our forces being repulsed with fearful slaughter. Our division was not engaged. Gens. Stewart and Loring were both slightly wounded. [6]

After the fight of the 28th unusual quiet reigned all a-

round our lines till about five o'clock p.m. Monday, August
1st, when a furious shelling of our entire line came off. The
day previous had been rainy. About this time a regular series
of religious [meetings] was inaugurated, and which was
kept up as long as we remained at that place.

On Tuesday August 2d our regiment went on the picket
line and remained three days. The picket line here was a
regular line of breastworks something like a quarter of a
mile in front of our main line, and we had a line of videttes
some one hundred and fifty yards in front of this. On
Thursday 4th I was on the vidette line with a detail from the
regiment. Three others occupied one post with me. The
woods all around us were so thick that we could see but a
few yards in any direction. These vidette posts were some
fifteen or twenty yards apart, wholly out of sight of each
other and consisted of flimsy piles of rails or rotting logs, or
anything that would stop a bullet.

About 3 o'clock p.m. the firing at our post became so
much hotter than usual that I became satisfied the enemy
was approaching. In a minute or two they were nearly upon
us, and judging by the direction of the bullets that they were
on both flanks, we slowly retired, being the last to leave our
position. About half way to the picket line was the edge of
the woods, the rest of the distance being an open field. At
the edge of the wood I halted while the others went on.
While my stop was less than two minutes it enabled the
others to reach the shelter of the picket line, and when I
started across the open field I drew the fire of seemingly
several scores of Yankees. I did more than "double-quick" –
I fairly ran across the open field with the bullets cutting the
dirt all around me and singing about my ears. I reached the
picket line in safety but I was completely winded.

The 4th Regt. came to our support and our regiment
charged into the woods, retook our lost line and secured a
few prisoners. The regiment lost 21 men – our company
having lost F.M. Howell wounded and W.T.J. Bass missing.
Among the badly wounded was Capt. D.C. Durham of
Company K and among the killed was Sergt. Caughman of
Company G. In speaking of this incident one of our com-

[Valentine Museum]

Gen. William W. Loring

pany remarked, "I always said, if I ever went into a charge, I wouldn't holler. But the very first time I fired off my gun I hollered as loud as I could, and I hollered every breath till we stopped!" [7]

On Friday 5th we were relieved, and Saturday 6th our division pressed the enemy's line in our front, the brigade losing about thirty men.

On Sunday 7th, S.J. Harper of our company with several others was baptized in the name of Christ. I was truly glad the Lord had touched his heart and constrained him to take this step. For several days there was little activity displayed on either side.

On Sunday August 14th occurred the saddest event of the whole campaign. On that day my messmate, Stephen Robertson, was killed. The circumstances were briefly these: The regiment had been detailed the night before to work on the picket line, the right wing working from midnight till day. The men had just returned to the main line, and re-marking that he was hungry my friend set to work to prepare his breakfast. As he was thus engaged, a minié ball, fired from some point a mile away perhaps, struck him. It entered just below and behind the right arm and ranged downward, lodging near the skin just above the left hip. The only rational words he uttered were "Lay me down!" addressed to Lt. Buchanan who caught him as he staggered on being struck. He twice muttered incoherently, once saying "want to live!" and at another time "my poor family!" He died without a struggle some ten minutes after being shot and as we bore him on a litter to the surgeon's tent. He was buried as decently as possible under the circumstances. His grave is about a mile southwest of Atlanta on the farm of Mr. Jett. It is about two hundred and fifty yards south of the dwelling and is on the east side of the road. I marked the spot by putting up a durable board, with full name, company, regiment and date of death upon it, and upon the center of the grave I placed a white stone about as large as a man's head. His brother, W.C.R., was present at the burial and Brother Lattimore made a talk and offered prayer at the grave. Sleep on, comrade, friend and brother, till the Lord shall call sleeping ones to meet him in the clouds!

That night we went on picket again and remained till the night of Wednesday 17th. There were no casualties of importance in the regiment and no unusual occurrence along the lines.

On Saturday 20th we again went on the picket line. This was an exceedingly unpleasant trip. It was raining all the time and the fire of the enemy was very close and very heavy. The 35th Regt. had permanently lost the vidette line the day previous, and the enemy's pickets had advanced their position till they could pour a hot fire into our main picket line.

On Monday 22d, Z.F. Duckworth of Company B was wounded while assisting in carrying a wounded comrade to the rear. The wound, though slight, resulted in his death some days afterward. Orderly Sergt. James Garrett of Company A and Private Thos. Stewart of Company G were both killed that day, and Rev. John Fletcher of Company H was severely wounded. We were relieved Tuesday 23d.

On Thursday 25th, and the day following, the enemy withdrew from our immediate front. Our division made a reconnoissance in force on Saturday 27th. We went till we encountered a strong Federal force on the east bank of the Chattahoochee River at Pace's Ferry. After some skirmishing we returned to the ditches at Atlanta, leaving one brigade about two miles out as pickets. On this day W.C. Robertson of Company I, 7th Miss. Regt., having effected an exchange with John R. Barnes of our company, came to us.[8]

As we passed outside of our lines on this occasion the woods between our picket line and that of the enemy presented a strange appearance. The undergrowth was very thick (there was but little else) and had been cut away by bullets about the height of a man's breast almost as evenly as the stubble in a grain field after the grain has been cut.

Sunday 28th we enjoyed the first rest we had had for some weeks. That day a Presbyterian preacher named Markham from New Orleans preached in our encampment. His remarks were founded on Isaiah 53:3, "He was a man of sorrows and acquainted with grief." It was one of the most eloquent sermons I ever heard in my life. Lt. A.H. McLaurin and others united with his church that afternoon.

Monday 29th our regiment went on picket alone. I was on vidette night duty, and though no danger was apparent yet I felt more lonely and apprehensive than usual. Four men were placed under me and we were sent to occupy an isolated hill on the right of the line. This hill was covered with deserted Federal works, and since there were no troops on our right I felt an unaccountable uneasiness. Sometimes an undefinable dread comes over one with no apparent cause. In ninety-nine cases out of every hundred, perhaps, it passes away as unaccountably as it came. In this instance, however, the danger that seemed so imminent all night as to keep me wide awake came in the early morning. We were relieved at daylight, but by the time we had reached the regiment the enemy appeared and drove our videttes from their position. We fought him so stubbornly from our regimental line that he soon withdrew to a more healthy locality. Immediately after this encounter we were relieved and went back to the ditches. The weather for some days had been very pleasant and beautiful.

Gen. Sherman's movement on Jonesboro had so far developed by this time that Hardee's and Lee's corps had been sent against him, leaving our corps and the State troops to man the works about Atlanta. We busily occupied ourselves in strengthening our works.[9]

CHAPTER 16

Atlanta Lost

On Thursday Sept. 1st was fought the disastrous battle of Jonesboro, which necessitated the evacuation of the "Gate City." By 12 o'clock midday we were informed that this step would have to be taken, and although our regiment had been on fatigue duty all day, we were dispatched about 2 o'clock p.m. to the depot in the city to destroy an ordnance train and other Government stores.[1]

I never witnessed such wholesale destruction of property before. The ordnance stores alone that we destroyed were said to be valued at *six million dollars.* Finding a lot of fine new English Tower rifles, we armed ourselves with them and equipped ourselves better than we had ever been e-quipped before. We broke our old guns at the breach, bent the barrels and threw them into a pond of water, into which we also threw several car loads of ammunition. After wreck-ing several R.R. locomotives by running them together we returned to the ditches, arriving there about dark.[2]

About 9 o'clock p.m. our brigade was put in motion. Our corps moved on the lower McDonough Road while the State troops and most of the wagon trains moved on the upper or left hand road. As our line of march was nearly southeast, the enemy was on our right flank. George and W.C.R. both being unwell did not march with the command and did not join it till the 6th.

After turning our backs on Atlanta our progress was ex-ceedingly slow, but there was no stop through the night. The road was thronged with men, women and children, and all sorts of vehicles with all sorts of loads, trying to get away from the abandoned city. A fire also had broken out in the city as we supposed, for the northern sky was lighted up and we frequently heard explosions as though ordnance stores were burning.

At daylight we were not over six miles from the city, and

yet we had not stopped five minutes at a time since we started. Nor did we halt now. Throughout the entire day the slow tramp was kept up, the only halt being made at one point where we formed a battle array on the right and parallel with the road till our wagon trains had passed a certain threatened point. We halted here about forty-five minutes after which the monotonous march was resumed. Already the men were falling from exhaustion, some even dying where they fell. But all through the afternoon and into the night we plodded on.

It was shortly after 10 o'clock p.m., some twenty-five hours after starting, that I fell in the road. I remember a slower movement caused by some obstruction ahead of us, and the next thing I remember was a horse's foot striking my face. At the same time the rider said to a companion, "Here lies another man." I crawled to the side of the road and by the starlight I saw that I was in a lane. I climbed over a fence and lay down under an apple tree. At daylight I awoke and found that Isaac and Henry Hester of our company were under another tree a few yards distant. We followed the trail of the command about a mile and found where they had bivouacked.

The roads forked here and my two companions insisted on going the left hand route. As the army had gone on the other road I followed it. In an hour or two I overtook Jones and Everett of Company H who, like myself, were "straggling." We traveled all that day (Saturday 3d), but failed to overtake the command. In the afternoon we learned from some scouts that the enemy were in the road just ahead of us. We made a masterly flank movement through the woods to the left till we found another road. Stopping for the night we started early next morning and pretty soon found ourselves again headed off by the enemy. A repetition of yesterday's flank movement became necessary, which we executed at once. All that day we tramped along crooked settlement roads, and at night slept in an unused dwelling-house. Starting from there next morning we soon came to a Confederate picket post and were informed that the Federal pickets were only a short distance beyond where we slept. That day (Monday 5th) we overtook the command. The brigade was in line of battle behind some breastworks, while there was picket fighting in front. We soon learned that our regiment was on the picket line, but as it was then late in the afternoon and we were informed that the pickets would be relieved at dark, we proceeded no further. I soon found two or three of Company B, however. They had brought Z.M. Rodgers from off the picket line. A minié ball had struck him in the mouth, slightly cutting his upper lip and knocking out two or three teeth. His uncle removed the ball with his finger, but the poor boy never moved or spoke again and died two or three days afterward. He was a steady boy, a brave soldier and an earnest Christian.

This was the most extensive, and really, the only "straggling" I had ever done. I felt ashamed of it but I was quite weak, having been rather indisposed for some time. We fared pretty well in our straggling, as we found plenty of field peas and potatoes (both Irish and sweet) on the farms as we passed. These farms had been abandoned by their owners with very few exceptions. On this trip I learned to eat tomatoes.

The army was now entrenched near Lovejoy Station, some thirty miles, I think, south of Atlanta on the Macon R.R. That night the enemy withdrew from our front, returning to Atlanta. Our regiment followed a few miles next morning, but succeeded in capturing one solitary straggler only, who informed us that the Federals were "going back to Atlanta to elect a President." [3]

Most of the other stragglers came in this day (Tuesday 6th). We occupied the trenches until Friday 9th, when we went into camp near the depot. This was really the first "rest" we had had all summer. We understood that a ten days' armistice was to begin on the 12th, and we made preparations for a stay of several days. Of the object of this armistice I know absolutely nothing; indeed, I very much doubt that any such thing was ever proposed, much less agreed upon. I know that many families [that] left their homes in Atlanta were driven out, we understood, by the torch of the captors. [4]

Our chaplains chose this opportunity to labor in the Master's vineyard, and an interesting series of meetings commenced at once. Many professed conversion and were baptized, and Christians generally enjoyed an abundant outpouring of the Holy Spirit in their midst. It was indeed a gracious revival and afforded the people of God an opportunity to sit together. Thursday 15th was set apart as a day of fasting and prayer, which was generally observed in the army, especially by Christians.

In a day or two after going into camp, we began a regular routine of drills, dress parades and inspections. On Wednesday 14th our division was reviewed by Lt. Gen. A.P. Stewart, and on Friday 16th Gen. Hood reviewed our corps. The removal of Gen. Johnston in July caused great indignation in our part of the army at least, and the reverses that had since befallen us had tended neither to allay nor mollify the feeling. On the contrary, it seemed to be intensified, and hence it was with distrustful glances we looked upon our brave but rash commander-in-chief.

We received orders to march on Saturday 17th, and on Sunday 18th at 2 o'clock p.m. we started. Our course was due west, and as usual speculations were rife as to our destination. The few days rest had wrought a wonderful change in the spirits and outward appearance of the men. They hardly seemed like the same troops that had come out of Atlanta two weeks before. It had rained before we started and was still raining, rendering the road we moved on exceedingly heavy and disagreeable. After a march of about ten miles we halted for the night. Next morning we passed through the village of Fayetteville, where the Federals had intercepted and destroyed one of our wagon trains during the summer. It is beautifully situated and is the seat of Fayette County. [5]

About an hour before sunset we passed the ruins of Palmetto, once a flourishing village on the West Point railroad, about thirty miles west of south from Atlanta. It had been burned by the Federals some months previous. Marching some four miles further we halted for the night, having traveled in all that day some eighteen or twenty miles.

[Valentine Museum]

Gen. Alexander P. Stewart

Starting again next morning we marched till 10 o'clock a.m. when we halted, formed a line of battle and at once began to strengthen our position by throwing up breastworks. This was done probably as much to keep the men employed as for any other purpose; for it certainly prevented a great deal of promiscuous foraging, or *stealing* to call it by its right name. For unfortunately, we had some men who seemingly preferred stealing an article to getting it any other way. Whether an attack was ever apprehended or not, we fortified a line some ten miles long facing Atlanta, the right of which rested on the West Point R.R. and the left on the Chattahoochee River.

Having completed the work assigned us, we went into camp Friday 23d. On the same day we held an election in Company B for junior 2d lieutenant. Major Constantine Rea, having died on the 14th of September as the result of the wound received July 9th, Capt. T.D. Magee was immediately promoted to the rank of major. This should have been done last April; but from some cause Major Rea failed in his examination for lieutenant colonel. Magee, however, was assigned to duty as major, leaving 1st Lt. Buchanan in command of the company. Rea's death opened the way for Magee's and Buchanan's promotions, and hence the vacancy. F.E. Collins, our orderly sergeant, was elected.

Monday 26th we were reviewed by President Davis. His reception was much less cordial than usual. To a large extent he is held responsible for the reverses the Army of Tennessee has sustained since Johnston's removal.[6]

As indicative of the spirit pervading the army I will relate a single incident. As the presidential party passed in front of our brigade, Col. Clarke, who was a small man with a thin voice, cried out, "Three cheers for President Davis and Gen. Hood!" Waving aloft his sword, he, with one or two others, raised a feeble yell. Instantly someone in the ranks in ringing tones cried out, "Three cheers for Gen. Joe Johnston!" They were given with a will, the other regiments caught on and in twenty-five seconds the whole line of Sears' brigade was "making the welkin ring" with the regular "rebel yell." For once in his life, Mr. Davis turned to look back as if to see whence this unseemly demonstration originated.[7]

CHAPTER 17

Disaster at Allatoona

We received marching orders Wednesday 28th, and at 2 o'clock p.m. next day we started. Owing to some unexplained delay it was 9 o'clock at night when we reached the river. A pontoon bridge with a great sag in the center spanned the stream. The night was very dark, but there were men with torches to give us light at intervals along the bridge and at each end. The swaying of the structure as we walked made it feel like an insecure crossing.

After reaching the western bank we marched about five miles further and halted till morning. Next day, Friday 30th, we marched about fifteen miles by 2 o'clock p.m. and halted for the night near a little hamlet called Brownsville. We did not move from our position on Saturday Oct. 1st, it being a day of almost incessant raining. Sunday 2d we moved at 10 o'clock a.m. and marched about twelve miles. The direction of our route had so changed that we were traveling a little east of north, and when the air was clear we could [see] the bulk of Kennesaw mountain in the distance. That night there was more heavy raining, yet we were in motion again at an early hour on Monday 3d. About the first feat we performed that day was to wade a wide, deep creek. About noon we came to the village of Lost Mountain, or rather where the village was last May. Now all the fences and every house save two or three had been burned. It was a desolate looking spot. Soon after passing this place the rain again set in, and there was no intermission till near nightfall, when it changed to a heavy mist. About sunset we struck the railroad about a mile below Big Shanty, and at once began tearing up the track, burning the cross ties and heating and bending the rails.

Loring's division was in advance of ours. They had captured about forty prisoners at Big Shanty, and the next morning at Acworth, the next station above, they captured a-

[Mass. MOLLUS, USAMHI]

**Confederate artillery firing on Allatoona Pass,
October 5, 1864. From a sketch by Alfred R. Waud.**

bout two hundred more. The other two corps, Hardee's and
Lee's, were at and below Lost Mountain and did not reach
the railroad east of the Etowah River at all.[1]

We labored at this work of destroying the track till about
3 o'clock a.m. Tuesday 4th, when we desisted till daylight. It
was still raining, but we managed to get some two or three
hours' sleep. Next morning skirmishers from Cockrell's
brigade met the Federals who were moving up from
Marietta in considerable force. A detachment of skirmishers
from our brigade also became engaged.

We remained in the vicinity of the depot at Big Shanty
till about 1 o'clock p.m. when we moved in the direction of
Acworth, which place we reached about dark. All the
forenoon we had been filling a deep cut at Big Shanty with
logs, trees, stones and dirt.

From Acworth to Allatoona is about seven miles by
railroad, yet our route was so crooked and our progress so
slow that we were practically all night in traversing the
distance. We arrived in the vicinity of Allatoona an hour or

two before day on Wednesday 5th, and lay down in the mud and slept a little.

As soon as daylight we began to put ourselves in position for the assault. Gen. French, it is said, should not have fought this battle. True, Gen. Stewart had ordered him to take the garrison, but it is claimed that this order was given under the belief that the garrison did not exceed one thousand men and that Gen. French should have discovered the excess sooner and not sacrificed his men.[2] But wherever the blame, if any, should properly lie it was certainly a disastrous affair. Our division consisted of not over two thousand effective men, and nearly one half of these were lost. Prisoners who were captured said the garrison numbered twenty-eight hundred; some of their newspapers said a corps was engaged. They were strongly fortified and a formidable line of obstructions in their front rendered an approach to their works exceedingly difficult.[3] In the face of these odds and difficulties an assault was ordered after a demand for the surrender of the place had been treated with silent contempt.[4]

Our division only was engaged, and it is probable that our brigade sustained the greatest loss. Three of Company B were killed on the field, viz: Sergt. J.P. Williamson and Privates Adelbert McNair and J.V. Reddock. The first was a member of a Baptist church, and I believe he tried to live a consistent Christian life. The other two had never professed religion at all. George Robertson was missing, W.P. Sullivan was slightly wounded in the knee, and these with our wounded made up the casualties of Company B. I have never ascertained the loss in the regiment, but it was very heavy. Col. William H. Clarke was killed while gallantly leading the third and last charge. Capt. B.D. Anderson of Company H and 1st Lieut. G.D. Davis of Company G were also killed.[5]

The assault lasted over three hours, and as we failed to dislodge the enemy we were drawn off, he making no effort to follow us. His loss in killed and wounded was doubtless heavy. We captured about two hundred prisoners and two stands of colors. The flag of the 35th Miss. Regt. was unfor-

[Mass. MOLLUS, USAMHI]

Gen. John M. Corse, Federal commander at Allatoona.

tunately lost.[6]

I hope I may be pardoned for a more minute and circum-
stantial account of this fight.

I felt assured all the morning that it was a more serious

["Southern Battlefields"]

Confederates storming the outer line of Federal works at Allatoona. From a sketch by Alfred R. Waud.

undertaking than many seemed to think it was, and when an officer remarked that taking the place was only "a breakfast task," I assured him that anybody was welcome to *my* share of *that* breakfast. As the danger began to thicken around me the words of the Psalmist came vividly into my mind: "Yea, though I walk through the valley of the shadow of death, I will fear no evil; for thou art with me; thy rod and thy staff they comfort me." Relying on God's protecting mercy I went forward.

The first charge was down a hillside facing the enemy's position. At the base was the railroad. We made a slight halt here, reformed our lines and started forward again. This time we were going up the hill on which the enemy was posted. There were acres of obstructions to be passed, mostly of timber that had been felled for that purpose, then a heavy skirmish line and behind them a line of palisades or timbers, one end in the ground and the upper end projecting forward. Over and through these obstructions we made our way in the second charge. Our loss was heavy, Reddock being killed a few paces from the railroad. We killed or captured nearly all their pickets, and after passing the palisades we halted under the crest of the hill where we were partially sheltered from the storm of bullets that were whistling over our heads.

The obstructions had been so difficult to overcome that all order was lost, the men of the different regiments being thrown promiscuously together. A few steps in front of us were the Federal tents and beyond them, thirty yards perhaps, was the line of breastworks, the intervening space being almost as smooth and level as a floor. A sharp rise of about four feet was between us and the tents.

After a slight effort to reform the lines, the command "forward" was given and somebody called out, "The 46th goes ahead." Inwardly, commending my soul to my Savior, I mounted the crest of the hill, and turning and waving my hat I shouted at the top of my voice, "Come on, boys! The 46th goes ahead!" With a wild yell a few of us, some twenty-five or thirty perhaps, dashed through an opening between the tents. Oh! what a devastating hailstorm of bullets met us! In thirty seconds or less only two of us were left – Lt. R.B. Henderson of Company K (than whom no braver soldier or more earnest Christian ever lived or died on "freedom's field of honor") and myself. Already a ball had struck my gun, flattening the barrel, cutting the stock and the rammer entirely in two, and taking out a small bit of my right forefinger. Thinking my gun would still do for a club, I did not throw it away. Henderson staggered and began falling, crying as he did so, "Brother Chambers, I am gone!" I caught him, and easing him down dropped on my knees beside him, grasping his hand in mine. Both hands were bleeding freely. "My dear brother," I said, "what is the ground of your hope?"

"My only hope is Christ," he replied, and then added, "Pray for me."

There amid the roar of the battle, and the shouts and groans of the wounded, I lifted my heart and my voice to God in behalf of the dying saint beside me. He slightly pressed my hand, and as another ball struck him, he exclaimed, "Oh, brother, I have received my third wound!" I felt the bullet cutting my clothing and equipments, and felt a

[Mass. MOLLUS, USAMHI]

With regiments intermingled and all alignment gone, French's troops reach their furthest point of advance at Allatoona. It was near here that the author was wounded in the finger and shoulder. From a painting by Thure de Thulstrap.

stinging, bounding blow on my shoulder. "Good bye!" he exclaimed. It was the last word he ever spoke, for there was a spasmodic clasp of his fingers, then their grasp relaxed. I glanced at his face; a ball had entered his brain. He was dead.

Finding I could not use my arm, I lay down behind the body of my friend. I could hear and feel the balls as they struck the corpse. I saw a Federal line advance on my right and pour a volley at short range into the faces of our men, and I saw an officer jump up and wave his sword in exultation over the result of the volley. I wanted a gun that would shoot so that I might try to bring him down and stop his foolishness. Realizing how helpless I was, I resolved to leave the field. A bar of soap was lying on a stump near me, and I thought of taking it with me. There were also two or three magazine rifles lying near me on the ground, and I thought of securing one or more of these. I was between the Federal tents and the breastworks, and could see the color of the eyes of the men as they raised up to fire.[7]

When there seemed a sort of lull in the firing I arose and ran back to where the crest of the hill afforded some protection to our men. Finding I was about to fall I lay down, after vainly looking for someone of my company. A man gave me a drink of water. I think I fainted, for the next thing I remember was that James Maxey of our company was pulling at me as I lay on my face, asking if I were badly hurt. Assuring him that my hurt was "very slight," I raised myself to a sitting posture and removed my cartridge box, which I found had been pierced by a minié ball, about half the ball protruding on the side next to my body.

After resting a minute or two more, I started to the rear. I passed Col. Barry and his regiment (the 35th). Col. B. had his arm in a sling and I saw it was bloody. "Sergeant, are you hurt?" he inquired as soon as he saw me. "A little," I replied. "The rascals have shot my shoulder all to pieces," he said, and I passed on. Two or three others asked me if I were wounded, and one man said he saw the hole in my coat. After resting two or three times I reached the brigade surgeon's post. There, someone removed my coat and I saw that the sleeve was full of blood. Up to that time I had no thought the ball had penetrated the flesh.

After a hasty examination Dr. Dunn said I must go to the division hospital to have the ball extracted. I started alone, and after a great deal of suffering and two or three fainting spells, I reached the place to find them already in the act of leaving. Feeling unable to walk another step I despaired of getting off the field. I requested Lt. McLaurin, whom I found there to write to my father when he could and tell him of my condition and where he saw me last. About that time the driver of a hospital wagon said, "We can take one more wounded man from Sears' brigade." "Here he is," sang out McLaurin, and he and one or two others lifted me into the wagon. As we turned into the road, our own brigade was filing by.

I had been hauled less than half a mile when some men on horseback rode up, one of whom was wounded in the foot. I exchanged conveyances with him, but after riding half a mile further I found that the horsemen were ordered on a different road. Dismounting, I waited till my own command came up, and Capt. Buchanan kindly ordered W.C.R. to remain with me till we got to some place where I could be taken care of. We were ordered to New Hope Church, but we failed to keep up with the command. Before night I was delirious, and W.C.R. and I lay in an old cabin on the road side that night. I was in great pain all night. Next morning I could hardly stand on my feet, and the rain was falling in torrents. A negro came by leading Col. Barry's horse; W.C.R. hailed him and I was placed on the horse and rode to New Hope Church, distant about four miles.

The command was in line to move when we arrived and again I could have no medical attention. By this time my wound was so painful that I could not ride on horseback or in a wagon, and the ambulances were all filled with men more severely wounded than myself, and so I walked the balance of the day. Gen. Sears after kindly inquiring as to the nature of my injury, advised me not to report to any hospital, but to go directly home and remain there until I was entirely well.

We moved in the direction of Rome, and after a march of about six miles halted for the night. Dr. McCormick examined my wound at dusk and probed in it for the ball, but it was so badly swollen and was already beginning to suppurate, that he could not trace the ball after it struck the bone. For the first time it was dressed.[8]

The next morning (the 7th) my attendant returned to the command, but we were frequently together all that day and the next. On the 7th we traveled about eighteen miles and spent the night near a place called Van Wert. I rode in a wagon a little once or twice, but the pain was so excruciating that I chose to walk. Saturday 8th we reached Cedar Town after a march of about twelve miles. Houses to stay in were procured here. About three hundred wounded men and a number of attendants and ten days' rations were left.

Sunday night, however, orders were received for all who were able to walk to go to Cave Springs twelve miles further. Monday 10th we started and reached Cave Springs a little after noon, to find that no arrangements whatever had been made for our reception. We were informed, however, that we must try to make our way to Jacksonville, Ala.

J.S. Addy of Company H, W.P. Sullivan of our company and I formed a squad of our own and started. We traveled about seven miles and stopped at a man's house that night where we slept on the floor, using blankets for bedding. Tuesday 11th we traveled about eighteen miles and staid all night at the home of Mrs. Griffin, near Cross Plains, where we were most kindly treated. Two men of Cockrell's brigade, one of whom was wounded, also stopped there that night.

Wednesday 12th we started quite early and about noon reached Jacksonville, where we found a large train of army wagons on the way to Blue Mountain. Mounting one of the wagons and clinging to it despite the jolts, we reached Blue Mountain about dark where we found no preparations at all, not even a stick of firewood on the ground. We were ordered, however, to have our names, ranks, commands and the nature of our wounds registered. Seeing that this was an all-night job, I called all our regiment together, made out the list myself, and told them to go and try to sleep. Placing myself in the line, I got into the tent at last and handed in my list. It was now midnight and beginning to rain. Returning to the depot I found that thrifty Joe Addy had secured an ear of corn. We divided and parched it, and slept some around the depot in the rain.

About 7 o'clock next morning (Thursday 13th) the train pulled out for Selma, where we arrived about 3 o'clock p.m. Another registration here took till night. At the "Wayside Home" a slight supper was given us, which was very acceptable to most of us.

An incident of this day's travel was pleasing to contemplate. As we rode on the train I was eating a grain of parched corn occasionally to allay the pangs of hunger. Some one from behind touched my shoulder and looking around I saw a big Texan holding out a handful of "cracker dust," which he had fished from the bottom of his haversack. I took it and added it to the few grains of corn on hand, invoking a blessing on the donor.

At 5 o'clock p.m. we went on board the steamer *Coquette,* ready to start to Montgomery. Here, for the first time, I heard music played by steam. The steamer *R.B. Taney* preceded us a few minutes and her calliope executed several pieces, among them "Dixie" which I thought was fine. We reached Montgomery about 8 o'clock a.m. Friday 14th. One hundred of us were sent to St. Mary's Hospital and the remainder were distributed among the other hospitals in the city. We were in the first detachment. After registering again we were bathed, clean clothes were put on us and we were shown our beds. Dinner, the first regular meal since leaving Mrs. Griffin's at Cross Plains, was served at 2 o'clock p.m. It was ample, however, and we did it ample justice.

Addy and I were placed in a room on the second floor with Capts. Alexander Archer, 30th Miss. Regt., W.N. Noakes, 31st Miss., and J.H. Wakefield, 25th Arkansas, as room-mates. They were all nice men, especially Archer and Wakefield, who remained there as long as I did. Our lodgings were good, nurses attentive, and there was nothing to complain of, only the fare was not always suitable for sick men.[9] We could get passes to go out in the city, and I one day went out with Addy and ate dinner at a private house. I was in great pain, however, and did not enjoy the trip.

On the night of the 24th I suffered intensely, and when the surgeon examined the wound next morning he found a swollen, inflamed place some two or three inches from where the bullet entered. Requesting the nurse to bring up his case of instruments, he said to me, "You were soldier enough to get shot; I reckon you are soldier enough to have the ball cut out." I told him I had no choice in the matter of getting shot, but I guessed the ball would have to come out. After everything was prepared and Capts. Wakefield and Archer sat one on each side holding my hands, the surgeon hesitated for some time, looking first at the wounded shoulder and then at the other. At last he said, "Chambers, I don't like to cut there." Then, as if pulling himself together, he said, "Well, turn your head away. I don't want you to look at me!"

The first stroke of the scalpel struck the bullet. It proved to be only a part of the original missile. Dr. Britts, the surgeon, indulged in considerable profanity when he saw this, and he probed for the rest which hurt much worse than the cutting did. It was just twenty days after being shot that the bullet was extracted.

About the 27th, Addy was transferred to the hospital at Columbus, Ga. I wished to go too, but the surgeon said I was too weak to stand the trip. On Sunday 30th Addy came back on his way home with a sixty-day furlough. I spent the afternoon with him on the streets, and saw him board the steamboat just at night. As soon as he was gone I went to the surgeon and asked for a transfer to Columbus, stating my reasons for the request. He informed me that he had just received orders to make no more transfers. Thus it seemed my last hope of obtaining a furlough was cut off. I "went and told Jesus," and soon a sweet spirit of resignation seemed to fill my whole heart.

Next morning, Monday 31st, I was ordered to go before

the examining board which was to meet that afternoon. As a result of the examination I was granted a sixty-day furlough beginning that very day. It was night Tuesday, Nov. 1st, however, before I left on the boat for home. The night was stormy and we had to stop a while on account of the weather. We were further delayed by an accident which befell the captain of the boat. Being intoxicated, he fell from the hurricane deck and, striking a cask, was so badly hurt that he died in a few minutes.

We arrived at Selma about sunrise, and I double-quicked all that I was able to the depot and arrived there just in time to see the train pull out of the station. So another day of my furlough was spent in Selma. I received good fare and lodgings at the "Wayside Home," however. Thursday 3d I was on the train before daylight and we left the station about 7 o'clock a.m. Soon after starting we were informed that dinner would be prepared at Uniontown for all soldiers; but when we reached that place the rain was pouring down and there was nobody in sight. We reached Demopolis, a town of some size and very deep mud, situated on the east bank of the Tombigbee River, about 1 o'clock p.m. We at once went on board a little steamer named *Marengo,* and went down the river about four miles to McDowell's Landing. Here we boarded another train and pulled out for Meridian, which place we reached about 9 o'clock p.m.

At Meridian I met a Mr. McGill of Smith County, and made arrangements to travel with him from Enterprise (where his wagon was) to Taylor[s]ville. About 11 o'clock p.m. the train on the M. & O. R.R. arrived, and boarding it I reached Enterprise about 1 o'clock a.m. Friday 4th. Both Meridian and Enterprise were burned last February by Gen. Sherman. We left Enterprise about 8 o'clock a.m. and found the bridge across Suenlovie Creek washed away, so we had to go back a few miles and try another road. All this took time and I ate dinner with a Mrs. Jennings to whom I paid the last dollar I possessed.

When we reached the creek again its banks were over-flowed, and I waded ahead of the team for more than a hundred yards. The night was cold and we camped in the woods about six miles east of Paulding. Saturday 5th I traveled with the wagon till nearly night, when I went on ahead and spent the night with a gentleman named Thigpen where I was well treated. Next morning, with shame, I confessed that I had no money, but Mr. T. informed me that he did not charge soldiers.

Sunday 6th I parted with Mr. McGill and spent the night with Mrs. Rhoda Easterling. Not till that afternoon had I learned that her son and my former messmate was dead. The arm was amputated, he recovered, went home and became able to handle tools with his left hand. He cut his knee with an ax in September. The wound inflamed, became gangrenous and killed him. Thus, only I am left of our mess as we constituted it at Vicksburg in May 1862.

Monday 7th I arrived at home.

December 30th. Meridian, Miss. This cold day I am seated in the sunshine to resume my journal.

I left home last Monday 26th, accompanied by John Self who was to go with me one day and lead back the horse I rode. The morning was cloudy and I felt sad at leaving home. I had heard nothing definite from my command while at home, and had suffered greatly nearly the whole time with aching teeth. I had learned, however, through a letter to his wife that G.G.R. was in prison at Camp Chase, Ohio, and that W.T.J. Bass was there also. Vague rumors were afloat of reverses on the field of battle, and a general gloom seemed to pervade the very air.

After traveling three or four miles we suddenly came upon a squad of deserters. The first intimation I had of their presence was as I was fording a very small creek. On the opposite bank, partly screened by bushes and less than fifteen feet away, stood four men with double barrelled shotguns cocked and pointed full at my breast. I was personally acquainted with every one of them; in fact, one of them belonged to my company and until after the fall of Vicksburg made a good soldier. I looked them squarely in the face as I rode by them, and though each one addressed me by name I made no response whatever. As the day wore on the clouds dispersed and we reached Raleigh, some thirty miles from our starting point, about nightfall.

Tuesday morning my companion started on his return home, and after seeing him mounted and on his way I also took up the line of march. I had quite a heavy knapsack to carry, having some clothing for one or two others. The road was muddy, and after a tramp of nineteen miles I was fairly tired out. I stopped for the night at the hamlet of Homewood in Scott County and put up at the tavern where I was well fed and lodged, for which I paid two dollars. I here met a Dr. Pardue, a relative of Lt. Col. Pardue of our brigade, who was killed last June, whom I found to be an interesting companion. I also read some in a book called "Moses and the Prophets," which I had long wished to see.

Starting early next morning (Wednesday 28th) I reached Forest about noon after walking nine miles over the worst road I ever saw. The train came about 1 o'clock p.m., and I was soon traveling over the same road where I had taken my first ride. Things appeared quite differently now from what they did then. This was especially true in regard to a certain hill which, at first sight, I thought was almost a mountain; and I was thrilled at the bare idea of standing on its top. Now its "magnitude" was too insignificant to wake any enthusiasm at all. I suppose I am getting "traveled." I was depressed in spirits, too, for I had learned that the Army of Tennessee had sustained an overwhelming defeat, and I knew that it would be days before I could reach my command, if indeed any of them were left.[10]

We reached Meridian about dark. It was understood that the enemy had possession of the railroad in North Mississippi, and I have as yet made no effort to go any further. Major Parton of the 36th Miss. Regt. is here and will probably take charge of all of Sears' brigade. He expresses the opinion that Gen. Hood will never be able to recross the Tennessee River with his army, but that all will be killed or captured in a few more days. I think the major is demoralized. But surely the prospect is a gloomy one. I daily thank God that I have been led to trust Him and that I can realize that every interest of nations as well as individuals is safe in His hands.

I observe today that Government property is being moved from this place in anticipation, I suppose, of a visit from the enemy. It is rumored this afternoon that he has left the vicinity of the railroad above here. The weather is quite cold, and I find the vicinity of the depot a sorry resting-place after the comforts of home. The *cause,* however, demands this hardship at my hands, and there *is* a pleasure in suffering in the discharge of duty.

1865

CHAPTER 18

In the Company of Strangers

Sunday, January 1, 1865. One mile west of West Point, Miss. I *must* write a little tonight, for my heart is full of *tears!* I have been told today, on seemingly good authority, that only one hundred and sixty men are left of all Sears' brigade. If this be true, how can I convey the mournful tiding to the waiting hearts at home. I can hardly refrain from shedding tears when I think of all the noble lives that have been sacrificed in vain. I can only pray to my God and trust that the calamity may not be as sweeping as it is represented.

I remained at Meridian until Saturday, Dec. 31st. On Friday night I went to the "Wayside Home," where I had good fare and lodgings. While there I listened to a sermon on the New Birth by a man named James, who is a missionary to the Confederate hospitals. It was an able sermon. During the night we were visited by a storm of wind, rain and hail, and next morning the air was bitterly cold.

Learning that a train would go up that day I got ready and sure enough we started at 9:30 o'clock a.m. I saw but little of the country and do not know the names of all the stations we passed. As I remember them, however, they are as follows: After leaving Meridian the first station is Marion Station, some three miles from the old town of that name, and which is the seat of Lauderdale County. It was burned last winter. The next station is Lockhart, which was also burned. Then we reach the famous "Lauderdale Springs." I think the village as well as the springs are some distance from the railroad; at least, if we could see the whole place. The name and the reputation are bigger than the thing itself. The next is Tancola and then Sucarnatchie, then Gainesville Junction, where a branch road leading to Gainesville, Ala., intersects the main line of the M. & O. R.R. Then comes Scooba, a nice little town, then Wahalak and then Sugualak, and then we reach Macon, the seat of Noxubee County and at this time the capital of the State of Mississippi.[1]

In consequence of numerous delays it was 9 o'clock p.m. when we reached Macon, and we lay over until 8 o'clock this morning. The night was cold but I slept some in my seat. It was not a restful night, however, for there was a battalion of "galvanized Yankees" aboard who were, without exception, the lowest and most debased looking set of men I ever saw. They are Federal prisoners who have enlisted in our army. They are ignorant, noisy and thievish, and are a discredit to any civilized army. It is said they fight well, but somehow I feel that I would rather have them in the Federal army than in our own, for such men have no lot in the South and no place among its defenders.

I did not see the town of Macon at all, as it is a mile off the railroad. I saw several church spires, however, and heard the bells calling to worship before we started. All soldiers belonging to the Army of Tennessee, it is said, were ordered to stop at Macon, but failing to learn anything definite in regard to such an order I came on.

After leaving Macon the first station I remember is Brooksville, which is a nice place, then Crawford where there is no town at all. Then comes Artesia, where the branch road leading to Columbus intersects the main line. The next is Mayhew, then Tibbe and then comes West Point, which seems to be a place of some importance, is more nicely built than many railroad towns, and is dryer than any place we have passed since leaving Lauderdale Springs.

All soldiers are temporarily detained here, though the trains run to the third and fourth station above here. I reported to Major Durr of the 39th Miss. Regt., who is in command of the "First Regiment of Consolidated Veterans." It is made up of odds and ends. I find one of my regiment here, William Youngblood of Company G. We have formed a mess composed as follows: M.P. Harbison, 4th Louisiana Battalion (my bed-fellow); C.C. Champion, —th Regt.; Dick Champion, Wm. McLeod and F.J. Carlisle, Company H, 57th Alabama Regt.; a man named Hinton, 39th Miss. Regt.; Youngblood and myself. It is uncertain when we can go to our respective commands. It seems to be pretty well understood that the remnant of Hood's army is at Corinth, Miss., and Major Durr thinks we can go on in less than a week. It is said to be about one hundred miles to Corinth and about twenty miles of the track has been destroyed. I trust it may soon be repaired.[2]

Tonight I am among strangers. One year ago I attempted a review of the principal events of the year just closed. This also has been a disastrous one for the Confederacy. In May began the terrible struggle that culminated in the fall of Atlanta. The Army of Tennessee is almost among the "things that were."

The campaign inaugurated by Gen. Hood in September has proven the most disastrous of any we have yet sustained. In addition to the loss of an army and its equipments, a way was opened for Gen. Sherman to march through the entire state of Georgia, which he promptly did, leaving a broad trail of desolation behind him. Savannah is fallen, Charleston may soon follow, and Mobile's outer defenses are taken and a vigorous assault will carry the city. In Virginia much blood has been shed without any great advantage to either side. Richmond and Petersburg are both besieged.[3]

It may be that God deigns our overthrow as a separate government. If so, may He prepare us for the ordeal that awaits us as a conquered people. There is too much iniquity in the land, in high and low places too, for us to expect any interposition of Providence in our behalf. May He teach us our duty.

January 3d. We are at the same place yet, though there is some talk of our removal to a more suitable camping ground. Last night we had a blessed season in prayer-meeting. Brother Hutson of the 39th Miss. Regt., who is a Methodist preacher, read a portion of Matt. VII and commented thereupon.

Jan. 4th. One and a half miles north of Columbus, Miss. Yesterday we were notified that we would move to another camping place at 8 o'clock this morning. At night Brother Hutson preached from Heb. XIII:5. "I will never leave thee nor forsake thee." Ere the service was concluded it was understood that we would move at once, and about 9 o'clock p.m. we started to the depot. By the time we got there the order was countermanded, and after some delay we returned to our camp.

At 8 o'clock this morning we started to our new camp and had nearly reached it when we received orders to proceed to this place at once, as a Federal raid was moving this way from North Alabama.[4] We boarded the train at 9 o'clock a.m. and proceeded to Artesia and were switched off on the Columbus road. By one o'clock p.m. we reached the splendid little city of Columbus, and immediately came out to this camp. It is now said there is no raid coming this way at all.

From the brief view I had of the place I should say that Columbus is the most wealthy and aristocratic looking town I have seen. It stands on the east bank of the Tombigbee River and is the seat of Lowndes County – I think the most populous and wealthy county in the state.

Jan. 7th. No event of special importance has transpired since I wrote here last. We are at the same place, and so far as I can see we are likely to remain here for several days to come. It is rumored that Stewart's corps will come to this place and go into quarters. I trust it may be so. The past two days have been cold, wet and disagreeable. We have had no religious service in camp since leaving West Point, as Brother Hutson went home from that place on furlough.

Jan. 8th. I will write a little ere I go to sleep, for I may not have an opportunity of writing again soon. We have orders to march at 6 o'clock tomorrow morning. Our destination is said to be Tupelo where, we are informed, a portion of the Army of Tennessee is at this time, though it is still said that Stewart's corps will come to this place. I do not know whether we will go by railroad or "take it afoot." I am anxious to meet my command and yet I dread to learn all that may be in store for me.

I attended religious service in town today at the Methodist Episcopal Church (South). Col. Fountain E. Pitts of the 81st Tenn. Regt. was the preacher. It was a deeply interesting and impressive discourse founded on the words "But one thing is needful; and Mary hath chosen that good part that shall not be taken from her." The subject was very well handled, and this together with the imposing appearance of the venerable old man, tall, straight and wearing a colonel's uniform, made an impression that will not soon wear off.[5]

Jan. 12th. One and a half miles S.W. of West Point. We have just arrived at this place, and I will employ a leisure hour in jotting down notes of a few events that make up the history of my campaign. When I wrote here last we were under orders to march next morning. When the hour for starting came it was raining in torrents. After everything was packed ready to move, the orders to march were countermanded "until further orders." The rain was incessant, and though Mr. Harbison and I had one of my blankets stretched it was an inefficient protection, and we became thoroughly wet. Until daylight Tuesday the rain continued, at which time the wind suddenly veered round to the north and by night it was again very cold.

That night I again attended preaching at the Methodist church. Dr. J.B. McFerrin was the preacher. I have seldom heard a more powerful sermon in my life. It was founded on Matt. XXV:21 – "Well done, thou good and faithful servant; thou hast been faithful over a few things; I will make thee ruler over many things."

Next morning, Wednesday 11th, we had orders to move at once. We accordingly repaired to the depot where a train was made up, and into which we were crowded regardless of comfort. After running about three miles it was found that the engine was too weak to pull so heavy a train. So four cars were cut off and all with no seats were ordered off the other boxes. I was among the number thus left. We built fires and waited for the engine to return. It came in about two hours and soon hauled us the rest of the way.

Our part of the train arrived at Artesia about 1 o'clock p.m., and finding the rest of the command already in line we marched right away. It had been ascertained that no transportation could be had for some hours, that no rations were accessible, and no fuel was convenient. Therefore, Lt. Col. Wier of the 37th Miss. Regt., commanding the brigade, resolved to march to West Point. Accordingly, we started on the railroad, and after marching about seven and one half miles bivouacked for the night not far from Tibbee Station. Moving at an early hour this morning we arrived here about 11 o'clock a.m. It is said that a train will be in readiness to haul us further this afternoon or tomorrow morning. We are now "reliably" informed that Stewart's corps will go into quarters at Tupelo, and it is said that Sears' brigade draws rations for six hundred men. If this report be true I shall expect to meet many of my comrades again.

It is enough to discourage the stoutest and most hopeful spirits to listen to the conversation of the men who participated in the recent campaign in Tennessee. They are utterly despondent and would hail with joy the prospect of peace on any terms. It is well known that Georgia is taking the initiatory steps looking to *submission* — at least the matter is being discussed in primary meetings held for that purpose, and I know that her course is approved and even applauded in the army. It seems to be a fact, shameful though it be, that three-fourths of the Army of Tennessee, and perhaps as great a proportion of the citizens of Georgia, Alabama and Mississippi, are in favor of peace on any terms, no matter how ignominious they may be. It is hard to feel reconciled to such a state of things. When I reflect on all the woes and misery our people have endured already, on the thousands of slain and maimed heroes who have already poured out their blood as water, on the vast army of brave spirits who are dying in Northern prisons, and on the sacrifices *we* have made and the hardships we have undergone, I feel a wild spirit of resentment that bids me resist as long as *one* Southern soldier is left.[6]

But this is not the voice of Wisdom. Helpless grayhairs, frail women and innocent children are in the land. They cannot find rest in a soldier's gory grave. We owe to them a duty, for strong arms, broad backs and stern discipline will be needed when the end comes, even as they are needed now. It is an unpleasant thought, but one that often suggests

itself, that when the contest is ended in our defeat, hundreds
– nay thousands – of the Northern soldiers will find homes
in the South and make wives of our sisters and our
daughters. They have fought us bravely as only brave men
can, but their hands are red with Southern blood, and it
seems that no true Southern maid would ever desire to wed
one who had helped to subdue her people. But I know that
where one would remain true to principle and be faithful to
a memory, many will be ready to forget it all and place her
affections in the keeping of a stranger, though his hands be
reeking with a brother's or a lover's blood.

But turning from this maddening theme and beholding
the ragged, frozen and half-starved survivors of the terrible
campaign just ended, reflecting on what they have suffered
and the less than nothing gained, I ask myself, "Is there a
way to stop this wholesale slaughter?" I can blame no one,
be he soldier or civilian, for desiring *peace*. More ardently
than for anything else do I desire peace for our terribly
scourged land. Yet, as a people, we have not humbled ourselves under the hand of God that His chastening may be
stayed. Perhaps others are better prepared than I, since they
are ready *now* for submission to the demands of our foes.

And while I am dealing in generalities I will again refer
to the soldiers recently enlisted from among the Federal
prisoners. I don't think there is a native-born American
among them. There is a small battalion (about one hundred
and fifty men) attached to this brigade. They belong to the
criminal class, and more than twenty instances are reported
in the past few days in which both whites and negroes have
been robbed and in many cases personally assaulted. They
are scattered all over the country through which we have
passed, and are said to be committing all sorts of depre-
dations. Some of them are not fit to be called *men*. Many
have already deserted to the enemy and others say they will
do the same at the first opportunity. It was an unwise step to
enlist them, and if they still wore the Federal uniform they
would be less harmful to us. It is said some of them fought
bravely at Egypt a few weeks ago before they were captured
by Col. Grierson. Perhaps so. They do well to dread capture,

but I would rather they were safely locked in Andersonville prison than here.[7]

One other man named Chambers, of Company G, has been added to our mess.

Jan. 16th. One mile west of Verona, Miss. Once more I am with Company B, 46th Miss. Regt. I feel grateful to God that he so mercifully shielded my regiment, and especially my company. Of the latter none were killed. Lts. Duckworth and Collins were both captured at Nashville on the 16th of December, and some four or five others were wounded at Franklin, among whom was W.C. Robertson. None of the wounds were serious.

But I will begin at the beginning. About dark on the evening of the 12th we were informed that we would move at sunrise next morning, and that we would march all the way to Tupelo, distant about forty-five miles. The men were indignant at the idea of making this march, especially as it was understood that Col. Wier had an order for the transportation of nine hundred men. But indignation on the part of a common soldier generally cuts a small figure in the execution of an order. Accordingly, we started about 8 o'clock next morning. Before we had gone three miles perhaps one half the men had "played out." They had simply *stopped* to wait for a train. That day I marched with the regiment. We passed Lahatan about noon. There is no town here, just a small station house and one or two shabby buildings in the midst of a vast cornfield which extends some twenty miles along the road. We bivouacked for the night just below Prairie, the next station above Lahatan. As soon as dark came on I bade farewell to the "First Regiment of Consolidated Veterans," and "flanking" headquarters, I traveled two or three miles up the railroad when I came to a long line of rail pens filled with Government corn. I crawled up into one of these pens and went to sleep, and awoke two hours before day nearly frozen. Starting before daylight I soon passed the spot where the "Consolidated Veterans" had fought Grierson's raid some weeks before. By sunrise I was at Egypt. There is no town at this place, nor at Prairie Station. At Egypt, however, Col. Burke's regiment of Federal recruits and Major Phelps' battalion of Reserves had been captured by Grierson's raiders. Traces of the struggle were visible on the trees and fences, as well as in the carcasses of several horses. The depot had been burned and near where it stood were one hundred Austrian rifles, broken at the breach.

I reached Okolona about 11 o'clock a.m. This was a town of some importance before it was burned by the recent raiding party. One church house is, I think, the only public building left standing. The next station is Shannon, a nice little town, but it had shared the same fate as Okolona.

I had already learned that Stewart's corps was at Verona, the next station above Shannon. Before reaching the station I came to the encampment, and before dark had found my command. I did not see Verona at all.

I find my regiment, the whole army in fact, in a deplorable condition. Twenty besides myself of Company B are here, but there is not a gun in the company. The regiment numbers about one hundred and fifty men, about half of whom are barefoot. All are ragged, dirty and covered with vermin, some not having sufficient clothing to hide their bodies. There are perhaps twenty guns, but not a single cartridge box in the regiment. The men are jovial enough in regard to their condition and their environment, but when it comes to discussing the prosecution of the war they are entirely despondent, being fully convinced that the Confederacy is *gone.* Capt. Heslip is in command of the regiment. Major Nelson of the 4th Regt. commands the brigade, which is attached to Walthall's division. I do not think there is a stand of colors in the brigade.[8]

Nearly all my friends and acquaintances are safe, though some are absent who have probably gone home. Among them is Robertson. Yesterday we had brigade inspection at 11 o'clock a.m. and preaching in the afternoon. Prayer meeting at night.

Immediately on my arrival in camp I was ordered on duty as orderly sergeant. I see no way to get out of it, so I suppose I must accept the office. It is understood, however, that I am not expected to carry a gun or go on fatigue duty or anything of that sort, till my wound is more completely cured. It is said we will move down the road tomorrow, though I do not think orders to that effect have yet been received.

Jan. 17th. As I am doing nothing today I will say a little more about my recent messmate, M.P. Harbison. He is an agreeable companion, the greatest charm in his conversation being his powers of description. He is a native of Delaware, but has traveled over several states. He was an eye-witness of the terrible powder explosion in Wilmington, Delaware, in 1855 or '56 in which seventy-five persons were instantly killed and a large number of others wounded. His description of the scene was vivid in the extreme.[9] Among the places of historic renown he had visited was the field on which the battle of Brandywine was fought during the Revolutionary War. A house is still standing which has a hole through the wall, made by a British cannonball.

Jan. 18th. There is some excitement in camp growing out of orders received in regard to furloughs. I am afraid it will be a difficult matter to procure one, though a liberal system has been promised. Many applications have been forwarded, and I have done little else since my last entry here than to write applications. We had prayer meeting last night. I am quite unwell today. I fainted last night, and when I regained consciousness I was almost frost bitten.

Jan. 19th. Companies B and H were consolidated today, and are commanded by Capt. Buchanan. Company H has one commissioned officer, Lt. Rufus White. Three other companies were formed of the remaining eight. So the regiment has four companies and is commanded by Capt. J.B. Hart of Company E. (Lt. Col. Magee was wounded at Franklin, Tenn., and there is no other field officer. Hart is senior captain). There are rumors to the effect that our regiment will shortly be detached.

Jan. 21st. Rained incessantly last night and today. Fuel is scarce but the situation might be much worse than it is. A portion of the army is moving from this place. Lee's corps is gone to South Carolina, we are told. Cheatham's (Hardee's) is to follow. Ours, it is said, is ordered to Meridian.

Jan. 22d. Still cloudy and bitterly cold. I am very unwell. We had the usual Sunday inspection in the forenoon
and preaching at 3 o'clock p.m. by a Mr. Andrews, missionary chaplain of our division.

Jan. 25th. The weather is very cold indeed, a light fall of
snow occurring Sunday night which is still lying on the
ground. Yesterday we were moved to the east of the railroad
about one and a half miles. We are in a pretty location now
for a camp. Last night, however, about dark orders came for
us to march at 8 o'clock a.m. tomorrow. We will march to
West Point, it is said, where transportation will be furnished.
Meridian is understood to be our destination. Gen. Richard
Taylor is now in command of what is left of the Army of
Tennessee, Gen. Hood being in Richmond so the story goes.
I guess Gen. Taylor is a Department Commander. [10]

Several furloughs have been granted to members of the
regiment. S.M. Howell of Company B left yesterday on
furlough, and Brother Lattimore left this morning. Furloughs of ten days are granted to entire companies and regiments, but the homes of our company are so remote from
the railroad that we have not applied for such leave of
absence. If we stop at Meridian it is the intention to apply
for a more extended leave for the whole company. I have
been reading some in Dr. Gill's "Words and Works of God."

Jan. 30th. Near West Point. Since my last entry the
weather has continued very cold, the snow of last Sunday
night not having entirely disappeared until today. When I
wrote here last we were under orders to move at 8 o'clock
next morning. When the hour arrived the orders were countermanded. At dark Thursday orders came to move at
sunrise Friday morning. The column was put in motion
about 7 o'clock a.m. on the 27th, Loring's division marching
in front and Walthall's bringing up the rear. We marched on
the railroad, which was not pleasant walking. We traveled
about sixteen miles that day and halted for the night some
three miles south of Okolona. Moving at 7 o'clock next
morning we marched about the same distance as on the day
previous, and bivouacked about midway between Prairie
and Lahatan. Starting yesterday morning at 6:30 o'clock, we

arrived here about noon after a tramp of some twelve miles. This march was rather severe on my "delicate" feet, and I was compelled to make part of the trip without my shoes. After leaving the railroad track, the sharp fragments of ice and the rough frozen ground made my progress exceedingly painful. Yet it ill becomes me to complain at this, for I have seen others march barefoot day after day, while the print of nearly every step was stained with blood. In the expressive if not elegant phraseology of the camp, I am "going on three legs" today.

Our brigade is quite small now. All of two regiments, the 39th and 35th Miss., are furloughed, and many members of the remaining regiments are absent with leave, among them being Companies A, D, F and K of the 46th. So many of the officers are away that Capt. Buchanan is in command of the regiment. No other arrangement would suit him but for me to serve as adjutant, and as we have no sergeant major I am quite busy. There are about fifteen of the company here now, Lt. McLaurin starting home on furlough last night.

Jan. 31st. Quite warm and pleasant today, though as I am unable to walk I lose much enjoyment of the fine weather. I suppose we will move on as soon as transportation can be secured.

CHAPTER 19

Losing Ground on Every Side

Feb. 8th. Five miles south of Mobile, Ala. On the night of Wednesday, Feb. 1st, Brother Andrews preached. At the close of the service we received orders to move at 3 o'clock next morning. In compliance with said order we were at the depot on time, but as the transportation facilities were inadequate a portion of us did not leave until about 11 o'clock a.m. The box in which I rode was old and dilapidated, and as a cold rain was falling we all got wet and suffered some with cold. We had been ordered to Marion, Miss., so the officers said, but when we arrived at that place we made no stop at all. We lay over at Meridian till about 5 o'clock p.m. Friday 3d, not leaving the cars, however. When it became apparent that we would not stop at Marion the conclusion was reached at once that we would be rushed to South Carolina right away. [1]

I felt indeed sorry for my ragged comrades who, while I was at home, had undergone so much peril and hardship, and who were now likely to be dragged away from nearly in sight of home and sent hundreds of miles in the opposite direction. Several men left the regiment though all of Company B remain at their posts. At Meridian on the 3d, an effort was made to have the rest of our brigade granted furloughs. Gen. Taylor told us in person that he could not furlough us then, but pledged his word that as soon as those now absent returned we should be permitted to go home. He also stated in most unequivocal terms that French's division had been detached from the rest of the corps, and would certainly remain at Mobile. These assurances somewhat pacified the men, but did not by any means wholly satisfy them; in fact, the most devoted of us are inclined to question the "whys and wherefores" of many things just now.

Leaving Meridian at 5 o'clock p.m., we arrived at Mobile at noon on Saturday 4th. As it was still raining, Capt. Benoit, A.A.A.G. of Sears' brigade, secured an old warehouse where we were sheltered till 10 o'clock a.m. Sunday 5th. We also were fortunate enough to secure some old tents that had once belonged to Reynolds' brigade. They are the first tents we have had since the fall of Vicksburg.[2]

Before leaving the warehouse Sunday morning, Brother Andrews preached. During the service we were ordered to move to this encampment. It was still raining when we arrived here, and by the time the wagons came with our tents we were thoroughly wet. Yesterday was a fair day and we erected chimneys to our tents, so we are quite comfortable indeed. We have a pretty location, though it is rather small. It is a mile or so from the shore of the bay, and from a point near our camp we have a pretty fair view of the Federal fleet. I am still acting as adjutant. None of the furloughed men from our regiment have returned. It is time they were here.

Feb. 10th. Some of the furloughed men are coming in, among them Company F to this regiment.

Feb. 12th. We have been inspected twice today. Last night I was up writing till a late hour, preparing applications for furloughs for Companies B and H. All of the furloughed companies are again represented in camp, though none of Company K are here except Orderly Sergeant J.H. McDonald. Applications for the rest of us have been forwarded.

We are doing picket duty on the beach now, in sight of the Federal fleet. Lt. R.N. Rea of Company F is now acting adjutant. Capt. Barwick of Company D will assume command of the regiment tomorrow, and Col. Barry of the 35th Regt. will assume command of the brigade at the same time. Some cannonading today.

Feb. 17th. I have the "blues" this morning. I am depressed in spirit when I contemplate the condition of our country. A spirit of submission is rife throughout the land. Union meetings are being held, even in Mississippi, and submission is openly advocated and the further prosecution of the war is bitterly denounced. Some of us did hope for peace, but the Federal government will entertain no proposition but unconditional surrender, and so we must nerve our arms for another campaign. It seems a useless waste of blood. We have no armies to fight our victorious foes. Tens of thousands of Confederates are at home.

There is a cry to put negroes in the army, and I understand that our congress is considering the subject.[3] There will be a brigade meeting today and a division meeting tomorrow to adopt resolutions expressing the sentiments of this command in regard to the prosecution of the war. These resolutions are to be *for show,* I suppose. The time for *big talk* has passed. Disguise the fact as we may, the *real sentiment* of this brigade and this division is for peace on almost any terms. The proper course, I think, is not to ignore this fact but to face it at once, and set about rectifying the evil in a legitimate manner. If this be the aim of the proposed meetings I can bid them "God speed."

Evening. I attended the brigade meeting today. We had speeches from Rev. Andrews, Capt. Harris of the 7th Battalion and Col. Barry and Capt. Brack of the 35th Regt. Col. Barry's argument, "There is hope in fighting, in submission none," seems to have been the key note of the situation. The resolutions were good, breathing unflagging zeal in our effort to be free. The proposition to arm the negroes was discussed pro and con, and two votes were taken thereupon but the matter was left undecided. I do not consider the measure expedient, but I am opposed to it on higher ground than expediency – *it is not right.*

Our furloughs still hang fire. W.R. Gibbons started home on furlough last night. Capt. Durham of Company K is in our mess now. Four of his company are here. Many others are coming in. We have preaching nearly every night now.

Feb. 19th. A gloomy day of clouds, wind and thunder. I did not attend the division meeting yesterday. I understand several ladies were present and that everything passed off very nicely. Speeches were made by Col. Barry, Col. Coleman of Ector's brigade and by Gen. Cockrell; besides these Hon. Percy Walker and Judge W.G. Jones from the city also made speeches. I have not seen the proceedings yet. I understand some *bloody* resolutions were passed. It was resolved that the best interests of the country demanded that the negroes be placed in the field as soldiers. It was also resolved that this command places unlimited confidence in the wisdom, sagacity and purity of Mr. Davis as a statesman and general, and that his course merits our unreserved commendation.

I understand that Congress has at last made Gen. R.E. Lee commander-in-chief of all the Confederate armies. Another measure of Congress is recalling Gen. J.E. Johnston to the command of his old army. It is thought these two measures will do much to restore public confidence. I do not know what is best. I am simply resolved to do my whole duty as nearly as I can.[4]

Feb. 27th. Robertson came into camp a week ago. He had been at home for some time and brought me letters when he came. He and I have a tent to ourselves. Brother Lattimore is messing with us, but has a tent of his own to sleep and study in. When the rain does not interfere we have preaching every night and frequently during the day. A missionary named McMurtry is here. He, Andrews and the three regular chaplains – Foster, 35th; Gordon, 36th; and Lattimore, 46th (with Hutson of the 39th) – frequently alternate in conducting the services. Much interest is manifested and the baptismal waters are often stirred. Four of Company B started home on furlough yesterday.

Feb. 28th. I have made out a complete set of muster and pay rolls today, and we were paid two months' wages this afternoon. Rained last night.

March 3d. We are under orders to move at a moment's notice. Two or three transports of the enemy entered the bay last night through Grant's Pass. It seems to be certain that the Federals are moving out from Pensacola, and I suppose that our authorities anticipate active campaigning as all furloughs have been revoked and the men are ordered to return to their respective commands. From certain indications I think this city will be evacuated if a heavy force moves against [it]. Our prospects are growing more gloomy every day. On every side we are losing ground. I very much doubt whether the *morale* of this army or of the citizens of the land is equal to the emergency that confronts us. All of us are weary of this ceaseless turmoil and bloodshed – we long so much for peace. May God teach us patience and resignation, and may the rod of affliction soon be stayed.

Yesterday Robertson and I went to the city. We encountered nothing worthy of note. We found very small stocks of goods in any of the houses, though what was there was held at exorbitant prices. We paid five dollars for a dinner of baker's bread and butter. On our return, the bay presented a beautiful appearance. The wind had been blowing all day and the surface of the water lashed into foam. White-capped waves chased each other and were dashed into boiling foam on the shore. The Federal fleet was target shooting, we supposed, as we could plainly see the puffs of smoke rising out [over] the water, apparently to be followed by a heavy "boom."

March 4th. I am somewhat unwell as I had a chill and fever today. The excitement in regard to moving seems to have subsided. Cool today with strong north wind. I have read some in "Baxter's Saints' Rest."

March 6th. I am indisposed again today. Yesterday Brother Lattimore, Robertson and I went across the river to a small Baptist church I had visited in February 1864. Bro. Lattimore preached to a congregation made up almost entirely of soldiers from our brigade and the women living near the place. His discourse was an interesting one and was listened to with marked attention. On our return we passed the spot where our brigade was encamped a year ago. Not a vestige of our cabins remains. At 3 o'clock p.m. Bro. Andrews preached and Bro. Lattimore preached at night. After the sermon last night my messmate Robertson professed conversion and offered himself as a candidate for baptism. Bro. Lattimore baptized him at 10 o'clock a.m. today. I was too unwell to witness the administration of the ordinance. I am taking medicine prescribed by Dr. Catchings of the 39th Miss. The troops are in the ditches this afternoon.

March 7th. I am feeling much better today. This morning I witnessed the administration of the ordinance of baptism. Bro. Lattimore baptized two from our brigade. Capt. Ziegel, commanding the 10th Texas Regt., Ector's brigade, who is a Baptist preacher, baptized three from that brigade, and Bro. Andrews baptized four. Two of these were from Ector's brigade and the other two were members of Company F, our regiment. Both the latter were named Denton, and one was baptized as a Methodist and the other a Presbyterian.

There is a General Review in the city this afternoon and all the command is gone, except a few "sick folks" like myself.

I think the apprehensions of an immediate attack upon this place are subsiding. But if rumors can be depended on, some movements will doubtless soon be made that will affect the destiny of the Gulf City. We understand that a large Federal force under command of Gen. Thomas is at New Orleans, and that it will be landed at Pensacola and probably move upon Selma.[5] A movement of this nature would insure the fall of Mobile, if successful, and would entail less loss of life than a direct assault upon the works here. For this place is strongly fortified and its armament is formidable. With a force sufficient to man the works it would prove well nigh impregnable so far as direct assault is concerned.

March 8th. We had a heavy rain accompanied by a great deal of wind and thunder last night. Today, however, is spring-like. The command will be equipped today. We were armed with Austrian rifles immediately after we came to this place, but there has not been a cartridge box in the brigade since I joined at Verona. It seems hardly credible, yet it is true, that all the picketing we have done here, though in sight of the enemy, has been done with "empty guns." I understand from the newspapers that the exchange of prisoners has been resumed. I trust it may be true, for there are doubtless many sufferers in the prisons of both North and South.[6]

March 11th. Yesterday was "fast day" by proclamation of the President. It was observed throughout this division in so far as all business was suspended, but I suppose it was literally observed by but few, even of the professors of religion. We had prayer-meeting in the brigade at 10 o'clock

a.m. Bro. Foster conducted the exercises. At 3 o'clock p.m.
Dr. Hamilton of Mobile preached a powerful sermon in our
brigade from the Scripture – "Likewise I say unto you, there
is joy in the presence of the angels of God over one sinner
that repenteth." Luke XVI:10. Bro. Lattimore preached at
night. A cold north wind prevailed yesterday and there is a
white frost this morning.

March 13th. On Saturday afternoon two of the Federal
ironclads took position in range of the lower batteries, and
for about two hours a vigorous bombardment was kept up. I
think, however, no damage was done. The fleet had been
augmented to about fifteen vessels, but yesterday morning
only nine were in sight.

The enemy are bombarding Spanish Fort today. I know
nothing of its importance as a means of defense. It is on the
eastern shore of the bay some miles below the city. If it falls
I suppose a landing can be effected on that side and the river
can be more easily controlled, leaving only the M. & O.
Railroad as a source of supplies.

March 15th. Yesterday was a day of incessant rain. In
fact, I do not remember seeing so much rain fall in some
length as has fallen since we came here.

Bro. Lattimore has tendered his resignation as chaplain
of our regiment. This action is based on his appointment as
a missionary to the batteries in the Confederate armies. Bro.
Gordon of the 36th has already resigned, and the resignation
of Bro. Foster of the 35th has also been forwarded to the
Department. This will leave the brigade without a regular
chaplain.

March 19th. Day before yesterday Capt. Buchanan
started home on a detail of twenty-five days for the purpose
of securing recruits for the company. About a year ago he
started home on a similar errand. Our consolidated company
is now commanded by Lt. Rufus White of Company H. In
compliance with orders from regimental headquarters I have
been engaged for the past few days in writing a history of
Company B from its organization to the present time. It is
not completed yet.

March 21st. I expected to have gone to the city yesterday, but no passes were granted. About 10 o'clock a.m. an order was received to keep all the men in camp and be ready to move at any time. At 3 o'clock p.m. an additional order came requiring us to cook three days' rations *at once* and be ready to move at a moment's notice. It was reported [that the enemy] were landing in force at Cedar Point some thirty miles below here, and Gibson's Louisiana brigade was sent in that direction yesterday afternoon.[7] Later reports say it is only a cavalry force that is debarking at Cedar Point. They may attempt to reach the railroad at some point north of here. Heavy raining all night and today. There was more cannonading on the bay yesterday which was probably directed against Spanish Fort.

March 24th. The brigade that was sent in the direction of Cedar Point returned Tuesday afternoon and everything appeared quiet again. It transpires, however, that the bombardment of Monday resulted in driving our forces from "Fort Montrose" on the eastern shore, and its subsequent occupation by the Federals. They are reported to be moving on Spanish Fort from that place. On Wednesday drilling was resumed. On the same day I received from Demopolis the missing portion of this journal, or most of it at least – some twenty-five pages being lost.

Yesterday Robertson and I again visited the city. We spent a portion of the time in ascertaining the location of the different churches. We went into one Catholic church and witnessed part of a funeral service. While in the city, Gibson's brigade marched through on its way to the wharf where it went on board a steamer bound for the eastern shore. With it I met my "consolidated" bed-fellow, M.P. Harbison. I was glad to see him.

On our return to camp we found the men again cooking three days' rations. I don't know whether we will move this time or not.

CHAPTER 20

The Final Act

March 25th. One mile south of Blakely, Ala. We left the camp about 4 o'clock p.m. yesterday and proceeded to the city. Embarking on the *Magnolia* at about 8 o'clock p.m., we were landed at Blakely about midnight. We are now in the bivouac and may remain here all day. Blakely is a pretty village, resembling Pollard in being surrounded by pine woods. As we neared the landing at Blakely a soldier of Cockrell's brigade, while in a state of intoxication, fell overboard and was drowned. An hour or two later two boats collided on the river and one of them was instantly sunk. It was laden with Q.M. and commissary stores principally for our brigade. It is said several lives were also lost. The collision was the result of sheer carelessness it would seem, for it was a beautiful starlit night and the boats could easily be seen for several hundred yards. We left the sick in camp with Bro. Lattimore, who is in charge of the regimental quarters.

April 10th. Claiborne, Ala. While awaiting a boat to go to Mobile I will begin an entry, not knowing when I can finish it.

On Saturday 25th we remained in bivouac until 3 o'clock p.m. when we marched about eight miles south and staid all night. In going down we crossed a body of water called Bay Minette and were not far, I think, from Spanish Fort. Next morning we returned in the direction of Blakely, but leaving it to our left we bivouacked for the night near Sibley's Mill. On Monday 27th we returned to Blakely and took position in the trenches.[1] Our brigade was on the extreme left, our regiment being, I think, about a mile and a half from the village. Meanwhile the enemy had invested Spanish Fort, which in addition to its artillery forces was manned by Gibson's Louisiana brigade and a brigade of Alabama State Reserves.[2]

On Tuesday 28th Ector's brigade was detached and sent
to the beleaguered Fort. In the meantime we were busily engaged in strengthening our position. We had only Cockrell's,
Sears' and Holtzclaw's brigades to man the works at Blakely, Gen. Cockrell commanding the division and Gen. Maury
commander-in-chief. [3]

On Wednesday 29th our regiment, about one hundred
strong and commanded by Capt. J.B. Hart of Company E,
was sent out about four miles on the Stockton road to do
picket duty. Nothing of special interest occurred till Saturday April 1st. The siege of Spanish Fort was not inter-
mitted, and we knew the enemy were advancing upon us
from above. About noon he made his appearance in our
front. A well directed fire emptied several saddles and ef-
fectually checked his advance for the time.

*(Editor's note — See Appendix A for an extended post-
war account by Chambers of his experiences at Blakely).*

Gen. Cockrell directed Capt. Hart to fall back if pressed,
but the latter protested that he was able to hold the enemy in
check for an indefinite period. He seemed to take no account of the open country and his unprotected flanks. After
some two hours' waiting, during which an occasional shot
was fired, we suddenly discovered that the enemy was on
our left flank as well as on our front. Forming two sides of a
square we at once began a running fight, loading our guns
as we double-quicked and then stopped, taking a hasty aim
and firing. This was kept up for about two miles. Then, as
we neared the head of a mill-pond, the enemy (cavalry)
made a charge, having gained the road in our front. In a
moment they were all among us, crying out, "Surrender!
Halt, you d—d rebels!" and such expressions. [4]

Nearly all the right wing, our left as we retreated, dashed
away from them and ran through the undergrowth toward
the mill-pond. Volley after volley was fired at us, knocking
the bark from the saplings all about us, but so far as I could
see not a man was touched. When the firing had all ceased
and we heard no one in pursuit, we halted. There were four
of us together, viz: Sergt. Robert Leachman of Company F,
Sergt. Willis Pickering, Robertson and myself of Company

B. After resting a few minutes we concluded to "flank" the enemy and try to reach our lines at Blakely.

We were already in a gall-berry flat. Following this till we came in sight of the waters of the bay we emerged from the thicket to find ourselves about seventy-five yards in rear of a Federal line of battle. Making no effort to dislodge the enemy, or even attract his attention, we crept back into the thicket and returned to our stopping place. We soon learned that several others were near us. We held a council of war – several of the officers and our squad. I showed the impracticability of entering our lines by the direct route, and suggested that we remain where we were till dark and pass to the enemy's rear.

We collected at dark forty-seven men all told, nine or ten of whom were officers. Capt. Hart was either killed or captured, we supposed, and so was Capt. Heslip. Lt. Rea was known to have been wounded. Capt. J.A. Barwick of Company D was in command. Directing our course by the stars we started and traveled due east. We forded streams, crossed swamps and jungles, taking some of them endwise, and were sometimes in water to our hips. I brought up the rear, no word was spoken above a whisper and a command was passed from man to man as we marched in single file about five feet apart. Soon after starting we passed within a few yards of the Federals as they took the floor out of a mill house to cover a bridge.

Altogether it was a unique march. The crescent moon was going down behind us, the air was full of fireflies, the ponds and brakes were vocal with the cries of thousands of frogs, and on the low ridges the dogwood trees sheeted in white blossoms stood like ghostly sentinels in the uncertain light. Once, when a timid deer started up in our path, in obedience to a preconcerted signal, we all fell as dead men "till the danger was past." It was ludicrous, too, and I often wanted to laugh outright when some fellow would fall into water to his waist or measure his length in the mud, especially if he indulged in smothered grunts or imprecations during the performance. There was no lagging and no inclination to straggle. We traveled till about 3 o'clock a.m. Sunday 2d, when we halted in a reed-brake to rest and reconnoiter.

In the early morning I had a chill. This was followed by a burning fever and delirium which lasted all day. I can only dimly recall the fact that they all left me in the swamp late in the afternoon with no one but Robertson, who agreed to stay with me. I know I have sorely tried his patience in my feverish hours, but he has never uttered an impatient word. Unable to walk, I was partly carried and we traveled about a mile and a half that night.

Monday 3d we started in the late afternoon, but so many swamps were in the way and I was so weak that we had gone only two or three miles by midnight when we halted again. We started at daylight and walked till noon, covering some six or seven miles. At dark we started again and turned to the northeast in order to reach the railroad. It must be understood that all this time we had seen no sign of human habitation, had not even crossed a road of any sort. About 1 o'clock a.m. Wednesday 5th we again made a long halt when we again started on another weary tramp. Soon after dark we treed and killed an opossum. We had no means of starting a fire for they took our guns when they left us in the swamp Sunday, and we had not a pinch of salt, yet we were getting hungry enough to seriously consider the propriety of trying to eat the disgusting marsupial. About midnight we came to a cabin, the first we had seen since leaving Blakely, and from a woman and a little boy we learned something of our whereabouts. We were about a mile from Williams Station on the railroad.[5] We also learned that some Federal soldiers were in camp about a mile from there, and that they had been at the very cabin the previous afternoon.

We reached the railroad near Williams Station and followed the eastern end till we crossed Dyer's Creek, when we lay down in the woods till morning. Starting soon after daylight we soon found a road, and after following for about six miles came to the house of a man named Bryers. From him we heard of the rest of our regiment who had passed only two days before. Our effort to secure something to eat was an ignoble failure.

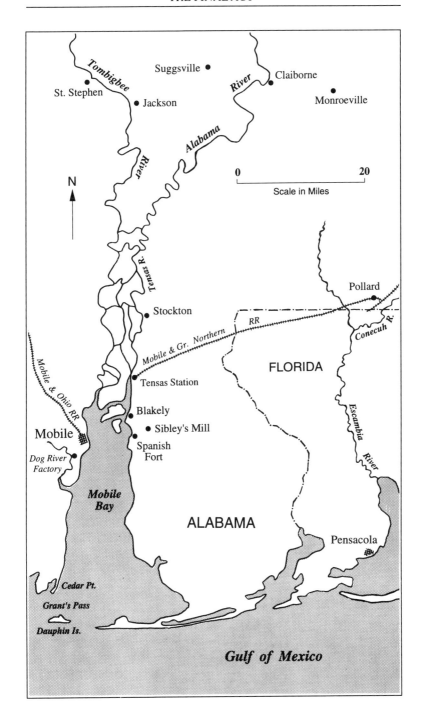

One and a half miles further brought us to the old Stage Road. The Federal army had traveled this road and had destroyed all the food-stuffs they could find, and had killed all the stock cattle and hogs. About 1 o'clock p.m. we came to the house of a Mr. McGill and asked for dinner. He was in the army and the Yankee soldiers had destroyed everything about the place, even breaking the dishes and destroying the bees. His wife, however, was a true Southern woman and declared she was not "near whipped." Out of her poverty she prepared us a meal that to us was a princely feast, for which she would accept no pay; but we each laid a dollar on the table and came away.

We soon left the route followed by the enemy and slept on the piazza of an unoccupied house that night. Next day (Friday 7th) it rained nearly all day and we ate dinner with a man named Lomax, who treated us very kindly. That night we slept in a school house. After traveling about two miles next morning we ate breakfast at Mrs. Parker's, who was very kind to us. We got a haversack of potatoes that day from a Mr. Robertson. Stopped in a church as it was raining, till nearly night, and then left the main road and slept in the woods.

We reached Monroeville about 9 o'clock a.m. on Sunday 9th. This is a pretty little town, the seat of Monroe County. As we rested on some benches near the hotel the proprietor, Mrs. Lewis, kindly invited us in, and she and her daughter, Miss Jane, set us a nice breakfast to which we did ample justice. They informed us that boats ran regularly between Claiborne and Mobile, and advised us to come here. We arrived [in Claiborne] about dark yesterday afternoon after a march of fourteen miles from Monroeville. We had understood that the 15th Confederate Cavalry Regt. was posted at this place, and hence were not surprised at being halted by some pickets some three miles from town. One of the men at our request escorted us to Lt. Col. Myers, who released us immediately and sent us to his regimental commissary. Capt. Davis bountifully supplied us with rations. We are awaiting a boat to take us to Mobile. We are told here that Selma is in the hands of the enemy and there are rumors that

Richmond has been evacuated.[6] Thus our prospects are growing more gloomy every day. May the Lord help us.

This is quite a pretty town. It is in Monroe County and is on the east bank of the Alabama River about [thirty-five] miles above its junction with the Tombigbee. It appears to have been a *fast place* before the war came on.

April 12th. Suggsville, Ala. We remained in the town of Claiborne all day Monday awaiting a boat. The time was spent pleasantly enough, yet it seemed at times like we were idlers. That night we slept in the Presbyterian church. We had about an inch of candle, and finding a note-book convenient we sang a few old pieces of music before going to sleep. The seats were cushioned and made for a soldier a most luxurious bed. We made an important purchase in Claiborne, viz: a plug of tobacco, for which we paid $10.00.

No boat having appeared by Tuesday morning, we decided to go across to the Tombigbee River as we were assured that boats were running on that stream all the time. Owing to unavoidable delays it was 11 o'clock a.m. yesterday when we crossed the Alabama River. Starting on the road to Point Jackson we reached this place about sunset. The intervening road was pleasant walking and several nice residences were passed. At one of these a lady handed us each a glass of milk which was much appreciated.

On our arrival here a gentleman furnished us with a haversack of potatoes, and we were intending to "camp out" as usual. An old gentleman, Dr. Rivers, learning our intention, insisted that we should spend the night at his house. We did so, and this morning his motherly wife insisted that we stop over today and have our clothes washed. This is a pleasant family and I pray that God may reward them for their kindness.

There is great commotion in town this morning. At a late hour last evening news was received that the 15th Confederate Cavalry had left Claiborne yesterday morning, had encountered the enemy a few miles from that place, and had sustained a severe repulse. It is said the enemy are on this side of the Alabama River and moving on Jackson. I am not at all desirous of being again "cut off." Advices from

Mobile, in which direction there has been heavy cannonading all day, are to the effect that Spanish Fort and Blakely
both are fallen. It is said they were evacuated; Mobile must
necessarily soon follow. The troops will probably come up
the river. It is also rumored that Gen. Forest [sic] has
checked a Federal column near Uniontown that was moving
out from Selma.[7]

This village is in Clarke County. There is some wealth
about here and the people seem very kind. As I close this
entry the tones of a piano are filling the house with music,
and a sweet young woman's voice is singing "When This
Cruel War is Over."

April 14th. Twelve miles west of St. Stephens, Ala. While
waiting for some potatoes to roast I will bring up my record
of events. We left Dr. Rivers at Suggsville about 4 o'clock
p.m. on Wednesday 12th, and after traveling five or six
miles we camped near the road. As the night was rainy it
was not really agreeable sleeping. Before daylight we were
aroused by mounted couriers who informed us that the
Yankees were within three miles of Suggsville. Not wishing
to get inside the Federal lines again, we resumed our march.
We found the citizens everywhere in great excitement, and a
thousand and one rumors were afloat as to the whereabouts
of the oncoming raid, all of which were probably untrue.

We arrived at Jackson about 11 o'clock a.m. and found
the excitement greater than on the road. Scores of wagons
loaded with furniture and with salt from the Oven Bluff Salt
Works, were awaiting to be ferried across the river, while
the whole landing and adjacent bluffs were thronged with
excited people. Several steamboats were in sight on the way
to Demopolis, but learning that the remnant of the Mobile
garrison were ordered to rendezvous at Meridian we
deemed it best to make our way to the M. & O. R.R. Hence
we gave a negro a dollar to put us across the river in his
skiff. The passage of the steamboats, however, had made the
water so rough that the skiff came near being swamped.
Jackson is a village on a high bluff on the east bank of the
Tombigbee River and is in Clarke County.

After crossing the river we were in Washington County,

Ala. It is ten miles from Jackson to St. Stephens, yet the road was so level and dry that we reached the latter place about 4 o'clock p.m. We passed some good farms, and at one farm house a lady gave us a canteen of milk. As we proceeded the country became more broken and sterile.

St. Stephens is the seat of Washington County. I must say I was sadly disappointed in the place. It is one of the oldest towns in the state, at one time was the State Capital, and is still the site of a Government land office, yet I found only a small, dilapidated village about as large and about as pretentious as Williamsburg, Miss. There must be an older town somewhere. We had expected to draw rations here but couldn't find any to draw.

We stopped for the night with a soldier named Dykes, two miles west of town. He was a very poor man who had been in the army about Mobile, and had stopped over with his family while being conveyed up the river to Demopolis. He bountifully fed us on substantial fare for which he would accept no renumeration. We found the wildest excitement among all classes, and rumors were rife as ever. We have traveled about ten miles today through a sterile region, having passed only three settlements. At one of these we got some potatoes, and from present indications we stand a good chance to lie out in the rain tonight.

April 15th. Four and a half miles north of State Line, Miss. Starting about 1 o'clock p.m. yesterday we marched nine or ten miles and camped with a family who are moving from Sparta, Ala. to Texas. They crossed the river at Claiborne just ahead of us and we have frequently passed each other since. They proved very agreeable companions. The family consists of Mr. Savers, formerly a Stock Commission merchant of New Orleans, his young wife, her mother, a Mrs. Robertson and a very beautiful young lady, a cousin of Mrs. Savers. They called her Miss Jennie. An Englishman, a soldier and about twenty-five negroes make up the party.

We started quite early this morning and reached the railroad nine miles distant a little before noon. We ate breakfast at a Mr. Williams' not long after starting. The entire distance from the Tombigbee River to the railroad is sterile pine woods and very sparsely populated. Just before reaching the railroad a man named Breland let us have some potatoes for which he would accept no pay. Finding that no rations were to be had at State Line, and that it was uncertain when a train would go up the road, we resolved to "walk on." We have come some four and a half miles, have eaten a primitive supper of roasted potatoes and are now seated by a pine knot fire. There is no town at all at State Line. It is about a mile from the Alabama line, and is on the line of Green and Wayne counties.

So we are in Mississippi again. The people of Alabama have treated us with great kindness during our tramp of two hundred miles in the last fourteen days. In fact, the state has earned the enviable reputation for hospitality to soldiers, and during the last two years has contributed more to feed the army of the West than any other state in the Confederacy.

Mobile is fallen! The Gulf City, our last seaport that for four years has stood proudly defiant, is now in the possession of our enemies. It is a sad story. Neither Spanish Fort or Blakely were evacuated. Both places were carried by assault. It is said that the latter place was carried by negro troops, that "Fort Pillow" was the battle-cry and that many of the garrison were slaughtered after they had surrendered. For the sake of American civilization I hope the rumor is not true. A feeble gleam of light comes from the East. It is said that Sherman has been beaten in North Carolina. May God have mercy upon us, and as a people direct us. [8]

April 17th. Shubuta, Miss. After an early start yesterday morning we found a train at Buckatunna Bridge on which we rode two miles to the station of that name, where we remained till about 11 o'clock a.m. Finding nothing to eat, and no hope of getting to ride any further, we walked up the track seven miles to Winchester, arriving there about 1:30 o'clock p.m. As there was no inducement to remain here, we halted only a few minutes and set out for Waynesboro, five and a half miles distant, where we arrived about 3:30 o'clock p.m. Being tired and both of us somewhat unwell, we stopped at the depot till nearly sunset. We had not tasted food all day, and every application had met with a cold refusal. Thinking we could fare better by leaving the railroad we made inquiry for a wagon road to Shubuta. We had gone a mile or two, and were passing a comfortable looking residence, when an old gentleman hailed us, and coming out to the road inquired where we were going and what command we belonged to. On hearing the number of the regiment he turned to another old gentleman, saying, "Isn't that the regiment that Jim is in?"

"I believe so," was the reply, and turning to me he asked, "Do you know anything of Jim Lampley?"

"If you mean Lt. James I. Lampley of Company A, 46th Miss. Regt., certainly I know him," I replied.

"Come in! Come in, boys!" he cried. "Jim is my son!" And the old man's voice was full of tears. We were royally treated that night. The family consisted of the father and mother and two beautiful girls, one of whom was grown into a young lady. Two Methodist preachers, S.R. Bankston and P.H. Napier, were spending the night there, and these with Mr. L. all came out to the road when they hailed us.

I have omitted to state that we heard of our regiment at Claiborne and at various places since leaving there. Lt. Lampley had spent a night at home a few days before we were there.

Leaving the Christian home of Mr. Lampley this morning with a nice lunch in our haversacks, we arrived at Red Bluff about seven miles distant by 10 o'clock a.m. We found Capt. Angus Taylor (first captain of Company A) posted there with a small company of State Troops. We came on to this place, arriving here about 1 o'clock p.m.

A gentleman gave us a few potatoes immediately on our arrival, and we found the Post Commissary willing to issue rations, though against orders, he says. Once more our haversacks are full and we are in no hurry to resume our tramp. There are more goods in the stores here than I expected to see. They are piling up hundreds of bales of cotton near the depot, ready for burning should the enemy attack this place.

News from Virginia is sad indeed. It is nothing less than that the Army of Northern Virginia has been surrendered to

Gen. Grant. If this rumor is true it seems useless to contend longer with the odds so against us. May God prepare us for what he has in store for us! [9]

April 19th. Near Meridian, Miss. We remained at Shubuta all day yesterday. We drew rations again, bought some molasses and potatoes, and a lady gave us some milk. We fared sumptuously for soldiers. About midnight a train came up from below. We boarded it and after a free ride of thirty-eight miles we arrived at Meridian at daylight. Starting to the office of the Post Commandant, we met Dr. Catchings of the 39th Regt. who had just arrived and knew as little as we did. We soon encountered Capt. Ziegel of Ector's brigade, who directed us to the camp.

All the officers of the regiment who escaped capture at Blakely are here. The brigade numbers about fifty-five enlisted men and ten or twelve officers. Our regiment numbers twenty-five. J.R. Powers of Company B and six of Company H, including Lt. White, are here. We are at present attached to Ector's brigade. Lt. Col. Shotwell of the 35th has made application to have this remnant of the brigade mounted. I trust he may succeed. Conflicting reports reach us from Virginia, but it seems certain that Gen. Lee surrendered himself and most of the Virginia Army at Appomattox.

Of a more sensational character, however, are the reports of the assassination of President Lincoln and Secy. Seward. Should these reports prove true, and they seem well authenticated, I am fearful the war will be prosecuted more barbarously than ever, for I have a poor opinion of the moderation of such a man as Andrew Johnson who, it is reported, was installed as President on the 15th inst.[10]

It appears that Capt. Hart reached the lines at Blakely and was captured with the rest of the garrison. There are not enough men for a regiment in our whole division.

April 20th. Today Col. Baylor and Mr. Sexton, congressmen from Texas, made speeches in town.

April 22d. Five and a half miles east of Meridian. "On the wing" again. Rained Thursday night. Yesterday we received orders to march at 10 o'clock a.m. today. Before starting this morning I was paid four months' wages, which came in good time.

I know nothing of our destination. It is said we will go to Cuba Station, Ala., but I suppose we will go further than that. The whole command is moving. I understand the infantry numbers about five thousand, including a regiment or two of heavy artillery which, since the fall of Mobile, is armed as infantry. I *think* our destination is the army of Gen. Johnston in North Carolina. It seems like following a "forlorn hope" and it is with extreme reluctance that the men will go. I feel despondent, yet I will try to do my whole duty, leaving the issue in the hands of Him who "doeth all things well."

April 23d. We have stopped for the night and I will write a line or two. We had preaching last night by Bro. Lattimore. The night was so cool that some of us did not sleep well. When the rolls were called this morning it was found that a great many had departed during the night. Some say three hundred men are gone. I know that five men of our brigade are not accounted for. We were ordered to move at 6 o'clock, but it was 9 o'clock before we started. We have marched twelve or fifteen miles and are said to be five or six miles from Cuba Station. We passed a hamlet called Why Not [Miss.] about 10 o'clock a.m. All the way from Meridian the land is generally poor.

April 24th. One and a half miles north of Cuba Station, Ala. We moved at 7:30 o'clock this morning and reached Cuba Station, a distance of six miles, about noon. Passing near the [Alabama & Mississippi Railroad] depot we kept on the Livingston road, and are bivouacked in the pine woods about a mile and a half from the station. At the depot we met Lt. Rea, who was wounded at Blakely.

It has been said ever since we started that we would remain here for some days at least, but our commissaries were ordered to issue two days' rations and we have orders to move at 8 o'clock a.m. tomorrow. We will go to Livingston I suppose. Several more of the command have deserted. About fifteen of our brigade are missing. I really doubt whether one thousand men of this whole force will cross the

Alabama River. It seems to be a settled fact that the days of
the Confederacy are numbered. Hard as it is to say it, *we
have failed.* It is painful, it is humiliating to write the record;
after all, we must give it up and own that *we are whipped!* A
thousand reflections are suggested by the facts.

The people of the South are *unworthy* of freedom, as we
sought it. Once it seemed we had the men and means to
achieve our independence, but a needless sacrifice of the
one and a prodigal waste of the other exhausted both in a
short time. Two hundred thousand of our best men, it is said,
have perished, and for *what?* To give the world another
proof that man is incapable of self-government. Right here
in America we have made the most stupendous failure that
has marked the history of our race. With all the light which
history has struck from the fallen republics of all the ages to
guide us, we reared a splendid fabric of Republicanism under the most favorable auspices the world has ever seen. In
less than a century we have miserably failed, in theory and
in practice. But I have the blues tonight.

April 26th. We are still at the same place and nothing
more is said of moving. On the contrary, it is said that an
armistice of sixty days has been agreed upon and that we
will remain here until its expiration. Evidently something is
up, for furloughs are being given in this command. Four
from our regiment started home on furloughs this morning.
Several other applications have been forwarded, and if Gen.
Taylor approves them I will endeavor to have Companies B
and H furloughed in a body.

We were paid six months' wages today and everybody is
"flush." I am acting as orderly sergeant, adjutant and adjutant general of this brigade which numbers thirty-five
men. There is preaching every night in Ector's brigade, to
which we are attached.

April 29th. Nothing of importance has transpired so far
as it affects us. It is rumored today that the Federal authorities at Washington have refused to ratify the terms agreed
upon by Gens. Sherman and Johnston, and that hostilities
will be resumed again on Monday. It may be a "grapevine"
dispatch. [11] I am somewhat unwell, having suffered with

tooth-ache a great deal during the last few days.

May 6th. A whole week has passed and nothing of special interest has occurred in our camp. Capt. Ogletree, who has commanded the brigade since Col. Shotwell left, has gone home and Capt. Pace of Company A, 46th Miss. Regt., is now in command.

An event of importance *has* occurred, however; one that is fraught with intense interest to us. Yesterday we were officially notified that we had been surrendered as "Prisoners of War." I do not, as yet, know when or where the terms of capitulation were signed. I suppose we will shortly be paroled.

Thus ends the Confederacy! I have loved it well and given my best service to establish it among the nations of the earth. But it has all been in vain so far as national independence is concerned. There are doubtless lessons in it for our good, as well as for the good of all the people of America, and I seem to realize more and more that God's hand is in it and that He has ordered it well.

May 9th. Meridian, Miss. In the hurry of other business I will write a little here, the last perhaps that I will ever write as a soldier of the Confederate States. And indeed I am a soldier no longer. This morning we formally laid down our arms. This act ends the "Rebellion" east of the Mississippi River.

The armies of both Lee and Johnston having both been surrendered to overwhelming numbers, there was no other course for Gen. Taylor to pursue. To have continued the struggle would have been madness – nay, it would have been murder. He therefore surrendered all the troops in this Department to Maj. Gen. E.R.S. Canby of the U.S.A. at Citronelle, Ala., on the 4th day of May 1865. No other army was surrendered on better terms than we are.[12]

But I will note a few events that have occurred. About the time of my last entry I made a short visit to Cuba Station. There is nothing to be seen except a Government bakery and a Government smoke-house. I never saw so much bacon at once as I saw there.

On Sunday May 7th we received orders at 5 o'clock a.m.

to move at 7 o'clock. Most of the men at once resolved that they would carry their guns no longer, so they filled the ordnance wagon with guns, piled them around it and leaned them by trees on the road side. We moved at the designated hour, returning by the same road we went out on. We marched sixteen miles that day and arrived here yesterday about 11 o'clock a.m. We found part of the garrison of Blakely here to be paroled. Capt. Durham of Company K, who was captured at Blakely and had already been paroled, kindly consented to assume command of our detachment to aid us. We have made out the rolls of the enlisted men, and the officers have signed their individual paroles. They are to sign paroles for the men.

Upon our arrival here yesterday I collected all the guns in Sears' brigade, numbering three, and taking one myself and two men with me, I marched them to the tent of the commanding officer and politely informed him that that was Sears' brigade, and asked *where* he would have it stack its arms. With a smile he pointed out a place. Thus my last act as a soldier is performed on nearly the same ground that I began my life in camp.

May 12th. Just before leaving I will write a last line in camp. Numerous delays occurred in paroling this command, at which nearly everybody found occasion to grumble. The delay was occasioned largely by the hundreds of *deserters* who are daily reporting and claiming paroles. At first no obstacle was thrown in their way, but they have become so numerous that Gen. Taylor advised that no more paroles be given them. He is reported as saying that he surrendered eight thousand men, and twenty thousand men are claiming paroles. I do not know what disposition Gen. Canby will make of the matter. Our paroles were received at noon today. Some had grown impatient and left without them. Powers will go out on the Vicksburg road, and Robertson and I will go to Enterprise.

May 16th. Fertile Glade, Miss. After an uneventful trip by way of Paulding and Oak Bowery Church, and after sleeping in the woods two nights, we reached our homes Sunday afternoon, May 14th, 1865.

And so the war is over. When I consider all that I have seen and heard, all that I have learned of men and motives, I am constrained to ask myself "What is it all for?" I have learned things of men that I wish I had never known, and I have learned things of God that I trust will secure my entrance into the rest that remaineth for His people.

I am weary trying to solve the problems that confront us. My heart is sick and sore, and I would fain shut my eyes to the painful picture. As a people we have failed. As Americans, it seems to me, we have demonstrated that we are incapable of governing ourselves.

Individually, we must address ourselves to the material problems of life. May the spirit of God guide and direct us in all our ways.

The Fight at Blakely

There was one fight during the War of the States of which I have never seen any record. Perhaps it was deemed too insignificant in results, in the numbers engaged, or in the casualties incident thereto to merit any notice; but inasmuch as it practically closed the career of a Mississippi regiment – obliterated it, in fact – I have thought that a short account of it might not be devoid of interest.

The last days of March, 1865, found Gen. F.M. Cockrell, of Missouri, in command of the remnant of French's Division of the Army of Tennessee and some other troops besides on the eastern shore of Mobile Bay, guarding the approaches of the Gulf City. Ector's Texas and North Carolina, Gibson's Louisiana, and one regiment of Sears' Mississippi Brigade were besieged in Spanish Fort. Cockrell's Missourians and the other regiments of Sears' Mississippians were at Blakely, a few miles north, where some breastworks had been hastily thrown up.

My own regiment, the 46th Mississippi, numbering about one hundred effective men, under the command of Capt. J.B. Hart, of Yazoo County, Miss., was about four miles east of Blakely on the Stockton road, doing picket duty. During the forenoon of Saturday, April 1, the scouts brought us word that the enemy was approaching. Using the rails of a little field around a deserted cabin, we hastily constructed a flimsy breastwork, behind which we awaited the attack. It was nearly noon when the head of the column came in sight over the brow of a little hill, and before it was near enough to suffer greatly our firing began. A few riderless horses in the hastily retreating column showed that somebody had been hit or badly scared. Before a second volley could be fired there was not a Yankee in sight.

For an hour or more we waited for the enemy to make a second advance. While thus waiting two men came to us from the swamp in our rear, stating that they were from a small picket detail of Missourians posted on another road; that they had heard the firing and had come to see what it meant and to ascertain what troops were engaged. I suspected at the time, and have often thought since, that they were spies.

It was during this lull in the fighting that the following is said to have occurred: A courier came from General Cockrell directing Captain Hart to bring in the regiment. Elated at the success already achieved, and perhaps overrating his own ability and resources, the Captain begged to be allowed to remain where he was, assuring the General that he could hold the enemy in check for an indefinite period. The courier promised to deliver the message and rode away.

Now, be it understood that we were in the open pine woods, where, on three sides at least, there was little or nothing to impede the movements of a body of cavalry, and when we next saw the enemy they were far more numerous than at first; and instead of being simply the head of a column on a single road, there were long lines on our front and left flanks. Judged by the number of flags in sight, there were three or four regiments bearing down on our little handful of men. Then began a running fight.

We formed two sides of a square. On the east and north were the lines of blue-coated horsemen, westward was the road to Blakely, while on the south, our left as we retreated, was a creek or a series of branches with undergrowth along the hillsides. We loaded our guns as we "double-quicked," stopped, aimed hastily and fired, and scampered off again. We kept this up for about two miles, when the enemy, having gained the road ahead of us, advanced at a gallop.

In a moment more they were among us, slashing with their sabers and with oaths and opprobrious epithets were calling on us to "halt" and to "surrender." A number of us refused to halt. Instead we dashed from among the rearing horses and shouting men and made for the cover of the friendly thicket close at hand. A storm of bullets was sent after us; but we were not pursued, and I, who purposely kept in the rear, did not see a single man who was struck.

In a minute, perhaps, the firing ceased, and after going about one hundred yards farther some of us stopped to get our breath. After resting for a time, four of us, Sergt. Robert Leachman of Company F, a good soldier, Sergt. Willis Pickering and Private W.C. Robertson, of my own company, and I, started to make our way into the lines at Blakely.

We were in a gall berry thicket, and we followed it toward the declining sun till the waters of the bay were in sight. Then we emerged from the friendly cover to find ourselves in the rear of a Federal line of battle, distant about seventy-five yards, occupying the ridge between us and the ditches we sought. Making no effort whatever to dislodge the enemy or even to apprise them of our proximity, we again sought the cover and sadly retraced our steps. Arriving at the point where we first stopped to breathe, we sat down among the trees. Sergeant Pickering, going in quest of water, soon returned with Captains Barwick and Pace and two or three lieutenants. They had come to hold a "council of war."

I explained the impracticability of reaching the rest of the brigade by a direct route, and after some discussion they all agreed that the plan I suggested was the most feasible. It was this: to remain quiet till nightfall and then pass to the rear of the advancing Federal army. The word was passed to the hidden boys, some of whom were said to be in water to their necks, and at deep dusk we came together, a forlorn-looking set. There were forty-seven all told, eleven of whom were commissioned officers and about the same number non-commissioned. J.A. Barwick of Company D was the senior captain. Hart, being mounted, as we afterwards learned, escaped to the lines at Blakely, and Captain Heslip of Company G, the next in seniority, was among the "missing." Lieut. R.N. Rea, acting adjutant, was known to have been wounded, but it was hoped that he had reached the Confederate lines. Only one of my company failed to show up. This was John W. Keyes who, being detailed to carry ammunition, made his escape.

The order of march was quickly made. The men were to march in single file about five feet apart and were to move in perfect silence. A command was to be passed from man to man in a whisper, and at certain signals all were to fall flat to the ground. I was unanimously chosen to bring up the rear.

Taking our course from a star which shone in the eastern sky, we started on the most unique march I ever made. The moon was at our backs and gave but a feeble light. On the ridges in the open woods the dogwood trees were clad in ghostly white, and in the brakes and bays millions of frogs piped forth their endless songs. Among it all nearly half a hundred men silently strode along with eyes and ears alert to every sight and sound.

The depressions between the hills had branches in them, with tangles of bamboo briers, shaky tussocks, rotten roots, and sullen pools. And to this good day I think we crossed some of these branches lengthwise. Sometimes when a comrade would fall in the water and mud almost to his waist, it was hard to keep from laughing, especially if he indulged in any grunts or groans or smothered imprecations.

Once when a timid deer started up in our path we fell as dead men and scarcely breathed till the danger was passed. The cry of a night bird thrilled us with a nameless sensation; it might have been fear. But there was real danger on the march, for soon after starting we passed within a short distance of the Federals as they tore out the floor of a mill house to cover a bridge that had been partly destroyed a day or two before.

Before daylight on Sunday, April 2nd, we halted in a swamp to rest and reconnoiter. In the early morning I was seized with a chill which soon developed into a burning fever, and I was delirious all day. I can but dimly recall the fact that the whole command, except one man left with me, came and bade me good-bye in the late afternoon and left us, so far as we could tell, miles away from any human habitation, for we had seen no sign of house or farm the night before.

I suppose it was thought unlikely that I would leave the spot where I lay; for when, nearly twelve months later, as I rode horseback through Rankin County and stopped one night with a Mr. Dent and the family learned after supper that I was the sick man left in the swamp to die, they all crowded around me to congratulate me on my recovery. The son and brother, who happened not to be at home, had often spoken of the sick man they had left.

Thus ended the career of the 46th Mississippi Regiment. When I and my companion ultimately reached Meridian, where the remnant of the Mobile garrison had gone, we found only one of Company B besides ourselves and about twenty-five of the regiment. All had gone home, for the end of the Confederacy was already at hand. And thus it came about that Privates John R. Powers, W.C. Robertson and I were all of Company B at the final surrender.

(The preceding account by William P. Chambers originally appeared under the title "One of the Unrecorded Battles," published in *Confederate Veteran*, Vol. XXII, No. 4, April 1914).

APPENDIX B

A Roster of the Officers of the 46th Miss. Regt.

(Author's note — I regret that I am unable to present a complete Roster of my regimental officers. The following is the list as it stood July 4th, 1863, the day of the surrender of Vicksburg. A few of the subsequent changes are noted).

F. & S.	Name	Rank	Remarks
	C.W. Sears	Col.	Promoted to Brig. Gen. Wounded at Franklin.
	W.K. Easterling	Lt. Col.	Resigned.
	W.H. Clarke	Major	Promoted to Lt. Col. and Col. Killed at Allatoona.
	P.J. McCormick	Major	Surgeon.
	R.L. Dunn	Capt.	Assistant Surgeon.
	W.R. Sheppard	Capt.	Quartermaster.

Co. A	W.R. McQuiston	Capt.	Best Statistician in Regiment. Resigned.
	Nicholas Pace	1st Lt.	Promoted to Capt.
	James White	2d Lt.	
	James I. Lampley	Jr. 2d Lt.	
Co. B	T.D. Magee	Capt.	Promoted to Maj. Lt. Col. & Col. Wounded at Franklin.
	G.C. Buchanan	1st Lt.	Promoted to Capt.
	M.M. Lott	2d Lt.	Dropped from Roll of Officers.
	T.G. Crawford	Jr. 2d Lt.	Dropped from Roll of Officers.
Co. C	J.M. Sublett	Capt.	Most enterprising Regt. officer.
	W.L. Stanford	1st Lt.	
	C.M. White	2d Lt.	
	J.M. Wiles	Jr. 2d Lt.	
Co. D	J.A. Barwick	Capt.	
	J.S. Easterling	1st Lt.	Bro. of Col. Easterling. Resigned.
	L.C. Alliston	2d Lt.	
	W.H. Barnett	Jr. 2d Lt.	
Co. E	James B. Hart	Capt.	
	Edwin H. Smith	1st Lt.	
	Geo. W. Tiller	2d Lt.	
	S.H. Childress	Jr. 2d Lt.	
Co. F	Constantine Rea	Capt.	Promoted to Major. Wounded and died.
	W.F. McKinnon	1st Lt.	Resigned.
	T.P. Wiggins	2d Lt.	Promoted to 1st Lt. & Capt.
	S.T. Williams	Jr. 2d Lt.	Resigned.
Co. G	D.D. Heslip	Capt.	
	Geo. D. Davis	1st Lt.	Killed at Allatoona.
	John A. Epting	2d Lt.	Wounded at Nashville and died.
	Jasper Boykin	Jr. 2d Lt.	Dropped from Roll of Officers.

Co. H	W.A. McAlpine	Capt.	Resigned.
	Geo. W. Stubbs	1st Lt.	Promoted to Capt. Resigned.
	A.L. Bratcher	2d Lt.	Resigned.
	B.D. Anderson	Jr. 2d Lt.	Promoted to 1st Lt. & Capt. Killed at Allatoona.
Co. I	John Watts	Capt.	Resigned.
	Timothy Burgess	1st Lt.	Promoted to Capt.
	S.R. Martin	2d Lt.	Promoted to 1st Lt.
	T.H. Creel	Jr. 2d Lt.	Dropped from Roll of Officers.
Co. K	D.C. Durham	Capt.	
	D.C. Chamberlain	1st Lt.	
	John McRae	2d Lt.	Resigned.
	D.D. Durham	Jr. 2d Lt.	

Muster-Roll of Company B, 46th Miss. Regt. From Oct. 31, 1864 to Feb. 28, 1865

(Author's note — Last one made out).

No.	Names	Rank	Present or Absent	Remarks
	G.C. Buchanan	Capt.	Present	
	J.T. Duckworth	1st Lt.	Absent	Captured at Nashville, Dec. 16, 1864.
	A.H. McLaurin	2d Lt.	"	On Furlough.
	F.E. Collins	Jr. 2d Lt.	"	Captured at Nashville, Dec. 16, 1864.
1	W.P. Chambers	1st Sergt.	Present	
2	S.J. Harper	2d Sergt.	"	
3	Thomas Biglane	3d Sergt.	Absent	In Hospital since Nov. 30, 1864.
1	Willis Pickering	Corporal	Present	
2	J.C. Dykes	"	Absent	In Hospital since Nov. 30, 1864.
3	J.M. McRaney	"	Present	
1	Bond, Jasper	Private	Absent	In Hospital since Nov. 30, 1864.
2	Bass, W.T.J.	"	"	Captured Aug. 4, 1864.
3	Clark, L.C.	"	"	In Hospital since Feb. 3, 1865.
4	Eaton, S.J.	"	Present	
5	Freeman, F.M.	"	Absent	In Hospital May 24, 1864. Absent without leave.
6	Gibbons, W.R.	"	"	On Furlough.
7	Gibbons, F.M.	"	"	On Furlough.
8	Gentry, A.	"	"	On Furlough.
9	Howell, F.M.	"	"	In Hospital. Wounded Franklin Nov. 30, 1864.
10	Howell, S.M.	"	"	On Furlough
11	Keyes, J.W.	"	Present	
12	Lott, N.J.	"	Absent	Without leave, Aug. 4, 1864.
13	McPhail, Joseph	"	Present	
14	McPhail, Jno.	"	Absent	Captured at Atlanta, Sept. 1, 1864.
15	McMillan, J.S.	"	"	Detailed as Teamster.
16	Moore, W.L.	"	"	In Hospital since Nov. 30, 1864.
17	Maxey, James	"	"	In Hospital since Nov. 30, 1864.
18	Powers, J.R.	"	Present	
19	Prine, A.	"	Absent	Captured near Smyrna Church, July 5, 1864.
20	Pickering, John	"	"	On Furlough.
21	Robertson, G.G.	"	"	Captured at Allatoona, Oct. 5, 1864.
22	Robertson, W.C.	"	Present	
23	Rodgers, Timothy	"	Absent	On Furlough.
24	Rodgers, Norvell	"	"	In Hospital since Nov. 30, 1864.
25	Rodgers, S.	"	"	In Hospital since Feb. 7, 1864.
26	Sullivan, T.J.H.	"	Present	
27	Sullivan, L.	"	Absent	Detailed as Wagon Escort.

No.	Names	Rank	Present or Absent	Remarks
28	Sullivan, W.P.	Private	Absent	In Hospital since Oct. 5, 1864.
29	Sullivan, H.	"	Present	
30	Sullivan, C.	"	"	
31	Speed, B.F.	"	Absent	In Hospital since July 17, 1864.
32	Ware, J.H.	"	Present	(Cook).
33	Wilkes, A.J.	"	"	
34	Watts, Ellis	"	Absent	In Hospital since Feb. 9, 1865.
35	Wilkes, S.H.P.	"	Present	
36	Wilkes, J.A.	"	"	

Transferred

| | Herrin, S. | Private | | To Co. G, 7th Miss. Battalion. |

Died

| | Duckworth, Z.F. | Private | | Died of wounds rec'd Aug. 22, 1864. Died Sept. 23, 1864. |

Deserted

1	Baker, Joseph	Private		Deserted, Tuscumbia, Ala., Oct. 30, 1864.
2	Cole, J.F.	"		Deserted, Chattahoochee River, July 9, 1864.
3	Hester, Henry	"		Deserted, Tuscumbia, Ala., Oct. 30, 1864.
4	Hester, Isaac	"		Deserted, Tuscumbia, Ala., Oct. 30, 1864.
5	Lott, Arthur	"		Deserted, Tuscumbia, Ala., Oct. 30, 1864.

The following were enlisted as recruits but never reached camp because of the surrender.

1 Dykes, Dennis
2 McNair, R.
3 Smith, W.P.
4 Smith, J.C.
5 Speed, J.M.
6 Sullivan, Alex.

APPENDIX D

Muster-Roll of Company B, 46th Miss. Regt. As Compiled From Memory

(Author's note — This roll is accurate so far as regards the officers, and is nearly accurate all the way through).

Date of election

Feb. 22, 1862	T.D. Magee	Capt.	Promoted to Maj. Lt. Col. and Col.
Feb. 22, 1862	G.C. Buchanan	1st Lt.	Promoted to Capt.
Feb. 22, 1862	Archie Fairley	2d Lt.	Defeated at Reëlection.
May 14, 1862	M.M. Lott	2d Lt.	Dropped from Roll.
Feb. 22, 1862	J.A. Graham	Jr. 2d Lt.	Resigned.
March 13, 1863	T.G. Crawford	Jr. 2d Lt.	Dropped from Roll.
Dec. 8, 1863	J.T. Duckworth	Jr. 2d Lt.	Promoted to 2d and 1st Lt.
Dec, 29, 1863	A.H. McLaurin	Jr. 2d Lt.	Promoted to 2d Lt.
Sept. 23, 1864	F.E. Collins	Jr. 2d Lt.	

Names	Remarks	Names	Remarks
Atwood, G.W.	Died	Gibbons, W.R.	
Baker, Joseph	Deserted	Gibbons, F.M.	
Barnes, John	Transferred	Gibson, Joseph	
Bass, J.H.	Killed	Graham, F.M.	
Bass, W.T.J.		Harper, S.J.	
Biglane, Thomas		Hathorn, G.R.	
Blackwell, J.W.		Herrin, S.	Transferred
Bond, Jasper		Hester, Henry	Deserted
Braddy, A.E.	Died	Hester, Isaac	Deserted
Braddy, John	Died	Howell, F.M.	
Broom, Thomas		Howell, J.T.	Died
Carr, John		Howell, S.M.	
Carr, Thomas		Keyes, Joshua	
Carter, N.H.	Died	Keyes, J.W.	
Carter, C.R.	Died	Lee, W.W.	Died
Carter, J.W.	Died	Lott, Arthur	Deserted
Carter, W.E.	Died	Lott, Thomas	
Chambers, W.P.		Lott, Cullen	
Clark, L.C.		Lott, A.J.	Died
Cole, J.F.	Deserted	Lott, N.J.	
Cole, C.P.		Magee, H.R.	
Cook, Marion	Died	Magee, G.W.	
Duckworth, Z.F.	Died of wounds	Magee, T.J.	
Dyes, W.P.		Magee, W.I.	
Dykes, J.C.		Manning, W.J.	Killed
Dykes, Irving	Died	Mathews, John	
Easterling, Z.A.	Died	Matthews, W.A.	
Eaton, S.J.		Maxey, James	
Freeman, E.G.	Died	Milloy, John	Died
Freeman, Harvey	Died	Moore, W.L.	
Freeman, F.M.		Morris, Winston	Died
Gentry, A.		McLane, D.R.	Died

Names	Remarks	Names	Remarks
McMillan, J.S.		Speed, B.F.	
McNair, A.	Killed	Speed, W.R.	Died
McPhail, J.R.	Died	Speights, E.L.L.	Died
McPhail, John		Stuckey, Elisha	Died
McPhail, Joseph		Sullivan, H.	
McRaney, J.M.		Sullivan, W.P.	
Pace, W.M.	Died	Sullivan, Lotan	
Pickering, John		Sullivan, T.J.H.	
Pickering, Willis		Sullivan, C.	
Powers, J.R.		Turnage, F.D.	Died
Prine, A.		Ware, J.H.	
Reddock, J.V.	Killed	Watts, J.A.P.	
Robertson, F.A.	Discharged	Watts, Ellis	
Robertson, G.G.		Watson, John	
Robertson, J.S.	Died	Whitehead, Daniel	
Robertson, Stephen	Killed	Whitehead, Thos.	
Robertson, W.C.		Wilkes, A.J.	
Rodgers, B.F.	Died	Wilkes, S.H.P.	
Rodgers, Josiah	Died of wounds	Wilkes, J.A.	
Rodgers, Norvell		Wilkinson, M.M.	Died
Rodgers, S.		Wilkinson, D.L.	
Rodgers, Timothy		Williams, John	Killed
Rodgers, Z.M.	Killed	Williamson, J.P.	Killed
Rowell, John		Williamson, J.H.	Died
Rowell, William		Yawn, Green.	
Short, Archy			

A List of Deaths in Company B

Names	Place of death	Date of death	Cause
N.H. Carter	At Home	March 15, 1862	of Disease
C.R. Carter	At Home	March 15, 1862	of Disease
W.W. Lee	Meridian, Miss.	May 5, 1862	of Disease
G.W. Atwood	Smedes Point, Miss.	June 18, 1862	"
A.E. Braddy	Smedes Point, Miss.	July 6, 1862	"
A.J. Lott	Smedes Point, Miss.	July 7, 1862	"
John Milloy	Brandon, Miss.	July 12, 1862	"
F.D. Turnage	Camp Tupelo, Miss.	July 12, 1862	"
Benj. Rodgers	Camp Tupelo, Miss.	July 15, 1862	"
Elisha Stuckey	Miss. Springs, Miss.	July 4, 1862	"
J.T. Howell	At Home	July 16, 1862	"
D.R. McLane	Clinton, Miss.	July 26, 1862	"
Marion Cook	Miss. Springs, Miss.	Aug. 1, 1862	"
W.M. Pace	Monticello, Miss.	Aug. 7, 1862	"
Irving Dykes	Clinton, Miss.	Aug. 14, 1862	"
J.R. McPhail	Clinton, Miss.	Aug. 25, 1862	"
Winston Morris	At Home	Aug. 23, 1862	"
Harvey Freeman	Hazelhurst, Miss.	Aug. 29, 1862	"
J.S. Robertson	Vicksburg, Miss.	Nov. 21, 1862	"
John Braddy	Crystal Springs, Miss.	Dec. 19, 1862	"
E.G. Freeman	Vicksburg, Miss.	March 19, 1863	"
W.R. Speed	In Camp, Vicksburg	April 10, 1863	"
E.L.L. Speights	Lauderdale Spgs, Miss.	April 14, 1863	"
J.H. Williamson	In Camp, Vicksburg	May 1, 1863	"
John Williams	Vicksburg, Miss.	May 19, 1863	Killed
W.E. Carter	Vicksburg, Miss.	June 8, 1863	of Disease
W.J. Manning	Vicksburg, Miss.	June 10, 1863	Killed
M.M. Wilkinson	At Home	July 5, 1863	of Disease
J.W. Carter	New Orleans, La.	July 15, 1863	of Disease

Sergt. Jonathan H. Bass was killed at Kennesaw Mountain, Ga., June 27, 1864.
Private Josiah Rodgers was wounded at New Hope Church, Ga., June 3, 1864.
    Died at home July 14, 1864.
Private Stephen Robertson was killed at Atlanta, Ga., Aug. 14, 1864.
Private Z.M. Rodgers was wounded at Lovejoy Station, Ga., Sept. 5, 1864.
    Died at Macon, Ga., several days later.
Private Z.F. Duckworth was wounded at Atlanta, Ga., Aug. 22, 1864.
    Died at Barnesville, Ga., Sept. 23, 1864.
Private Z.A. Easterling died at home Sept. 23, 1864,
    from the effects of a self-inflicted accidental wound.
Sergt. J.P. Williamson was killed at Allatoona, Ga., Oct. 5, 1864.
Private Adelbert McNair was killed at Allatoona, Ga., Oct. 5, 1864.
Private Jas. Virgil Reddock was killed at Allatoona, Ga., Oct. 5, 1864.

BIBLIOGRAPHY

Albaugh, William A. III and Simmons, Edward N., *Confederate Arms,* Harrisburg: The Stackpole Co., 1957.

Bearss, Edwin C., *Decision in Mississippi,* Jackson: Mississippi Commission on the War Between the States, 1962.

———. *The Campaign for Vicksburg,* 3 volumes, Dayton: Morningside House Inc., 1985.

Bergeron, Arthur W. Jr., *Guide to Louisiana Confederate Military Units 1861-1865,* Baton Rouge: LSU Press, 1989.

Bettersworth, John K., *Confederate Mississippi,* Baton Rouge: LSU Press, 1943.

Bevier, R.S., *History of the First and Second Missouri Confederate Brigades 1861-1865,* St. Louis: Bryan, Brand & Co., 1879.

Biographical and Historical Memoirs of Mississippi, 2 volumes, Chicago: Goodspeed Publishing Co., 1891.

Civil War Naval Chronology 1861-1865, Part III, Washington, D.C.: Government Printing Office, 1963.

Confederate Military History, Vol. IX, Wilmington, N.C.: Broadfoot Publishing Co., 1987.

Confederate Veteran, 40 volumes, Wilmington, N.C.: Broadfoot Publishing Co.

Connelly, Thomas L., *Autumn of Glory: The Army of Tennessee, 1862-1865,* Baton Rouge: LSU Press, 1971.

Cox, Jacob D., *Atlanta,* New York: Charles Scribner's Sons, 1882.

Davis, Reuben, *Recollections of Mississippi and Mississippians,* Boston: Houghton, Mifflin and Company, 1890.

Hall, Winchester, *The Story of the 26th Louisiana Infantry in the Service of the Confederate States,* Gaithersburg, Md.: Butternut Press Inc. 1984.

Kirkland, Edward C., *The Peacemakers of 1864,* New York: MacMillan Co., 1927.

Lee, Stephen D., "The Siege of Vicksburg," *Publications of the Mississippi Historical Society,* Vol. III, Oxford, Miss., 1900.

Lindsley, John B., *The Military Annals of Tennessee: Confederate,* Nashville: J.M. Lindsley & Co., 1886.

List of Field Officers, Regiments & Battalions in the Confederate States Army 1861-1865, Bryan, Texas: J.M. Carroll & Co., 1983.

Long, E.B., *The Civil War Day by Day: An Almanac 1861-1865,* Garden City: Doubleday & Co., 1971.

McCain, William D., *The Story of Jackson: A History of the Capital of Mississippi, 1821-1951,* Vol. I, Jackson: J.F. Hyer, 1953.

Pemberton, John C., *Pemberton: Defender of Vicksburg,* Chapel Hill: University of North Carolina Press, 1942.

Publications of the Mississippi Historical Society, Vol. V, Centenary Series, 1925.

Rietti, John C., *Military Annals of Mississippi,* n.p., n.d.

Scharf, J. Thomas, *History of the Confederate States Navy,* New York: Rogers & Sherwood, 1886.

Sherman, William T., *Memoirs of Gen. W.T. Sherman,* 2 volumes, New York: Webster & Co., 1891.

Stern, Philip Van Doren, *The Confederate Navy: A Pictorial History,* Garden City: Doubleday & Co., 1962.

Strayer, Larry M. and Baumgartner, Richard A., eds., *Echoes of Battle: The Atlanta Campaign,* Huntington: Blue Acorn Press, 1991.

Sykes, E.T., *Walthall's Brigade, Army of Tennessee C.S.A.,* Columbus: Mississippi Historical Society, 1905.

Taylor, Richard, *Destruction and Reconstruction,* New York: Longmans, Green & Co., 1955.

The War of the Rebellion: A Compilation of the Official Records of the Union and Confederate Armies, 128 volumes, Washington, D.C.: Government Printing Office, 1880-1900.

Tunnard, W.H., *A Southern Record: The History of the Third Regiment Louisiana Infantry,* Baton Rouge, 1866.

Urquhart, Kenneth T., ed., *Vicksburg: Southern City Under Siege,* New Orleans: The Historic New Orleans Collection, 1980.

Warner, Ezra J., *Generals in Gray,* Baton Rouge: LSU Press, 1959.

Wilkinson, Norman B., *Lammot du Pont and the American Explosives Industry 1850-1884,* University Press of Virginia, 1984.

Winters, John D., *The Civil War in Louisiana,* Baton Rouge: LSU Press, 1963.

NOTES

1862

CHAPTER 1

1. Brandon, seat of Rankin County, Miss., is located about 12 miles east of Jackson. The Southern Railroad ran through the town during the war. Brandon was the home of Lieutenant Colonel William K. Easterling and Colonel William H. Clark, both of whom commanded the author's regiment.

2. Just a rumor. By April 3, Major General Ulysses S. Grant had some 33,000 Federal troops at Pittsburg Landing on the Tennessee River, 18 miles northeast of Corinth, and was awaiting 25,000 reinforcements from Major General Don Carlos Buell's Army of the Ohio. Confederate General Albert S. Johnston planned to attack Grant before Buell's arrival, and Johnston's Army of the Mississippi left Corinth on April 3 for that purpose.

3. By April 5, Flag Officer David G. Farragut's fleet of Union men-of-war and mortar gunboats threatened New Orleans' defenses below the city on the Mississippi River. It was not until April 18 that Forts Jackson and St. Philip, 75 miles below the city, were attacked by Commander David D. Porter's gunboats. [Winters, 86-87].

4. The battle of Shiloh or Pittsburg Landing, April 6-7, 1862. In the first day's fighting, furious but disjointed Confederate assaults pushed back the surprised Federals under Grant to the Tennessee River. Reinforced during the night, Grant's army stubbornly retook most of the ground lost the previous day, and the Confederates slowly withdrew toward Corinth. Federal casualties amounted to 13,047 killed, wounded and missing, while the Confederates lost more than 10,600. [Long, 194-196].

5. An unfounded rumor. Chambers also was in error. The 13th Mississippi Regiment contained no company named the "Laurence Rifles." However, Company C of the 12th Mississippi — raised in Lawrence County and organized at Brookhaven in May 1861 — was known as the "Lawrence Rifles." Its first serious engagement was the battle of Seven Pines near Richmond, Va., on May 31, 1862. [Rietti, 157, 158].

6. Johnston was mortally wounded at Shiloh on April 6, and died before nightfall from loss of blood. Buell was not killed or wounded. Brigadier General Benjamin M. Prentiss of Illinois, commanding a division in Grant's Army of the Tennessee, was captured on April 6 along with 2,200 of his men (many of them wounded) in the Hornet's Nest.

7. Brigadier General Charles Clark, a native Ohioan, commanded the 1st Division, 1st Corps, Army of the Mississippi at Shiloh, and was wounded severely in the right shoulder on April 6. [O.R., S.1, vol. 10, pt. 2, 415]. He was badly wounded again in July 1862 at Baton Rouge, La., and disabled from further active service. In late 1863 he was elected Mississippi's governor. [*Confederate Military History,* vol. 9, 246-247].

8. Brigadier General Adley H. Gladden of South Carolina commanded a brigade of Alabama and Louisiana troops at Shiloh. Early on April 6 he was struck by a shell fragment, forcing amputation of an arm on the field. He died at Corinth six days later. [Warner, 107-108].

9. On April 16, the Confederate Congress passed the first Conscription Act, which authorized "to call out and place in the military service of the Confederate States, for three years, unless the war shall have been sooner ended, all white men who are residents of the Confederate States, between the ages of eighteen and thirty-five years at the time the call or calls may be made, who are not legally exempted from military service." [O.R., S.4, vol. 1, 1095].

10. With 11 vessels from his fleet, Farragut anchored off New Orleans' blazing waterfront, set afire by local citizens, on April 25. The fall of New Orleans meant the loss of the South's largest city and most vital port, and the city soon became a new base of Federal operations against the Confederacy's heartland. [Long, 203].

11. The Mobile & Ohio Railroad.

CHAPTER 2

1. On May 18, 1862, the first division of the Federal fleet, along with transports carrying some 3,000 soldiers, appeared at Vicksburg and the naval commander, Captain S. Phillips Lee, immediately demanded the city's surrender. This was promptly refused, and Confederate authorities quickly reinforced infantry and artillery units already stationed there. [O.R., S.1, vol. 15, 6-7].

2. William C. Smedes owned a plantation near the river about three-fourths of a mile west of the Warrenton Road. [O.R. Atlas, plate 36, No. 2].

3. Governor John Jones Pettus was elected in November 1859, and characterized by one of his political contemporaries on the eve of war as "a disunion man of the most unmitigated order." [Davis, 378].

4. Vicksburg's population was 4,591 in 1860. The Warren County courthouse was built between 1858 and 1861 at a cost of more than $100,000. St. Paul's Catholic Church, a large Gothic structure with a central tower, was the place of worship for a large number of Roman Catholics living in and around antebellum Vicksburg. The Methodist church, built in 1850, was a combination of Roman, Gothic and Colonial architecture. [Biographical and Historical Memoirs of Mississippi, vol. 2, 151-152].

5. Martin Luther Smith was appointed brigadier general on April 11, 1862, and major general the following November. A native of New York state and West Point graduate (class of 1842), he used his engineering skills to improve Vicksburg's defenses from May to November 1862. During the 1862-63 Vicksburg operations and siege, he exercised brigade and division command, and supervised construction of the city's interior defenses. [Warner, 282-283].

CHAPTER 3

1. The Federal bombardment of Vicksburg from the river between June 20-28, was

described in the report of Brigadier General Martin L. Smith, commanding the city's defenses:

"From the 20th to the 27th the bombardment was pretty constant during the day-time, at times very heavy, but generally ceasing at 10 or 11 o'clock at night.

"On the evening of the 27th the firing began to increase in fury, and for some hours a shower of bomb-shells was rained upon our batteries that severely tried the nerve and courage of both officers and men. Still the damage was quickly repaired, and the men held their places at the guns.

"At daylight on the 28th the enemy recommenced with the same fury, and it was soon perceived that the entire gunboat fleet was in motion, moving rapidly up in front of the batteries and city, and it became apparent that the decisive struggle was at hand. Some thirty-five vessels were soon firing as rapidly as was possible, the mortars filling the air with shells, and the sloops of war and gunboats delivering broadside after broadside of shot, shell, and grape, according to their distance. Our batteries opened as soon as the vessels were within range and for the first time in full force. The roar of cannon was now continuous and deafening; loud explosions shook the city to its foundations; shot and shell went hissing and tearing through trees and walls, scattering fragments far and wide in their terrible flight; men, women, and children rushed into the streets, and, amid the crash of falling houses, commenced their hasty flight to the country for safety. This continued for about an hour and a half, when the enemy left, the vessels that had passed the lower batteries continuing on up the river, apparently as the quickest means of getting out of range, those that had not passed rapidly dropping down.

"The result of this effort on the part of the enemy was most satisfactory; not a single gun was silenced, none disabled, and, to their surprise, the serious bombardment of the preceding seven days had thrown nothing out of fighting trim. It also demonstrated to our satisfaction that how large soever the number of guns and mortar-boats, our batteries could probably be successfully held; consequently that the ultimate success of our resistance hinged upon a movement by land. The enemy evidently came to the same conclusion, as, after one week's bombardment with their mortars and the final attempt on the morning of June 28 to silence and take our guns, the attack sensibly decreased in vigor and persistency." [*O.R.*, S.1, vol. 15, 8-9].

2.   Uncertain. Chambers may have been referring to fighting of the Seven Days' campaign in Virginia, June 25-July 1, 1862, in which Richmond was saved from capture.

3.   Major General Earl Van Dorn officially assumed command of the District of the Mississippi on June 28, which charged him with the defense of Vicksburg and surrounding country east to the Pearl River. [*O.R.*, S.1, vol. 15, 769]. Major General John C. Breckinridge commanded a division comprising four brigades at the time. [*Ibid.*, 1121].

4.   The newly completed ironclad *Arkansas*, under Commander Isaac N. Brown, passed through the Union fleet on July 15 in a running battle on the Yazoo and Mississippi rivers. Although the *Arkansas* was damaged and Brown lost 10 killed and 15 wounded, the Federals suffered heavier losses of 18 killed, 50 wounded and 10 missing. [Long, 240]. Three Union vessels were badly damaged, including *Queen of the West*, flagship of Lieutenant Colonel Alfred W. Ellet, commander of the ram fleet. [*O.R.*, S.1, vol. 15, 38]. "It was the first and only square, fair, and equal stand-up and knock-down fight between the two navies that the Confederates came out first best," wrote Lieutenant George W. Gift of the *Arkansas*. "From the beginning our ship was handled with more pluck, decision, and judgement than theirs." [Scharf, 315].

5. Colonel Henry Watkins Allen, 4th Louisiana, was appointed brigadier general on August 19, 1863. He was wounded at Shiloh and again on August 5, 1862, while commanding a brigade in the battle of Baton Rouge, La. Personally carrying the colors of the 4th Louisiana in a charge, he was struck by grape-shot in the legs and severely wounded. [*O.R.,* S.1, vol. 15, 100-101]. During the last year of the war he served as governor of Louisiana.

6. On August 6, the *Arkansas* was attacked by the Federal ironclad *Essex* and four other vessels at Baton Rouge. After its engines failed, the *Arkansas* made an easy target, but its crew fought back despite a raging fire on board. After the crew was ordered to abandon the *Arkansas,* it was blown up. [Long, 248].

A battle was fought at Baton Rouge on August 5, after which Confederate commander John C. Breckinridge pulled back to the north and began fortifying Port Hudson. [Ibid., 248].

7. Between August 16-27, a Federal gunboat expedition augmented with two infantry regiments, 100 cavalrymen and six field guns, left Helena, Ark., captured the steamer *Fair Play* at Milliken's Bend early on August 18, and caused other destruction up the Yazoo River. Of the *Fair Play's* capture, ram fleet commander Lieutenant Colonel Alfred W. Ellet wrote: "The steamboat was loaded with arms — some 5,000 and more of Enfield rifles and muskets — a large amount of ammunition, and a great many boxes filled with accouterments, &c., most of which was said to have been destined for Little Rock, Ark. We captured the camp equippage, tents, arms, horses, mules, and wagons for a camp of 1,000 men, besides other supplies, and took about 40 prisoners." [*O.R.,* S.1, vol. 13, 244-245].

8. Two days later (September 7) the *Essex* engaged the batteries guarding Port Hudson, La. [*O.R.,* S.1, vol. 15, 2].

9. DeWitt Clinton Durham was commissioned captain when the Kemper Guards joined the 6th Mississippi Battalion (46th Mississippi) as Company K. In 1861 he was elected second lieutenant of the Guards, which were attached to Wise's Legion (59th Virginia Infantry), commanded by Henry A. Wise. After seeing action in western Virginia at Sewell Mountain, Durham and the Legion were transferred to Roanoke Island on the coast of North Carolina. [*Confederate Veteran,* vol. 29, 149]. There, on February 8, 1862, Wise's force under the command of Colonel H.M. Shaw was defeated by Union General Ambrose E. Burnside. The Confederates suffered only 85 casualties, but more than 2,000 troops were surrendered. [Long, 168].

10. Colonel John F. Girault had been commander of the Confederate Guards, Louisiana Volunteer State Troops. [Bergeron, 184]. During the summer of 1862 he served as assistant adjutant general on the staff of Brigadier General Martin L. Smith. [*O.R.,* S.1, vol. 15, 11].

CHAPTER 4

1. After previous service as a staff officer and artillery commander in the eastern theater of operations, Stephen Dill Lee was appointed brigadier general on November 6, 1862, and given brigade command. This initially consisted of the 4th and 46th Mississippi, the 17th, 26th, 27th, 28th and 31st Louisiana, and Drew's and Bowman's batteries of light artillery. But before the end of December 1862 Lee's command was increased by three

infantry regiments, two cavalry companies and another artillery battery. [Hall, 34; *O.R.,* S.1, vol. 17, pt. 1, 671].

2. After visiting the Army of Tennessee at Murfreesboro, Tenn., President Jefferson Davis arrived in Vicksburg late on December 19 and spent the next two days inspecting the city's troops and defenses. From Jackson, Miss., on the 23rd, he wired the War Department in Richmond and urged that more heavy guns and long-range field pieces be rushed to Vicksburg. [*O.R.,* S.1, vol. 17, pt. 2, 802].

3. On December 4, General Joseph Eggleston Johnston assumed command of the Confederate Department of the West. Accompanying President Davis to Vicksburg between December 19-22, he was unimpressed with the city's defenses and placement of heavy ordnance overlooking the Mississippi River. At the time, only 5,900 infantry and artillery troops were fit for duty to defend a 10-mile line. [*O.R.,* S.1, vol. 17, pt. 2, 801].

4. Union Generals Ulysses S. Grant and William T. Sherman met on December 8 in Oxford, Miss., to discuss plans concerning Sherman's movement to capture Vicksburg from the rear via the Yazoo River. Preparations for this movement began on December 12 from Memphis. Sherman's expedition consisted of four divisions totalling 31,000 men, and disembarked on December 26 about 13 miles up the Yazoo River at the mouth of Chickasaw Bayou. [Sherman, 309-317].

5. Captain Paul Hamilton served as assistant adjutant general on the staff of Stephen D. Lee. According to Lee, the popular Hamilton was killed "by the explosion of a caisson by a shell from the enemy, while executing an order. He was the most promising young officer it has been my fortune to meet. He was but twenty-one years of age, but had been in thirty battles." [*O.R.,* S.1, vol. 17, pt. 1, 683].

6. At Chickasaw Bayou on December 28-29, Sherman's force suffered casualties of 208 killed, 1,005 wounded and 563 missing, compared to Confederate losses of only 63 killed, 134 wounded and 10 missing out of 14,000 troops engaged. [Long, 301]. Chambers' regiment served in S.D. Lee's provisional division during the battle, and Lee lauded the "admirable service" of the 46th Mississippi and gun crews of the 1st Mississippi Artillery Regiment it was supporting at Blake's Levee. [*O.R.,* S.1, vol. 17, pt. 1, 682]. Colonel William T. Withers, commander of the artillery regiment, was in charge of this important section of the Confederate line, and his defense merited particular praise from Lee. [*Ibid.,* 683]. One of Withers' cannoneers, Private W.T. Moore of Company A, later wrote of his experiences at Chickasaw Bayou as a member of Lieutenant Frank Johnston's section of two 12-pound Napoleon guns:

"The [Federal] infantry was landed and made a demonstration to attack us, while the gunboats engaged our batteries and shelled our works. Our company was engaged all along the line, when suddenly a courier appeared with orders for Johnston's section to proceed with all possible haste and report to Gen. S.D. Lee at Chickasaw Bayou.

"In a few minutes we were on the way, and for two miles we were exposed to a heavy fire from the enemy's infantry and gunboats, but without accident to men or horses. Arriving at the designated place, we were met by General Lee and assigned to a position somewhat in advance of our infantry upon a knoll which had been leveled and dirt thrown up in front about eighteen inches high. Both men and guns were exposed from the knees up. General Lee told us that we held the most important position; that the enemy would make an effort to cross the bayou at a ford about two hundred and fifty or three hundred yards to our left front, and for us to mow them down as they came across and up

[*Harper's Weekly*]

Queen of the West **engages the CSS** *City of Vicksburg* **under the guns of the Hill City's defenses, February 2, 1863.**

the bank. To this our commander, Lieut. Frank Johnston, replied: 'All right, General, we will do the best we can.'

"In our front, about four hundred yards, was a heavy, thick growth of timber, also McNutt Lake, and to the right of the lake also there was timber. In a day or so the enemy placed two heavy eight-inch guns to our left front across the bayou about six hundred yards distant and also a six-gun battery, supported by infantry, besides the lake to our right front, and began a heavy crossfire upon us. We opened fire upon the six-gun battery and soon disabled some of them and drove the rest back, but paid no attention to the two heavy guns on our left. The next day this battery was brought back to about the same place and opened fire upon us, as did the siege guns, mortars, and everything else that could be brought to bear upon us. And in a few minutes their infantry was advancing, with the main body crossing the ford.

"We paid no attention to the enemy's batteries. Our whole aim and efforts were directed to the ford on our left. Every man nobly stood to his post, and such rapid fire from muzzle-loaders I don't believe was ever surpassed. We used up all of our own ammunition and had begun to use howitzer shells when the enemy broke in confusion, and the day was won. None of us were hurt, but several were whirled around and around by the force of the eight-inch shots coming so close.

"The night after the battle was cold, with sleet and rain falling. We built a big fire in a soldiers' hut close by, and while some were in there drying and talking of the battle there came a knock upon the door. It was General Lee all alone. In his right hand he held a water bucket about half full of whisky. He said: 'Gentlemen, I have come especially to congratulate you and also to bring something along to warm you. I don't approve of drinking whisky, but you have been exposed to so much cold and disagreeable weather that I think a little of this will do you good. It is my treat, gentlemen; drink, but don't get drunk. I want to say to you that I asked Colonel Withers to send me the best section of artillery he had for this important position. He sent you. I saw the effect of every shot you made. Not one failed of its mark. I have been in a good many battles and never saw better work done by artillery than you did today. Your colonel was not mistaken. He sent the right men. It is a mystery how you all escaped. I am glad you did.' He bade us good night and was gone. Of course we considered it a great compliment.

"The next day we were ordered to cross the bayou at the same ford we had defended. We were halted a few minutes at Lake Plantation, where Sherman had his headquarters. We continued our march upon the levee and very soon came in full view of Sherman's army on their transports, making haste to get down the river. General Lee was riding alone just ahead of us, and we were about three hundred yards from the enemy, with a clear, open space between us. Their gunboats began to send ricochet shots toward us. General Lee motioned us to halt and rode farther on up the levee and stopped, deliberately took out his field glasses, and began observing the enemy. While doing so his horse was shot down under him. He motioned to us to get behind the levee and to bring him another horse. A little later Sherman and all his army were gone without our having fired a shot at them. Undoubtedly we could have done great execution, and why we were not ordered to fire was always a mystery to me." [*Confederate Veteran,* vol. 22, December 1914, 553].

1863

CHAPTER 5

1. Claudius Wistar Sears, a native of Massachusetts and graduate of West Point, was 45 years old when commissioned colonel on December 11, 1862, and appointed to command the 46th Mississippi. A mathematics professor and college president before the war, he saw previous service in the 17th Mississippi as captain of Company G. [Warner, 271].

2. On February 2, 19-year-old Colonel Charles Rivers Ellet took the steam ram *Queen of the West* past the Vicksburg batteries and attacked the Confederate steamer *City of Vicksburg* in broad daylight. Both vessels caught fire, but the flames were quickly extinguished. *Queen of the West* absorbed 12 cannon shots before heading downstream. [*O.R.,* S.1, vol. 24, pt. 1, 336]. The following day Ellet captured three Rebel steamers — *A.W. Baker, Moro* and *Berwick Bay* — two of them laden with supplies and provisions destined for the garrison at Port Hudson, La. All three were burned. [*Ibid.,* 338].

Pleased with Ellet's success, Acting Rear Admiral David D. Porter sent the new ironclad *Indianola* downriver to meet him. On February 14, Ellet, without waiting for the *Indianola,* steamed up the Red and Black rivers, and captured the steamboat *Era No. 5,* whose pilot he pressed into service as a guide. Encountering a battery of 32-pounders at a sharp bend near Gordon's Landing, the Rebel pilot ran *Queen of the West* aground shortly before shells slammed into the ram, severing the steam pipe and penetrating the boilers. *Queen of the West* was abandoned to the Confederates, and its survivors, including Ellet, escaped by drifting downstream on a small ferryboat. [*Ibid.,* 342-343].

3. After blockading the mouth of the Red River between February 17-21, the *Indianola,* under Lieutenant Commander George Brown, was attacked on the Mississippi River below Warrenton during the night of February 24 by four Confederate vessels, including the ram *William H. Webb* and the recently captured and repaired *Queen of the West.* During the close-quarters, one-and-a-half hour battle the *Indianola* was rammed seven times and crippled when the paddle wheel and rudder were crushed, and water began pouring into the hull. Brown ordered the ironclad run on to the western shore and surrendered his entire crew of more than 100 officers and men. [Stern, 133; *O.R.,* S.1, vol. 24, pt. 1, 361].

"The fire of the enemy was terrific," reported Major J.L. Brent, commander of the Confederate expedition. "Their huge shot and shell came whizzing by us, directed wide of the mark in every instance, except two shots that struck the *Queen* and one that passed through the bulwarks of the *Webb,* while the far-darting flames of their enormous guns [two 11-inch and two 9-inch Dahlgrens] almost licking our bows, and the loud thunder of their reports (heard as far away as Vicksburg, 30 miles off), added unusual sublimity to the scene." [*O.R.,* S.1, vol. 24, pt. 1, 367].

The Confederates towed the *Indianola* across the river to the eastern shore, where she sank in 10 feet of water. Salvage work immediately commenced. *Queen of the West* was sent upriver to Vicksburg to obtain a pump and other materials, but soon was seen returning below Warrenton. She brought news of a large Union "gunboat" passing the Vicksburg batteries and approaching the small Rebel squadron. According to Colonel Wirt Adams, commander of Adams' Mississippi Cavalry, "all the vessels at once got underway in a panic, and proceeded down the river, abandoning without a word the working party and fieldpieces on the wreck. The Federal vessel did not approach nearer than two-and-a-half miles, and appeared very apprehensive of attack." [*O.R.,* S.1, vol. 24, pt. 1, 370].

After making further fruitless efforts to free *Indianola* of water, the next evening the working party fired the heavy 11-inch Dahlgren guns into each other and burned her to the water line. A clever Union hoax had worked. The "gunboat" was actually a barge camouflaged to give the appearance of a formidable ironclad, which Rear Admiral Porter had floated downriver. [*Civil War Naval Chronology,* pt. 3, 34-35]. On April 14, three Federal gunboats engaged and destroyed *Queen of the West* in Grand Lake, La. [*Ibid.,* 66].

4. William Edwin Baldwin had been colonel of the 14th Mississippi Infantry and was captured at Fort Donelson in February 1862. Following his release that August he was commissioned brigadier general to date from September 19, 1862. [Warner, 16].

Winfield Scott Featherston, a Mississippi congressman from 1847 to 1851, served during 1862 with the Army of Northern Virginia as colonel of the 17th Mississippi Infantry. His commission to brigadier general dated back to March 4, 1862. He was transferred to Vicksburg in January 1863. [Ibid., 86].

5. For the same date, Private William H. Tunnard of the 3rd Louisiana Infantry wrote shortly after the war: "On the 6th, the whole brigade attended the execution of a deserter from the First Louisiana Heavy Artillery, who had been captured in Federal uniform. His bearing was firm, and he met his death most courageously." [Tunnard, 220].

6. Before daybreak on March 25, the Union rams *Switzerland* and *Lancaster* got underway to run past Vicksburg to join Rear Admiral David G. Farragut below with U.S.S. *Hartford* and *Albatross.* After noise from the rams' escape pipes alerted the Rebel batteries to their presence, Colonel Charles R. Ellet on board *Switzerland* ordered both vessels to continue under full steam — directly into concentrated fire from the Confederate works. A shell penetrated *Switzerland's* boiler and stopped the engines, but the pilots kept the ram in the river and she floated downstream to safety. The *Lancaster* was not so fortunate. Two heavy shells pierced her steam drum and hull, the latter causing an enormous leak. She sank within minutes. A planned joint attack on Warrenton was canceled because of the extensive repairs required by the *Switzerland.* [*Civil War Naval Chronology,* pt. 3, 53].

7. This march to north of Vicksburg was a response to Federal movements of the Steele's

[*Harper's Weekly*]

In running past Vicksburg's batteries on March 25, 1863, the Federal ram *Switzerland* (above) was heavily damaged. *Lancaster,* accompanying her, was sunk.

Bayou expedition. In a series of unsuccessful efforts in early 1863 to take Vicksburg from the rear, Union land and river forces were stymied by nature, terrain and a stiff Confederate defense. Launched on March 14, Grant's and Porter's plan relied upon a naval force navigating a connecting series of waterways above the city — Steele's Bayou, Black Bayou, Deer Creek and Rolling Fork — and gaining the Big Sunflower River. Having reached this stream, it was believed it would be easy for a task force to enter the Yazoo River above Haynes' Bluff, and strike Vicksburg from the rear with a minimum of losses. [Bearss, *The Campaign for Vicksburg,* vol. 1, 549]. The expedition did not succeed and was terminated on March 27.

8. Brigadier General Stephen D. Lee was ordered to take charge of an expedition "to obstruct the creek [lower Deer Creek], throw up works, and, if advisable, make a diversion in the enemy's rear." [*O.R.,* S.1, vol. 24, pt. 1, 461]. He arrived at Wilson's plantation six miles above the mouth of Deer Creek on March 24 with the 3rd Louisiana Infantry, whose men had just been issued new uniforms of white jeans-cloth and were "arrayed as if for a summer's day festival. What an expedition this was, comprising a perfect fleet of flats, flat-boats, skiffs, canoes, and every conceivable small floating craft. The men were wild with excitement and fun, and made the swamps re-echo with their shouts and laughter. They preceded the little steamer [*Dew Drop*] in their flotilla of small craft, cutting down trees, whose interpolated branches obstructed the passage." [Tunnard, 220, 221].

9. Brigadier General Louis Hébert, originally colonel of the 3rd Louisiana Infantry, commanded a brigade of Mississippi and Louisiana infantry in Major General Dabney H. Maury's division.

CHAPTER 6

1. On April 16-17, gunboats under Rear Admiral D.D. Porter engaged and ran past Vicksburg's batteries while shepherding army transports to New Carthage below the city.

The force included the *Benton, Lafayette, Louisville, Pittsburg, Mound City, Carondelet* and *Tuscumbia. General Sterling Price* was lashed to the starboard side of *Lafayette* for the passage, as was the tug *Ivy* to *Benton*. Each ship, except *Benton,* also towed a coal barge containing 10,000 bushels of coal. *Lafayette,* hampered by the ship lashed to her side, received nine shots through her casemate and had her coal barge sunk. Transport *Henry Clay* was sunk with no loss of life and another, *Forest Queen,* was temporarily disabled. [*Civil War Naval Chronology,* pt. 3, 67].

2. On April 17, Colonel Benjamin H. Grierson of the 6th Illinois Cavalry left LaGrange, Tenn., with 1,700 Illinois and Iowa troopers in a raid south through Mississippi that was intended to draw attention away from Grant's operations against Vicksburg. In 17 days Grierson's command marched 800 miles, repeatedly engaged Confederate forces, ruined two railroads and destroyed vast amounts of property, before riding into Baton Rouge, La., on May 2. For this feat Grierson was appointed brigadier general to date from June 3, 1863. [Warner, 190].

On April 22, a Federal flotilla of six transports and 12 barges attempted to pass Vicksburg's batteries. One transport and six barges were sunk, but the remainder carried their supplies to Grant's men below the city. [Long, 340].

3. Settled in the early 1790s by South Carolina native Samuel Gibson, Port Gibson received its name by an act of the Mississippi legislature in 1803 and became the seat of Claiborne County. Before the war the town was noted as the home of a large number of Mississippi's most wealthy cotton planters. It is situated on the south fork of Bayou Pierre about 26 miles southeast of Vicksburg. [*Biographical and Historical Memoirs of Mississippi,* vol. 2, 213, 214].

4. Federal losses on May 1 at Port Gibson were reported as 131 killed, 719 wounded and 25 missing. [*O.R.,* S.1, vol. 24, pt. 1, 585]. Confederate casualties were reported by Brigadier General John S. Bowen, commanding, as 68 killed, 380 wounded and 384 missing. [*Ibid.,* 667]. Chambers' brigade commander, William E. Baldwin, reported eight days after the fight: "The command reached Vicksburg at 5 o'clock Monday evening [May 4], having in less than five days marched over 100 miles, besides being engaged with the enemy more than ten successive hours. The men marched in better order and with less straggling than I ever before observed in any troops ... their patient and cheerful endurance of fatigue and an unusual march bespeaks the highest quality of soldiers." [*Ibid.,* 677].

Another observer, however, watched Bowen's troops pass Brigadier General John C. Moore's brigade camp near Warrenton on their way back to Vicksburg. Chaplain William L. Foster of the 35th Mississippi, a former private in Company F, wrote to his wife: "In a few days after Bowen's defeat, some of his troops passed our camps worn down & exhausted from repeated forced marches ... It always makes me feel sad to behold a retreating army. There they go — covered with dust — with a swinging gait, hungry, thirsty, tired, sleepy & discouraged." [Urquhart, 1].

5. Soon after General Bowen issued orders about midnight on May 2 to evacuate Grand Gulf, a dispatch from Lieutenant General John C. Pemberton also ordered the abandonment of the position. On May 3, after the last of Bowen's troops cleared the post, heavy guns were spiked and all magazines destroyed. [*O.R.,* S.1, vol. 24, pt. 1, 666].

6. Colonel Robert Richardson, 17th Louisiana. His regiment was heavily engaged on May 1 at Port Gibson. [*O.R.,* S.1, vol. 24, pt. 1, 677].

[*Harper's Weekly*]

Federal gunboats of the Mississippi Squadron bombard Grand Gulf, Miss., on April 29, 1863.

7. Baldwin reported his brigade's losses at Port Gibson as 12 killed, 48 wounded and 27 missing. [*O.R.,* S.1, vol. 24, pt. 1, 678].

8. Because Pemberton had been born in the North (Philadelphia, Pa.), many Southerners — including a sizeable number in the army — doubted his devotion to the Confederate cause. Lieutenant Colonel R.S. Bevier of the 5th Missouri, Cockrell's Brigade, later wrote of the army's sentiment in mid-May 1863: "An uneasy and ominous feeling of distrust imbued the minds of both men and officers, combining a fear of those troops who fled so readily at Baker's Creek [Champion's Hill] and Big Black [River], and a suspicion of the motives and patriotism of General Pemberton. Many expressed the belief that he had betrayed the army, and that his movements since assuming active command all tended to that result. So firm was this conviction that numbers doffed their dust-begrimed garments and donned their holiday apparel in anticipation of speedy capture, whilst gloomy visions of Northern prisons flitted through their imaginations. But they judged their General wrongly — he was incapable of harboring a thought of treason; he may not have been an

able commander, but he was brave and true, and they soon found that he would surrender to nothing but starvation." [Bevier, 199-200].

CHAPTER 7

1. After capturing Jackson, Miss., on May 14, Grant's forces advanced from the capital toward Vicksburg, threatening to cut communications between Pemberton near Edward's Station and Johnston to the north. After refusing to attempt to join Johnston on May 15, Pemberton now responded to a second order and marched out to effect a link-up in order that together they might fight Grant. [Long, 353-354]. The effort was blocked at Champion's Hill, or Baker's Creek as the May 16 battle was called by the Confederates. Rebel losses amounted to 3,851 (nearly 1,700 captured or missing) out of 20,000 engaged, while Grant's 29,000-man force lost 2,441. [Long, 354].

2. Brigadier General Lloyd Tilghman commanded a brigade of Mississippi troops in Major General William W. Loring's division. On May 16 at Baker's Creek, while directing artillery fire, Tilghman was struck in the chest by a shell fragment and fatally wounded. [*O.R.*, S.1, vol. 29, pt. 2, 77]. His body was taken to Vicksburg and buried there.

3. The Vicksburg & Jackson Railroad bridge crossing the Big Black River was fired by Pemberton's chief engineer, Major Samuel H. Lockett, using piled rails and loose cotton soaked with turpentine. [*O.R.*, S.1, vol. 29, pt. 2, 73].

     The "burning steamboat" referred to by Chambers may have been the *Charm* or *Paul Jones*, whose remains were found in the river and identified in 1962 and 1965, respectively. [Bearss, *The Campaign for Vicksburg*, vol. 2, 678].

4. The 4th Mississippi was detached from Baldwin's brigade and forwarded on May 16 as a support to Brigadier General John C. Vaughn's East Tennessee brigade, entrenched 1,500 yards east of the Big Black railroad bridge. The 4th, commanded by Lieutenant Colonel T.N. Adaire, was placed on the far right of Vaughn's line, and when the Federals attacked on May 17 Adaire's regiment was located immediately north of the railroad embankment. The unequal fight lasted less than five minutes when Vaughn's troops, including the 4th, gave way and scrambled for the safety of the Big Black's western bank, or surrendered. A large, though undetermined number of soldiers in the 4th were captured, including Major Joseph J. Gee. [Bearss, *The Campaign for Vicksburg*, vol. 2, 674, 689]. Overall, about 1,700 Confederates were taken prisoner.

5. Brigadier General Francis A. Shoup commanded the 3rd Brigade of Martin L. Smith's division. Shoup had sent the 27th Louisiana, which he accompanied, down the Graveyard Road to cover a foraging party outside Stockade Redan, when the regiment was halted by Federal skirmish fire. Sharpshooting was maintained on Shoup's brigade front for the next seven hours. [*O.R.*, S.1, vol. 29, pt. 2, 405-406].

     Among the casualties of the day's sniping was Captain Julius Pitzman, General William T. Sherman's chief engineer, who was shot in the hip by one of Shoup's marksmen. [Sherman, vol. 1, 352].

CHAPTER 8

1. Pemberton's division commanders were Major General Carter L. Stevenson, Major General John H. Forney, Major General Martin L. Smith and Brigadier General John S.

Bowen. Stevenson's four brigades were commanded by Brigadier Generals Seth M. Barton, Alfred Cumming, Stephen D. Lee and Colonel Alexander W. Reynolds. Forney's brigade commanders were Louis Hébert and John C. Moore, while Bowen's were Colonel Francis M. Cockrell and Brigadier General Martin E. Green (succeeded by Colonel Thomas P. Dockery after Green's death on June 27). [*O.R.,* S.1, vol. 29, pt. 2, 326-327].

The Mississippi State Troops, placed under Vaughn's command, were led by Brigadier General J.V. Harris and consisted of the 5th Regiment and 3rd Battalion. [*Ibid.,* 327].

2. The left flank of the Confederate fortifications guarding Vicksburg's land approaches was anchored on the Mississippi River, one and a half miles north of the city. Between the river and Stockade Redan two defensive lines were laid out. The outer rifle pits followed the ridge north of Mint Spring Bayou and the inner works ran along Fort Hill Ridge, south of the bayou. [Bearss, *The Campaign for Vicksburg,* vol. 3, 740].

3. Grant hoped a sudden assault would prevent Pemberton from completing his defensive arrangements. All three Federal corps investing Vicksburg attacked on May 19, but were repulsed after incurring about 1,000 casualties. [Long, 355].

4. Baldwin's shoulder wound forced him to relinquish brigade command to Colonel Robert Richardson, 17th Louisiana, until June 13. [*O.R.,* S.1, vol. 29, pt. 2, 402].

5. On May 22, the Federals attacked along a three-mile section of Vicksburg's defenses, including the right of Chambers' brigade. Union casualties were staggering. More than 3,200 soldiers were killed, wounded or captured compared to total Confederate losses of less than 500. The end of the bloody day marked the real beginning of Vicksburg's siege. [Long, 356].

6. "One of the most striking incidents of the horrors of war occurred after the failure of the Federal assault on May 22nd," recalled brigade commander Stephen D. Lee. "The dead and many wounded of the gallant Union army remained unburied and uncared for from the time they fell until the afternoon of May 25th at 6 p.m., over three days, under the burning sun and damp dews, in full view, and close up to the Confederate works, and in view of the Union army. Incessant artillery and infantry firing prevented both sides from attending to this matter. Many wounded died. A flag of truce was sent out by Gen. Pemberton on the 25th, protesting against such a scene and asking for a cessation of the strife for two hours and a half to bury the dead, and care for the wounded, offering to do it himself if necessary. Two and one-half hours were agreed on, and the two armies met on the line and chatted, and performed this sad duty. The bodies of the gallant soldiers from Iowa and Illinois in the ditch of the railroad fort were so decomposed that dirt was thrown on them in the ditch. The wounded left in the ditch had died. They could not be moved. This was the case nearly everywhere on the field, and they had to be buried generally where they fell." [*Publications of the Mississippi Historical Society,* vol. 3, 63-64].

Chaplain William L. Foster, 35th Mississippi, also wrote of the truce a short time after it took place: "On Monday morning the 25 of May, a flag of truce was sent from our General to the enemy requesting that they would bury their dead, for their dead bodies were becoming very offensive, since some of them had been killed nearly one week & the weather being hot decomposition was very rapid. The enemy did not seem to be very anxious to inter their slain, hence we were under the necessity of making this request. The flag of truce was received & the request granted. Presently the firing began to cease on the centre of the line & gradually extended from right & left until quiet reigned along the whole line. What a relief! For nearly a week our ears had been greeted by the continual sound of small arms & cannon. Not a moment in the day passed but brought with it some report. The stillness seemed unnatural, but was very welcome. Now the enemy make their appearance, coming out of their trenches & hiding places. They are as numerous as a swarm of black-birds in the winter season. They come out as numerous as the ants from a freshly stirred up nest. Some of them with spades & shovels approach to perform the solemn work of burying their fallen comrades. They dig ditches near the dead & then roll the putrid bodies in — sometimes with a blanket for the winding sheet — sometimes with nothing but the clothing in which they fell. A little earth is thrown over them & there they are left unmarked, unknown ..." [Urquhart, 20-21].

7. This incident actually occurred during the morning of May 27. Although protected by logs and hay bales, the *Cincinnati* was riddled by upper-battery shells from 8-inch rifles and 10-inch smoothbores. One shell exploded in the *Cincinnati's* magazine, and the ironclad sank after a 30-minute fight with its colors nailed to the mast. Twenty-five men aboard were killed or wounded and another 15 drowned. [*O.R.,* S.1, vol. 24, pt. 2, 337-338; *Civil War Naval Chronology,* pt. 3, 86].

8. Though Johnston's 35,000-man Army of Relief between Canton and Jackson posed a grave threat to the Federal position in front of Vicksburg, he stalled making a serious effort to reach Pemberton. On June 15 Johnston telegraphed Richmond that he considered "saving Vicksburg hopeless." Secretary of War James A. Seddon replied the next day: "Vicksburg must not be lost without a desperate struggle. The interest and honor of the Confederacy forbid it. I rely on you still to avert the loss." [*O.R.,* S.1, vol. 24, pt. 1, 227].

Pemberton believed "that every charge of ammunition on hand should be hoarded with the most jealous care. [*Ibid.,* 274]. After the siege Captain Frederick E. Prime, chief engineer of the Federal Army of the Tennessee during May and early June, wrote: "At the assaults of May 19 and 22, the [Confederates] used artillery fire freely. Afterward, as our batteries were built and opened, their artillery fire slackened, until toward the close of the siege it was scarcely used at all, the enemy contenting himself with occasionally running a gun into position, firing two or three rounds, and withdrawing it again as soon as our fire was concentrated on it. We attributed during the siege the silence of their artillery to the lack of ammunition, but on the surrender of the place over 40,000 rounds of captured artillery ammunition were reported to the chief of ordnance of General Grant's army. A small portion of this, judiciously used, would have rendered our approach much slower." [*O.R.,* S.1, vol. 24, pt. 2, 175].

9. Major Samuel H. Lockett, Pemberton's chief engineer, was responsible for construction and maintenance of Vicksburg's physical defenses during the siege, as well as counter-mining efforts. "The engineers were engaged in general repairs," he reported, "strengthening the parapets, extending the rifle-pits, placing obstructions in front of the exposed points, consisting of abatis, palisades, ditches, and entanglements of pickets and telegraph wire. Sand-bag loop-holes were also made along the whole line to protect our sharpshooters. These sand-bags were made from tent-flies and old tents turned over to me by the quartermaster's department, and from the same source I obtained a supply of material during the whole siege." [*O.R.,* S.1, vol. 24, pt. 2, 331].

10. Colonel Edward Higgins, commanding Vicksburg's river batteries, wrote of this incident: "June 1, a large fire broke out in the city, close upon the magazine of the Whig [newspaper] Office battery, which was at one time in great danger. The ammunition was taken out and placed in a more secure position. All the men of my command that could be

spared from the guns were ordered out immediately to assist in arresting the progress of the conflagration." [*O.R.,* S.1, vol. 24, pt. 2, 338].

11. The artillery supporting Baldwin's brigade very early in the siege was described in his July 1863 report: "... the following pieces of light artillery were placed in position on my line: One 30-pounder Parrott gun, manned by a detachment from a Missouri battery (this gun burst, and was replaced by a 32-pounder smooth-bore, served by a detachment from Captain J.P. Lynch's company, First Tennessee Artillery); one Whitworth gun, which also burst; one 24-pounder howitzer, two 12-pounder howitzers, two 6-pounder guns, and two 3-inch rifled guns, served by Wofford's company, Withers' regiment light artillery, and three 6-pounder guns, served by a detachment of Guibor's artillery company, the whole under the immediate direction of Captain J.L. Wofford as chief of artillery for the brigade. One of the 3-inch rifled pieces was disabled by a trunnion being knocked off early in the siege. With the exception named, no other damage was done to my artillery during the siege except such as was immediately repaired." [*O.R.,* S.1, vol. 24, pt. 2, 402].

12. By June 14, soldiers of Sherman's 15th Corps had dug three approach trenches toward the Stockade Redan complex, shared by the Confederate brigades of Martin E. Green and Francis A. Shoup. Shoup's Louisianans were located to the immediate right of Baldwin's brigade, in which the author served.

On the morning of the 14th, Federal cannoneers hammered the redan with a withering barrage of shot and shell. In addition to damaging the parapet, they dismounted and disabled an Arkansas battery's 12-pounder howitzer. That night the Arkansans armed themselves with grenades (6- and 12-pound shells with shortened, hand-lit fuses) and infiltrated the area between the lines. The grenades were lobbed into the Union saps, inflicting some casualties. [Bearss, *The Campaign for Vicksburg,* vol. 3, 894, 895]. This may have been the noise Chambers heard. Springing a mine on June 14 was just a rumor.

CHAPTER 9

1. On June 25 the Federals, after digging for nearly a month, exploded four branch mines simultaneously under the 3rd Louisiana Redan about one and one-fourth miles east-southeast of the author's position. At 3:30 p.m. some 2,200 pounds of powder were ignited and blew out a crater 40 feet across and 12 feet deep. Fortunately for the Confederates, General Hébert had withdrawn the 3rd Louisiana from the redan before the mine was detonated, and positioned it behind a protective traverse in the rear. Six men from the 43rd Mississippi, working on a countermine, were killed in the explosion. Reinforced by the 5th and 6th Missouri of Cockrell's brigade, the Louisianans repelled five Illinois and Indiana regiments ordered to breach the Rebel line through the crater. Casualties for the day at the redan amounted to 34 Federals killed and 209 wounded, while Confederate losses were listed as 21 killed and 73 wounded. [Bearss, *The Campaign for Vicksburg,* vol. 3, 918-925; *O.R.,* S.1, vol. 24, pt. 2, 202].

Six days later, on July 1, 1,800 pounds of powder were exploded under the redan's northeast face and caused far greater damage and casualties. This time the Federals did not attack with infantry, but pasted the sector with accurate artillery and Coehorn mortar fire. [Bearss, *The Campaign for Vicksburg,* vol. 3, 928, 929]. An eyewitness recalled: "At first there was a general rush to escape the huge mass of descending earth. Then the survivors, without halting to inquire who had fallen, hastened to the immense gap in the works to repel the anticipated assault. The enemy, taught by a dearly-bought experience, made no attempt to enter the opening, not daring to assault the intrepid defenders. An immense number of 12-pounder shells, thrown from wooden mortars, descended among the troops, doing fearful execution. The fire was tremendous, rapid, and concentrated ... The wounded and dying were speedily conveyed to the hospitals for attendance. The spectacle was horrible in the extreme. Stretched out on the green-sward, with no shelter save the overshadowing trees, lay these men, suffering from every conceivable wound known in war. Some writhing in the agonies of death, others bruised, torn, mangled and lacerated by shell and shot, while others were blackened and burned from the effects of the explosion. Surgeons, with sleeves rolled up to their elbows, hands, arms and shirts red with human gore, hastened hither and thither, or were using their keen-edged instruments in amputating some shattered limb, extracting balls and fragments of shells from the lacerated bodies, or probing some ghastly wound of the sufferers. Such were the scenes of war on this hot July afternoon." [Tunnard, 266, 267].

2. General Baldwin, the author's brigade commander, reported that he was summoned on the night of July 3 "to a council of general officers and brigade commanders, to consider terms of capitulation offered by the commander of the Federal forces. I object[ed] to a surrender of the troops, and [was] in favor of holding the position, or attempting to do so, as long as possible." [*O.R.,* S.1, vol. 24, pt. 2, 403, 405]. Baldwin was the only one of Pemberton's brigade and division commanders who did not urge acceptance of Grant's surrender terms. [*O.R.,* S.1, vol. 24, pt. 1, 285].

3. Not every Confederate believed that Pemberton had "sold out." Years later Allen Thomas, colonel of the 28th Louisiana of Shoup's brigade, wrote: "In view of [the] facts, succor being hopeless — our capture was but a matter of time, and could be delayed but a few days at best — it was deemed unnecessary to sacrifice further the lives of the gallant men, who, from simple rifle-pits, had repulsed for forty-eight days, the combined attack by land and water of a force more than ten times their number, that was replete with every appliance of modern warfare ... The capitulation was, therefore, universally assented to; and I am sure that there was not an officer present — and there were not a few who were heroes of many hard-fought fields — but was convinced that General Pemberton had done all that the most exalted patriotism, or the most punctilious soldierly honor, could have demanded ..." [Pemberton, 233].
    Of the Vicksburg garrison, 31,600 soldiers were surrendered (only 11,000 comprised an effective fighting force), 172 cannon of all calibers, 60,000 muskets and a large amount of ammunition. [Ibid., 238].

4. The New Orleans & Jackson Railroad.

CHAPTER 10

1. After a day of heavy skirmishing on September 18, General Braxton Bragg's Army of Tennessee clashed with Major General William S. Rosecrans' Army of the Cumberland in wooded terrain near Chickamauga Creek, about 10 miles south of Chattanooga, Tenn. Two days of heavy, sometimes hand-to-hand fighting followed, and by nightfall on September 20 Rosecrans' army was in retreat to Chattanooga, having suffered 16,170 casualties. Although Bragg lost about 2,000 more men than Rosecrans, the battle was a great Confederate tactical victory. [Long, 410-412].

2. At Chickamauga the 7th Mississippi served in Brigadier General Patton Anderson's brigade, Hindman's division. Its colonel, W.H. Bishop, reported regimental losses of 10 killed, 64 wounded (three mortally) and 1 missing. [*O.R.,* S.1, vol. 30, pt. 2, 15, 322].

3. Davis left Richmond October 6 for an inspection tour of the Western departments. He first visited Bragg's Army of Tennessee besieging Chattanooga before heading to Selma, Ala., Meridian, Miss., and Mobile, Ala. Davis returned to the Confederate capital on November 9 after traveling through Atlanta, Savannah, Charleston, S.C. and Wilmington, N.C.

4. Imported by both sides from the Imperial Arsenal at Vienna, the .58 caliber Austrian rifle was 47 inches overall and took a saber bayonet on the end of its 32-inch barrel. They were furnished with steel mountings and a cheek piece on the side of the stock. [Albaugh & Simmons, 61, 199].

CHAPTER 11

1. This journey was via the Alabama & Florida Railroad.

2. West Point, Ga. was the eastern terminus of the Montgomery & West Point Railroad.

3. Big Shanty was a station on the Western & Atlantic Railroad. The large number of wounded soldiers passing south through the station was a result of the battle of Chattanooga, November 23-25. After being routed from Lookout Mountain and Missionary Ridge, Bragg's troops retreated southeast to Dalton, Ga., where they went into winter quarters.

4. Colonel William S. Barry, a native Mississippian, served in the Confederate Congress until early 1862, when he raised and organized the 35th Mississippi Volunteer Infantry. [*Confederate Military History,* vol. 9, 297].

5. On November 30, Bragg was relieved of command of the Army of Tennessee at his own request. He was replaced temporarily by Lieutenant General William J. Hardee, then by General Joseph E. Johnston on December 16. [Long, 441, 447].

6. Confederate losses on November 25 at Missionary Ridge totaled nearly 6,700 officers and men, with 4,146 of this number taken prisoner. [Ibid., 438]. Those captured represented about one-tenth of the Army of Tennessee's effective strength at the beginning of the fight.

7. Typical arrangement of a regiment's 10 companies when in line was, from the right: A, F, D, I, C (usually the color company), H, E, K, G and B. Such positioning placed the author's company on the regiment's far left, as he states, but Company D was immediately adjacent. It is not known what specific arrangement was used in the 46th Mississippi, but apparently the flank companies' positioning was based on seniority of their captains. Hence, when Capt. T.D. Magee became the regiment's senior line officer by December 1863, Company B moved from the far left to the far right.

1864

CHAPTER 12

1. In what became known as the Meridian Campaign, Sherman, on February 3, left Vicksburg with 26,000 troops to destroy Confederate-held railroads in Mississippi and

inflict damage in and about Meridian. An additional 7,600 cavalrymen operating from Memphis under Brigadier General William Sooy Smith cooperated with Sherman. The Federals were opposed by some 20,000 widely scattered troops under Lieutenant General Leonidas Polk. Yankee troops entered Meridian on February 14 and stayed for six days, wrecking rail trackage and supplies in the area. [Long, 460, 464].

Sherman's report described the destruction: "The immense depots, warehouses, and length of sidetrack demonstrated the importance to the enemy of that place. Through it he has heretofore transported his armies and vast supplies, and by means of the railroads large amounts of corn, bacon, meal, and produce have been distributed to his armies. For five days 10,000 men worked hard and with a will in that work of destruction, with axes, crowbars, sledges, clawbars, and with fire, and I have no hesitation in pronouncing the work as well done. Meridian, with its depots, store-houses, arsenal, hospitals, offices, hotels, and cantonments no longer exists. To General Hurlbut I intrusted the destruction north and east of the town, and to General McPherson south and west. The former reports to me officially the destruction of 60 miles of road, with ties burned and iron bent, one locomotive destroyed, and 8 bridges burned. The latter reports officially 55 miles of road destroyed, with 53 bridges and culverts burned, and 6,075 feet of trestle-work below Enterprise across a swamp burned, 19 locomotives, 28 cars, and 3 steam saw-mills destroyed and burned. The railroad is destroyed all the way from Jackson to Meridian, 100 miles; from Meridian to and including the large bridge over the Chickasawha below Quitman; north to and including a bridge at Lauderdale Springs, and east about 20 miles. The enemy cannot use these roads to our prejudice in the coming campaign." [O.R., S.1, vol. 32, pt. 1, 176].

Sooy Smith's part in the campaign was not as successful as Sherman's Although he also destroyed considerable railroad facilities, cotton and corn, Smith was prevented from linking up with Sherman by Major General Nathan Bedford Forrest's cavalry in northern Mississippi. [Long, 466-467].

2.   Although it was not part of Sherman's plan to march further than Meridian, Confederate military authorities were alarmed that he next would head for Mobile. [Long, 464]. Instead, he withdrew leisurely back to Vicksburg, and the evacuation of Mobile proved only to be a rumor.

3.   Major Constantine Rea earlier had commanded Company F, 46th Mississippi. In April 1864 he was assigned to command a battalion of Mississippi sharpshooters. Shot in the right leg on July 9 along the Chattahoochee River, he died September 14 following the leg's amputation. His 19-year-old son, Richard N. Rea, was first lieutenant of the 46th's Company F at the time. In September, after acting as regimental adjutant, Richard was promoted captain and commanded his father's old company until April 1, 1865, when he was wounded twice in a skirmish near Fort Blakely, Ala. [Confederate Veteran, vol. 33, January 1925, 22; vol. 30, July 1922, 265; vol. 30, August 1922, 289].

4.   On February 19 near Dog River Factory, Baldwin was killed in a freak fall from his horse. First buried in Mobile, his remains later were interred in Columbus, Miss. [Warner, 16].

5.   Williamsburg, Covington County, Miss. Chambers refers to William J. Hardee, author of Rifle and Light Infantry Tactics, commonly called Hardee's Tactics. First published in 1855, the original edition was in two volumes — Volume 1 being "Schools of the Soldier and Company's Instructions for Skirmishes." Hardee's Tactics was used widely by Confederates throughout the war and by Federal troops until the fall of 1862.

6. Fort Powell was located at Cedar Point opposite Dauphin Island, and about 25 miles south of Mobile. A heavy Federal bombardment of the fort on February 16 aggravated Confederate fears of an attack. Guarding a secondary entry to Mobile Bay, Fort Powell was evacuated during the night of August 5-6. [Long, 464, 552].

7. Chambers refers to the brigades of native Virginian William A. Quarles and native North Carolinian Evander McNair. At the time, McNair's brigade was commanded by Col. David Coleman, and shortly afterward by Daniel H. Reynolds, who was promoted brigadier general to rank from March 5, 1864. McNair had been severely wounded at Chickamauga on September 20, 1863. [Warner, 256; *O.R.*, S.1, vol. 30, pt. 2, 500].

8. Brigadier General James Cantey, a native of South Carolina, originally served as colonel of the 15th Alabama during the 1862 Shenandoah Valley and Peninsula campaigns in Virginia. In the subsequent Atlanta Campaign he reverted to brigade command. [Warner, 43].

9. Sears' commission to brigadier general ranked him from March 1, 1864. [Warner, 272]. Constantine Rea did not pass the examining board for promotion to lieutenant colonel.

10. On February 17, the Confederate Congress approved an act creating the office of ensign in each infantry regiment, "with the rank, pay and allowances of a first lieutenant, whose duty it shall be to bear the colors of the regiment, but without right to command in the field." [*O.R.*, S.4, vol. 3, 190]. This act was amended on May 31 to allow appointments of ensigns to infantry battalions as well. [*Ibid.*, 492]. The office was abolished on February 23, 1865 by another act of Congress, which stated: "Hereafter the officer commanding a battalion or regiment shall assign, to act as color-bearer, a non-commissioned officer or private from his command, who may be distinguished for meritorious or soldierly conduct, or for valor or skill; and said non-commissioned officer or private, while so acting, shall receive the pay of a first lieutenant." [*Ibid.*, 1167].

11. Brigadier General George B. Hodge.

12. Robert Lowry began the war as a private in Company B, 6th Mississippi Volunteer Infantry. After Shiloh, where he was twice wounded, Lowry was elected colonel of the regiment and led it with distinction at Corinth, Port Gibson and Baker's Creek. He succeeded to brigade command on November 30, 1864 at Franklin, following the death of Brigadier General John Adams, and was promoted to brigadier general to rank from February 4, 1865. Sixteen years after the war he was elected governor of Mississippi. [*Confederate Military History*, vol. 9, 262-263].

CHAPTER 13

1. Major General Samuel G. French, a native of New Jersey who became a wealthy Mississippi planter before the war, commanded the division containing Sears', Ector's and Cockrell's brigades. [*Confederate Military History*, vol. 9, 254].

2. King's Iron Works.

3. Sherman's Federals did not have balloons with them on the Atlanta Campaign. It is not known what Chambers and his comrades observed on May 16.

Originally colonel of the 14th Texas Cavalry (Dismounted), Brigadier General Matthew D. Ector commanded four Texas and two North Carolina regiments. [Warner, 81; *O.R.,* S.1, vol. 38, pt. 3, 653].

Brigadier General Francis M. Cockrell, at the time 29 years old, commanded the Missouri Brigade of seven regiments and a battalion. [Warner, 57; *O.R.,* S.1, vol. 38, pt. 3, 653].

French arrived in Rome, Ga. on May 16 and immediately forwarded Sears' brigade by rail to join Lieutenant General Leonidas Polk's corps south of Resaca. Ector's brigade was to follow on the 17th, but the appearance of Federals only two and a half miles from Rome preempted the move. Assisted by cavalry, Ector's and Cockrell's brigades skirmished while marching to Kingston, losing 100 men along the way to enemy bullets. [*O.R.,* S.1, vol. 38, pt. 3, 899].

4. Via the Rome Railroad the distance was about 20 miles.

5. After two days of heavy skirmishing, Sherman's and Johnston's armies clashed at Resaca on May 15. Although Johnston's entrenched line just north of the Oostanaula River was too strong for direct attack, his position was threatened when Sherman began flanking movements to gain the Confederate rear, especially at Lay's Ferry. Johnston withdrew that night, burning the Western & Atlantic Railroad bridge over the Oostanaula, and headed south toward Calhoun and Adairsville. [Long, 502].

6. Polk, as head of the Army of Mississippi, commanded one of Johnston's three corps during the second half of May and first two weeks of June. A close friend of President Davis, Polk was a graduate of West Point and an Episcopal bishop. [Warner, 242].

7. At the time, the 27th Mississippi was part of Brigadier General Edward C. Walthall's brigade, Hindman's division, Hood's corps. The regiment's commander, Lieutenant Colonel A.J. Jones, had been killed by a shell fragment on May 15 at Resaca. [Sykes, 567].

8. The May 25 battle of New Hope Church was fought in a thunderstorm, primarily between troops of Major General Alexander P. Stewart's division, Hood's corps, and Federals belonging to the 20th Corps under Major General Joseph Hooker.

9. Walthall was not promoted to division command until June, when he was transferred to Polk's corps to replace Brigadier General James Cantey. [Sykes, 572].

10. The 11 days of fighting along this line between May 25 and June 4 was styled the battle of Dallas by soldiers of both sides. Some of them referred to it as the "Hell Hole."

CHAPTER 14

1. While reconnoitering the Federal positions from the top of Pine Mountain, Polk was struck in the chest and instantly killed by a shell fired by the 5th Indiana Battery. He was replaced temporarily by General W.W. Loring. On June 23, A.P. Stewart was promoted to lieutenant general and given command of Polk's corps on July 7. [*Echoes of Battle,* 148; Warner, 294].

2. Lucien B. Pardue.

3. Major General Jacob D. Cox, an historian of the Atlanta Campaign and a division commander in the Federal 23rd Corps, described the weather this way: "The pouring rain had not ceased since the beginning of the month, and the whole country was a quagmire. Streams that were ordinarily dry at this season of the year were now formidable obstructions. The 'lagunes' in the hollows were dangerous quicksands in which artillery and horses were in peril of being utterly engulfed. The supply trains ... toiled painfully along wherever solid ground could be found, leaving the impassable roads for new tracks, which a few trains made in their turn impassable, until the whole country between Allatoona and the centre and right of the [Federal] army was a wilderness of mire in which the original roads could not be traced." [Cox, 104].

4. The battle of Kolb's Farm actually occurred on June 22. Without proper reconnaissance, Hood impulsively attacked two Federal corps (the 20th and 23rd) that were trying to slide by the Army of Tennessee's left flank south of Kennesaw Mountain. Casualties were highest in Major General Carter L. Stevenson's division, which lost 870 men. [O.R., S.1, vol. 38, pt. 3, 815].

5. While the Army of the Ohio threatened the Confederate left, troops from both the Armies of the Cumberland and of the Tennessee directly assaulted Johnston's Kennesaw Mountain defenses on June 27, and were soundly repulsed with losses of about 2,000 killed, wounded and missing. [Long, 529]
    French's division fought Federals of the 15th Corps belonging to Brigadier General Morgan L. Smith's division. French reported one day after the battle: "The enemy ... in my front advanced and attacked the line of intrenchments occupied by Brig. Gen. F.M. Cockrell, commanding the Missouri brigade, and a portion of the left of the line occupied by General Sears' brigade [commanded that day by Colonel William S. Barry, 35th Mississippi], and after a spirited contest of an hour were signally repulsed with severe loss. The killed of the enemy that fell nearest our lines were left on the field. So severe and continuous was the cannonading that the volleys of musketry could scarcely be heard at all on the line." He claimed his division's casualties on June 27 as 17 killed, 92 wounded and 77 missing. [O.R., S.1, vol. 38, pt. 3, 900, 901].

6. During its two-week occupation of Little Kennesaw Mountain, Sears' brigade lost 33 killed, 120 wounded and 125 missing. The 46th Mississippi's casualties for the same period amounted to 9 killed (the most in the brigade), 26 wounded and 20 missing. [O.R., S.1, vol. 38, pt. 3, 908].

CHAPTER 15

1. Between July 3 and 12, the 46th Mississippi's casualties were 2 killed, 4 wounded and 8 missing. [O.R., S.1, vol. 38, pt. 3, 908, 909].

2. Johnston received word of his dismissal on July 17 in a telegram from Richmond. Most enlisted men in the Army of Tennessee shared Chambers' sentiments regarding Hood and the change of commanders. "Old Joe was our idol," wrote Private J.B. Gracey of Company G, 51st Tennessee. "I can bear witness to the spirit of mutiny that filled the minds of the troops, who to a man were ready to throw down their arms and quit." [Confederate Veteran, vol. 26, September 1918, 385].
    "When Johnston was removed from the army his soldiers almost mutinied," wrote Private David B. Morgan, 5th Georgia Cavalry. "Not that they did not trust Hood, but their love for Johnston was so great, and they knew he had such consideration for their

welfare, that they felt no one else could take his place." [*Confederate Veteran*, vol. 26, July 1918, 302].

3. Hood's first attack after assuming Army of Tennessee command ended with 4,800 casualties at Peachtree Creek, with little if anything gained in return. Federal losses amounted to about 1,780 killed, wounded and missing. [Long, 542]. Sears' brigade did not take part in the battle, and the remainder of French's division (some 1,500 effectives) was only engaged in skirmishing. [*O.R.*, S.1, vol. 38, pt. 3, 902].

4. Of nearly 40,000 Confederates engaged July 22 in the battle of Atlanta, between 7,000 and 10,000 were killed, wounded or captured. Of slightly more than 30,000 Federals who fought that day, 430 were killed (including Major General James B. McPherson, Army of the Tennessee commander), 1,559 wounded and 1,733 missing or captured. [Long, 544]. As French's division was occupying the fortified line near Turner's Ferry west of Atlanta, it did not participate in the battle. [*O.R.*, S.1, vol. 38, pt. 3, 903].

5. Colonel William H. Young, 9th Texas Infantry, succeeded to command of Ector's brigade. Young (already wounded five times during the war, and who was to lose his left foot 10 weeks later at Allatoona, Ga.), described Ector's misfortune of July 27: "On that day, while in the redan occupied by [Captain John J.] Ward's battery and directing the fire of the same, General Ector received, by a piece of shell which exploded in the redan, a painful wound above the left knee, which caused the amputation of the left leg about midway the thigh. A piece of the same shell inflicted upon the gallant Captain Ward a mortal wound." [Warner, 349; *O.R.*, S.1, vol. 38, pt. 3, 910].

6. The battle of Ezra Church. S.D. Lee's and A.P. Stewart's corps attacked the 15th Corps, Army of the Tennessee (now commanded by Major General Oliver O. Howard) in a series of futile frontal assaults west of Atlanta, which caused as many as 5,000 Confederate casualties. [Long, 547]. In French's division, only Young's (Ector's) brigade saw slight action at the close of the battle. [*O.R.*, S.1, vol. 38, pt. 3, 904].

7. The report of Colonel William H. Clark, 46th Mississippi, supplies additional details of this engagement: "On the night of August 2 I was ordered to take the Forty-sixth Mississippi Regiment and 120 men of the dismounted cavalry and relieve the troops then occupying the picket ditches of Sears' brigade. I deployed my men at 9 p.m., covering a front of 1,200 yards with my vedettes, in groups of four men under the command of a commissioned officer. The picket-line was about 800 yards in front of the main line, and the vedette line still advanced farther 500 yards. The vedettes being required to be vigilant, reported on the morning of the 4th of August that the enemy was moving to our left. Hitherto nothing more than the usual sharpshooting had occurred.

"At 4 p.m. a sharp and sudden firing announced the fact that the vedettes were attacked, when soon after they appeared retreating and skirmishing with the enemy, who, having arrived within 250 yards of the picket-line, were received by a volley from the ditches, which caused them to fall back. In consequence of the thickness of the woods through which the enemy approached we could not determine the number, but they were reported by the lieutenant commanding the vedette line to be in one line of battle, preceded by a heavy skirmish line. Having after the retiring of the enemy thrown forward my vedettes as skirmishers, with orders to halt as soon as the enemy was felt, and unite with the picket-line when it came up, I dispatched a note to Colonel Barry, commanding brigade, desiring him to send me a regiment to hold the picket-line, fearing lest I might be flanked and cut off by a superior force, while I charged the enemy with my regiment and the dismounted cavalry.

"The support having arrived I assembled my command on the center in one rank in order that I might embrace the whole scope of woods in my front, the flanks resting on open fields. At the command forward every soldier stepped out with alacrity and confidence, although they were ignorant of what might be the additional strength opposed to them. My command advanced within sixty yards of the enemy before we were discovered, when they fired, the balls mostly passing over us, at which time I ordered, 'Fire and charge with a yell.' The men charged the enemy out of our original vedette line, passed beyond into the vedette line of the enemy, when I ordered them to fall back to our original vedette line. The enemy reformed behind some hills in our front, and advanced in two lines of battle with a heavy skirmish line in front, but the steady bearing, defiant shout, and galling fire of the troops under me drove them back. The officers of the enemy could be heard endeavoring to rally their men, but they could not succeed. Night coming on found us in possession of our original vedette line, when I doubled the sentinels on the vedette posts and withdrew the remainder of the troops to the picket-line.

"My command numbered in the aggregate 420 men. We lost in killed 7, and 25 wounded and 1 missing. We took 21 prisoners, some small-arms, among which were two fine [Henry] rifles, shooting sixteen times before reloading, knapsacks, intrenching tools, &c." [*O.R.*, S.1, vol. 38, pt. 3, 921-922].

8. On August 25, Sherman began withdrawing his troops from their entrenchments west of Atlanta, and sent them leapfrogging south in an effort to sever the city's two remaining rail supply lines. The Federal 20th Corps, meanwhile, pulled back to guard the Chattahoochee River rail and ferry crossings above Atlanta. It was troops of this corps that French's division encountered. [Long, 560; *O.R.*, S.1, vol. 38, pt. 3, 906].

9. The Georgia state troops were commanded by Major General Gustavus W. Smith.

CHAPTER 16

1. The battle of Jonesboro was fought August 31-September 1, and ended in a decisive Confederate defeat. Even before the fighting subsided, Hood ordered Atlanta's evacuation. With no time to remove them, extensive stores of munitions and supplies were torched, as well as five locomotives and more than 80 railcars. [Long, 564].

2. The rifle muskets confiscated by Chambers' regiment were .577-caliber Enfields. The lockplates of these weapons, manufactured in England, were stamped with the word Tower.

3. Lovejoy's Station lies about eight miles below Jonesboro on the Macon & Western Railroad.

On August 31, the Democrats nominated Major General George B. McClellan for president to run against incumbent Abraham Lincoln. The election was not held until November 8, but the fall of Atlanta virtually assured Lincoln's victory.

4. Between September 9 and 15, "quite an angry correspondence" was carried on by Generals Hood and Sherman regarding treatment and disposition of Atlanta's civilian population, as well as a general exchange of prisoners. The latter question was resolved at a neutral camp established at Rough and Ready, Ga., where details of a prisoner swap were worked out by officers of both generals' staffs. [Sherman, 112, 129]

5.   Federal cavalrymen of Brigadier General Edward M. McCook's division passed through Fayetteville on the night of July 29, 1864. One of his troopers, First Lieutenant Granville C. West of Company C, 4th Kentucky (U.S.) Mounted Infantry, later wrote: "The command tore through that country that night like the concentrated energies of the tornado, cyclone and a holocaust of fire. Everywhere along the route, and especially around Fayetteville, were the parks of tents and wagons loaded with quartermaster, commissary and ordnance stores of the enemy, General headquarters' and paymasters' wagons, and trains, and hundreds of the finest mules and horses I ever saw. Tents, wagons and stores of all kinds, wherever found, were given up to the torch, and fire completed the work of destruction. In fact, it was a trail of fire from Palmetto [Ga.], and the whole heavens were lighted up all night by the flames from burning stores and army equipments. About 300 prisoners, quartermasters, paymasters, commissaries and others were captured and taken along." [West, Granville C., "McCook's Raid in the Rear of Atlanta and Hood's Army, August 1864," *Military Order of the Loyal Legion of the United States, District of Columbia War Papers No. 29, 9*].

6.   Davis had left Richmond for Georgia on September 20 to see first-hand what could be done to retrieve the military situation there. He visited Hood's headquarters at Palmetto on the 25th. Three days later from West Point, Ga., Davis wired Hood to relieve General Hardee from the Army of Tennessee and send him to command the Department of South Carolina, Georgia and Florida. [Long, 572, 574, 575].

7.   Four months later, General Stephen D. Lee wrote: "As a corps commander I regarded the morale of the army greatly impaired after the fall of Atlanta, and, in fact, before its fall the troops were not by any means in good spirits." [*O.R.,* S.1, vol. 39, pt. 1, 810].

CHAPTER 17

1.   Brigadier General Francis A. Shoup, Hood's chief of staff, recorded in his journal on October 4 that 175 Federals were captured at Big Shanty, while another 250 surrendered to Loring at Acworth. [*O.R.,* S.1, vol. 39, pt. 1, 806].
     Major General Benjamin F. Cheatham was given command of Hardee's corps on September 28.

2.   Hood's reasoning for the Allatoona operation was stated in his report written four months later: "Hearing that the enemy had a quantity of stores at Allatoona, I determined, if possible, to destroy the bridge over the Etowah River, and directed Lieutenant-General Stewart to send a division also to Allatoona, instructing the officer in command [French] to destroy the railroad there and take possession of the place, if, in his judgment, when he reached there, he deemed it practicable." [*O.R.,* S.1, vol. 39, pt. 1, 802].

3.   Brigadier General John M. Corse, commanding the Federal garrison at Allatoona, listed his total infantry and artillery force as 1,944 officers and men on October 5. French claimed his division's effective strength as "about equal" to the Yankees. [*O.R.,* S.1, vol. 39, pt. 1, 763, 813].

4.   French's October 5 surrender demand to the "commanding officer U.S. forces" at Allatoona was worded as follows — "Sir: I have placed the forces under my command in such position that you are surrounded, and to avoid a needless effusion of blood, I call on you to surrender your forces at once and unconditionally. Five minutes will be allowed you to decide. Should you accede to this, you will be treated in the most honorable

Gen. Stephen Dill Lee

manner as prisoners of war."

Corse responded to French at 8:30 a.m. — "Your communication demanding surrender of my command I acknowledge receipt of, and would respectfully reply that we
are prepared for the 'needless effusion of blood' whenever it is agreeable to you." [*O.R.,*
*S.*1, vol. 39, pt. 1, 763].

5. On October 8, French reported his division's losses at Allatoona as 798 killed, wounded and missing. But revised lists compiled for Cockrell's and Sears' brigades a month later pushed the figure to 897 — nearly 200 more casualties than the Federals suffered. [*O.R.,* S.1, vol. 39, pt. 1, 813, 820].

Sears reported his brigade's losses as 425 killed, wounded and missing. The 46th Mississippi lost three officers (including Colonel William H. Clark, "who fell in the advance near the enemy's works with the battle-flag in his hands") and 15 enlisted men killed, 26 wounded and 56 missing or captured, for an aggregate of 100. With 147 casualties, the 35th Mississippi suffered the most heavily of any Confederate regiment engaged. [*Ibid.,* 820, 818].

The desperate nature of the five-hour battle was graphically illustrated in the report of Major Ezekiel H. Hampton, commanding the 29th North Carolina of Ector's brigade: "At 10 a.m. we were ordered forward upon the enemy. My regiment moved forward as a unit through the timber, which was very thick. The enemy were meanwhile pouring a heavy fire into our ranks. My regiment had to advance through the forest farther than the other regiments of the brigade, and not being able to see the brigade got separated from and in advance of the brigade. Upon arriving to where the timber was all felled I saw my regiment was separated from the other regiments, and being exposed to a heavy fire from the enemy, and supposing the remainder of the brigade to be in advance, I ordered my regiment forward at a double-quick to within forty feet of the enemy's outer works, where I halted, ordered my men to lie down, rest and load. After resting from three to five minutes, I ordered my regiment forward. They moved into the enemy's works, where they had a hand-to-hand encounter with sword, bayonet, butt of muskets, rocks, &c., killing a good many and capturing 25 or 30 prisoners and the enemy's intrenchments; thence the regiment moved forward to within twenty yards of the foe's last and strong fort, where they remained contending with the enemy until withdrawn by order of Major-General French ...

"I took 138 aggregate into the action and came out minus 12 killed, 39 wounded, and 3 missing. Sergeant John Rich was carrying the colors in front of the regiment crying 'come ahead, boys!' when he was severely wounded and fell. The colors were scarcely to the ground before they were hoisted by Lieut. E.B. Alexander, commanding Company C. He threw them to the breeze saying, 'come on, my brave boys!' but he did not get more than fifteen paces until he was killed. Sergeant W.J. Parker, of Company F, took up the colors and again threw them to the breeze, and carried them to and planted them on the enemy's inner works. Here he was severely wounded in the face. He then took up the flag, captured a fine horse, and came out with the flag, horse, and his first lieutenant, who was severely wounded in the leg." [*O.R.,* S.1, vol. 39, pt. 1, 820-821].

6. Federal forces engaged at Allatoona included the 39th Iowa, 4th Minnesota, 18th Wisconsin, 7th, 12th, 50th, 57th (two companies) and 93rd Illinois infantry regiments, and the 12th Wisconsin Battery. General Corse, wounded in the face during the battle, reported his total losses at 142 killed, 352 wounded and 212 missing. [*O.R.,* S.1, vol. 39, pt. 1, 766].

The eight companies of the 39th Iowa suffered the highest number of casualties. Of 284 men engaged, 165 were killed (including the regiment's commander and four lieutenants), wounded or captured. Only three officers passed through the battle unscathed. The 39th's entire color guard was killed or wounded, and the regiment's national flag captured by a lieutenant of the 10th Texas Cavalry (Dismounted). The other flag (state colors) captured belonged to the 93rd Illinois. [*Ibid.,* 785, 787, 814].

7. Chambers probably was referring to Henry repeating rifles, a magazine-fed weapon

capable of firing 16 rounds before reloading was necessary. Part of the 7th Illinois Infantry engaged at Allatoona was equipped with Henrys.

8. Doctor P.J. McCormick, a native of Roscommon County, Ireland, was surgeon of the 46th Mississippi. He had lived five years in Yazoo County, Miss., before his enlistment in early 1862. [*Confederate Veteran,* vol. 13, April 1905, 156].

9. The 30th Mississippi belonged to Brigadier General William F. Brantly's brigade, Johnson's division, Lee's corps. The 31st Mississippi was part of Featherston's brigade, Loring's division, Stewart's corps; while the 25th Arkansas belonged to D.H. Reynolds' brigade, Walthall's division, Stewart's corps. [*O.R.,* S.1, vol. 45, pt. 1, 664, 665, 666].

10. On November 30, Hood's Army of Tennessee directly assaulted Major General John M. Schofield's entrenched Federals at Franklin, Tenn., and during a six-hour battle lost more than 6,250 men — 1,750 of them killed or fatally wounded, including six generals — in some of the war's bloodiest fighting. [Long, 603]. Sears' brigade lost 30 officers and men killed, 168 wounded and 35 missing. Cockrell's brigade suffered nearly twice as many casualties; of 696 officers and men in the entire brigade who went into the fight, 419 became casualties, a loss of 60 percent. Cockrell himself was severely wounded, hit in three places. [*O.R.,* S.1, vol. 45, pt. 1, 716].

1865

CHAPTER 18

1. With the fall of Jackson in May 1863, the towns of Enterprise, Columbus and Macon became Mississippi's temporary seats of government. On May 20, 1865, the Legislature returned to war-ravaged Jackson and briefly met for the first time after the war's conclusion. [McCain, 204].

2. On Christmas Day 1864, the decimated Army of Tennessee reached the Tennessee River at Bainbridge, Tenn., nine days after its crushing defeat in the battle of Nashville. Crossing the river on the 26th, Hood led the army's survivors (less than 15,000 infantry officers and men) to Tupelo, Miss., arriving there on January 9, 1865. Hood resigned his command four days later. [*O.R.,* S.1, vol. 45, pt. 2, 780, 781].

3. Sherman's "march through Georgia" began at Atlanta on November 15, 1864. On December 9 his troops reached Savannah, which the Confederates evacuated 11 days later.
    The Army of Northern Virginia had been under siege in the trenches at Petersburg, Va. since June 1864.

4. On January 4, a skirmish flared at The Ponds, Miss., along the Mobile & Ohio Railroad. A brief fight near Mechanicsburg, Miss. occurred the previous day. [*O.R.,* S.1, vol. 45, pt. 1, 855].

5. The 61st Tennessee Infantry Regiment also was known as the 81st Tennessee. Its first colonel, Fountain E. Pitts, resigned in 1863 on account of age and medical disability. [Lindsley, 574].

6. As early as January 1863, Confederate Vice President Alexander H. Stephens, a Georgia native, was openly discussing peace possibilities, and by 1864 a so-called "Peace Society" had sprouted up in Georgia. Stephens became the "apostle of discontent" and the "wet nurse" of the Georgia group, to which state "all the greatest malcontents of the South seemed to have gravitated." They included General Robert Toombs, Georgia Governor Joseph E. Brown and Judge Linton Stephens. [Kirkland, 208]. In North Carolina, one of that state's leading peace advocates was unsuccessful 1864 gubernatorial candidate W.W. Holden, editor of the *Raleigh Standard* who formerly had been an ardent secessionist.. His newspaper was responsible for a great sway in public opinion in that state toward peace advocacy. [Ibid., 207]. See also *O.R.,* S.4, vol. 3, 393-398, for several interesting reports on the Georgia "Peace Society."

7. The engagement near Egypt, Miss. took place on December 28, 1864, during a Federal railroad-wrecking expedition led by Brigadier General Benjamin H. Grierson. His 3,500-man cavalry force consisted of the 2nd New Jersey, 7th Indiana, 1st Mississippi Mounted Rifles, 4th and 10th Missouri, 3rd and 4th Iowa, 2nd Wisconsin, 4th and 11th Illinois, and 3rd U.S. Colored. [*O.R.,* S.1, vol. 45, pt. 1, 845]. Grierson claimed taking 500 Confederate prisoners. [*Ibid.,* 846]. He reported: "Over 100 of the prisoners captured at Egypt formerly belonged to our army and were recruited from Southern prisons into the rebel service, and most of whom I believe were induced to join their ranks from a desire to escape a loathsome confinement. I commend them to the leniency of the Government." [*Ibid.,* 847].

8. Captain D.D. Heslip formerly commanded Company G, 46th Mississippi. He assumed temporary command of the regiment after the battle of Franklin, where Major T.D. Magee was wounded. Nelson superceded Col. Thomas N. Adaire, also wounded at Franklin, in command of the 4th Mississippi. At least 23 Confederate flags were lost in the battles of Franklin and Nashville, including the 4th Mississippi's colors, captured at Nashville on December 16 by the adjutant of the 5th Minnesota Infantry. [*O.R.,* S.1, vol. 45, pt. 1, 685, 646].

9. On May 31, 1854, three wagons loaded with 450 metallic kegs of gunpowder, produced by the E.I. du Pont de Nemours Gun Powder Manufactory, blew up on a cobblestone street leading to a wharf in Wilmington, Del. Three drivers, two passers-by and 18 mules were blown to bits, and 15 people were injured. A number of nearby houses were destroyed, and damage was estimated as high as $100,000. Immediate criticism of the Du Pont Company soon led to a city ordinance banning powder wagons from Wilmington's streets. The cause of the explosion was never determined. [Wilkinson, 34, 35].

10. Lieutenant General Richard "Dick" Taylor, only son of former President Zachary Taylor and commander of the Department of Alabama, Mississippi and East Louisiana, assumed command of the Army of Tennessee on January 23, 1865. [*O.R.,* S.1, vol. 45, pt. 2, 805]. At the time the army was reduced to slightly fewer than 18,000 officers and men. The same day, Hood left for Richmond to personally appeal for a plan to bring 25,000 troops, mostly Texans, east from the Trans-Mississippi as reinforcements. [*Ibid.,* 804].

Taylor later described his impressions after reaching Tupelo: "This was my first view of a beaten army ... and a painful sight it was. Many guns and small arms had been lost, and the ranks were depleted by thousands of prisoners and missing. Blankets, shoes, clothing and accouterments were wanting. Some men perished by frost; many had the extremities severely bitten." [Taylor, 266].

CHAPTER 19

1. By order of President Davis, Taylor retained Stewart's diminished corps (in which the author's regiment served) and the Army of Tennessee's remaining cavalry, while S.D. Lee's and Cheatham's corps (with the exception of R.L. Gibson's Louisiana brigade) were sent east to reinforce Confederate forces in South Carolina, then commanded by General Hardee. [Connelly, 514; *O.R.*, S.1, vol. 45, pt. 2, 795].

2. Captain James W. Benoit had served as assistant adjutant general on General W.E. Baldwin's brigade staff earlier in the war.

3. Although Major General Patrick R. Cleburne first advocated early in 1864 using Negroes to augment Southern military forces, a year passed before President Davis and General Robert E. Lee came to favor the idea. Fierce debate of the issue in the Confederate Congress' final session began in January 1865. In opposition to what became known as the Negro Soldier Bill, North Carolina congressman J.T. Leach on January 25 condemned the use of Negroes as soldiers in the Confederate armies as "wrong in principle, disastrous in practice, an infringement upon the States rights, an endorsement of the principle contained in President Lincoln's emancipation proclamation, an insult to our brave soldiers and an outrage upon humanity which, if carried into effect, will degrade us in the eyes of the civilized world, endanger our liberties, and jeopardize the lives of our wives and children." [Proceedings of the Second Confederate Congress, Second Session in Part, December 15, 1864-March 18, 1865, *Southern Historical Society Papers,* vol. 52, 226-227].

After nearly two months of debate, the Senate passed the bill on March 8 by a one-vote margin. The next day the House voted 39-27 in favor of passage. [*Ibid.,* 465, 470]. Davis signed the bill on March 13. As finally amended, the Negro Soldier Bill read:

The Congress of the Confederate States of America do enact, That in order to provide additional forces to repel invasion, maintain the rightful possession of the Confederate States, secure their independence and preserve their institutions, the President be and he is hereby authorized to ask for and accept from the owners of slaves the services of such number of able-bodied negro men as he may deem expedient, for and during the war, to perform military service in whatever capacity he may direct.

Section 2. That the General-in-Chief be authorized to organize the said slaves into companies, battalions, regiments and brigades, under such rules and regulations as the Secretary of War may prescribe, and to be commanded by such officers as the President may appoint.

Section 3. That while employed in the service the said troops shall receive the same rations, clothing and compensation as are allowed to other troops in the same branch of the service.

Section 4. That if, under the previous sections of this act, the President shall not be able to raise a sufficient number of troops to prosecute the war successfully, and maintain the sovereignty of the States and the independence of the Confederate States, then he is hereby authorized to call on each State, whenever he thinks it expedient for her quota of three hundred thousand troops, in addition to those subject to military service under existing laws, or so many thereof as the President may deem necessary, to be raised from such classes of the population, irrespective of colour, in each State, as the proper authorities may determine. *Provided,* That not more than twenty-five per cent of the male slaves between the ages of eighteen and forty-five in any State shall be called for under the provisions of this act.

Section 5. That nothing in this act shall be construed to authorize a change in the relation of the said slaves. [*Ibid.,* 452-453, 465].

The law was too late to be of much value, but a small number of black troops was raised and began training before war's end.

4.   On January 23, President Davis signed a bill providing for appointment of a general-in-chief of all Confederate armies. On the 31st, Robert E. Lee was named to the position and assumed command on February 6. But the measure came too late in the war to have any effect on the military situation. Lee primarily continued as commander of the Army of Northern Virginia. [Long, 628, 630, 635].

A congressional resolution requesting Davis to reinstate Johnston was approved on January 23, and the general was assigned officially by Lee on February 22 to command of the Department of South Carolina, Georgia and Florida, and the Department of Tennessee and Georgia. On March 6 the Department of North Carolina also was added to his responsibilities. [*SHSP,* vol. 52, 204; Long, 642, 648]. Johnston immediately began marshaling Confederate forces in and to South Carolina to confront Sherman's move north.

5.   The rumor that Major General George H. Thomas, recent victor in the battle of Nashville, was at New Orleans was false. He remained in Nashville through the winter of 1864-65 to the end of the war.

6.   In April 1864, General Grant refused continuing prisoner exchanges in an effort to further reduce Southern manpower. During the next eight months Confederate officials persisted with new exchange proposals, but it was not until late January 1865 that Grant relented, accepting a plan for man-for-man exchanges. [Long, 628, 716].

7.   Brigadier General Randall Lee Gibson, born in Kentucky, originally served as colonel of the 13th Louisiana and commanded the Army of Tennessee's Louisiana brigade from the 1863 Chattanooga campaign to the end of the war. [Warner, 104]. On March 25 he assumed command of Spanish Fort's incomplete defenses overlooking Mobile Bay at Minette Bay and Blakely River. Upon doing so, Gibson turned over command of the Louisiana brigade to Colonel Francis L. Campbell. [*O.R.,* S.1, vol. 49, pt. 1, 314].

CHAPTER 20

1.   Minette Bayou emptied into Minette Bay, on whose swampy southern shore was anchored the "left wing" of Confederate fortifications comprising Spanish Fort's defenses. Cyrus Sibley's Mill was located about four miles southeast of Fort Blakely. [*O.R. Atlas,* plates 79 and 147].

2.   Between March 25-27, Confederate forces at Spanish Fort were Gibson's 500 Louisianans, 950 Alabama reserves under Brigadier General Bryan M. Thomas, and 360 artillerymen commanded by Colonel Isaac W. Patton. Armament consisted of six heavy guns, 14 light fieldpieces and 12 Coehorn mortars. Other ordnance was added later [*O.R.,* S.1, vol. 49, pt. 1, 314].

Federal infantry forces poised to invest Mobile's defenses numbered 32,200 officers and men primarily belonging to the 13th and 16th Army corps, under overall command of Major General Edward R.S. Canby. [*Ibid.,* 92].

3.   Major General Dabney H. Maury commanded the Confederate District of the Gulf and was responsible for the defense of Mobile. [Warner, 215]. Brigadier General James T.

Holtzclaw's five Alabama regiments were under the immediate command of Colonel Bushrod Jones, 32nd/58th Alabama, while Holtzclaw personally commanded the "left wing" at Spanish Fort. [*O.R.*, S.1, vol. 49, pt. 1, 318, 1046].

4. The Federal horsemen fought by the author's regiment on April 1 belonged to the 2nd Illinois Cavalry, part of a "special cavalry expedition" under command of Lieutenant Colonel Andrew B. Spurling, 2nd Maine Cavalry. Spurling reported the next day: "I charged the enemy with [the 2nd Illinois]. It was a complete success. His whole force was routed and a portion of it captured. Two companies ... pursued the fugitives within half a mile of the enemy's works at Blakely, from which a sharp fire was opened with artillery. In all, 74 men were taken prisoners, including 3 commissioned officers. Nearly all of them were members of the Forty-sixth Mississippi Infantry. The colors of that regiment were also captured; 8 horses and mules were taken; 70 stand of arms captured and destroyed." Spurling claimed his own losses were only two men wounded (one mortally) from the 2nd Illinois, and four horses killed. [*O.R.*, S.1, vol. 49, pt. 1, 311].

5. Probably the Mobile & Great Northern Railroad, built in 1862, that ran between the Tensas River just below Hall's Mills northeast to Pollard, Ala. [*O.R. Atlas,* plate 147].

6. Late on April 2, Federal troops under Major General James H. Wilson entered Selma after successfully assaulting that important manufacturing center's thinly held works and capturing 2,700 prisoners, 40 guns and a large quantity of stores. [Long, 664]. By 11 p.m. the same night, President Jefferson Davis and most of his Cabinet evacuated Richmond upon hearing news of Petersburg's fall earlier in the day. [Ibid., 664, 663].

7. On April 11, Brigadier General Thomas J. Lucas' Federal cavalry brigade attacked a 15th Confederate Cavalry detachment of 450 troopers between Mount Pleasant and Claiborne, Ala. According to Lucas, his force broke the Rebel line "and they retreated in disorder in all directions. I pursued them four miles, capturing prisoners all the way. Among the results of the engagement were the capture of 2 commissioned officers and 70 men, 2 battle-flags, horses, arms, &c. Many of the enemy escaped on the flanks in consequence of the difficulty in pressing over the soft, spongy ground." [*O.R.*, S.1, vol. 49, pt. 1, 304].

The surviving defenders of Spanish Fort evacuated during the night of April 8-9. Blakely fell to Canby's Federals on the 9th. Three days later Canby entered Mobile after General Maury ordered its evacuation on April 11. Maury's remaining troops moved unopposed to Meridian, Miss., and began refitting with the slim hope of joining Confederate forces in North Carolina. [Long, 670, 672, 673].

8. Fort Blakely fell on April 9 after an all-out Federal attack began at 5:30 p.m. Some 3,200 Confederates were captured, including Gens. F.M. Cockrell, B.M. Thomas and St. John R. Liddell, the fort's commander. [*O.R.*, S.1, vol. 49, pt. 1, 283-284]. Among the assault troops was Brigadier General John P. Hawkins' division of U.S. Colored Troops. One of Hawkins' brigade commanders, Brigadier General William A. Pile, wrote four days after the battle: "To the Seventy-third U.S. Colored Infantry belongs the honor of first planting their colors on the enemy's parapet. Many of the enemy garrisoning these works threw down their arms and ran toward their right to the white troops to avoid capture by the colored soldiers, fearing violence after surrender." [*Ibid.,* 289-290].

The rumor of black soldiers slaughtering surrendered Confederates as a reprisal stemmed from an incident at Fort Pillow, Tenn., on April 12, 1864. Major General Nathan Bedford Forrest's Confederate cavalry overwhelmed Fort Pillow's 557 defenders, nearly half of whom were black. Federal casualties amounted to 231 dead, 100 wounded and 226 captured compared to Rebel losses of 14 killed and 86 wounded. Charges of numerous atrocities, including the wanton shooting and bayonetting of unarmed prisoners were vehemently denied by Confederate civil and military authorities. For the rest of the war the Fort Pillow "massacre" remained an emotional issue on both sides. [Long, 484].

The rumor of Sherman being beaten in North Carolina was untrue.

9. Lee surrendered to Grant near Appomattox Court House on April 9, eight days before this entry in the author's journal.

10. While watching a comedy at Ford's Theater in Washington, D.C., Lincoln was shot in the head by actor John Wilkes Booth the night of April 14. He died at 7:22 a.m. on April 15. The same night as Lincoln's shooting, Secretary of State William H. Seward was attacked and stabbed in his bed by a Booth accomplice, but survived. At 11 a.m. on April 15, less than four hours after Lincoln's death, Vice President Andrew Johnson, a Tennesseean, assumed the office of President. [Long, 675, 676, 677].

11. Sherman and Johnston first met to discuss surrender terms on April 17 near Durham Station, N.C. The following day they signed a controversial document calling for an armistice by all armies in the field; Confederate forces were to be disbanded and to deposit their arms in the state arsenals; each man was to agree to cease from war and to abide by state and Federal authority; the President was to recognize the existing state governments when their officials took oaths to the United States; reestablishment of Federal courts would take place; people were to be guaranteed rights of person and property; the United States would not disturb the people of the South as long as they lived in peace; and a general amnesty for Confederates. Both generals recognized that they were not fully empowered to carry out such far-reaching measures and that necessary authority would have to be obtained.

Sherman learned on April 24 that the agreement was disapproved by President Johnson, and he was ordered to give Johnston 48 hours to surrender before the resumption of hostilities. On the 26th Johnston capitulated, receiving terms similar to those given Lee at Appomattox. [Long, 678, 681, 682].

12. Dick Taylor's surrender involved Confederate forces in the Department of Alabama, Mississippi and East Louisiana. Although the surrender officially was May 4, Taylor regarded the capitulation as May 8 — the date the paroles of his men were accepted by General Canby's commissioners. [O.R., S.1, vol. 49, pt. 2, 573, 660]. Taylor himself described the final act: "The terms of surrender demanded and granted were consistent with the honor of our arms; and it is due to the memory of General Canby to add that he was ready with suggestions to soothe our military pride. Officers retained their side arms, mounted men their horses, which in our service were private property; and public stores, ordnance, commissary and quartermaster, were to be turned over to officers of the proper departments and receipted for. Paroles of the men were to be signed by their officers on rolls made out for that purpose, and I was to retain control of railways and river steamers to transport the troops as nearly as possible to their homes and feed them on the road, in order to spare the destitute people of the country the burden of their maintenance. Railways and steamers, though used by the Confederate authorities, were private property, and had been taken by force which the owners could not resist; and it was agreed that they should not be seized by civil jackals following the army without special orders from Washington. Finally, I was to notify Canby when to send his officers to my camp to receive paroles and stores." [Taylor, 276-277].

INDEX